T0100102

The Rise of Fog Computing in the Digital Era

K.G. Srinivasa
Chaudhary Brahm Prakash Government Engineering College, India

Pankaj Lathar
Chaudhary Brahm Prakash Government Engineering College, India

G.M. Siddesh
Ramaiah Institute of Technology, India

A volume in the Advances
in Computer and Electrical
Engineering (ACEE) Book Series

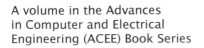

Published in the United States of America by
    IGI Global
    Engineering Science Reference (an imprint of IGI Global)
    701 E. Chocolate Avenue
    Hershey PA, USA 17033
    Tel: 717-533-8845
    Fax: 717-533-8661
    E-mail: cust@igi-global.com
    Web site: http://www.igi-global.com

Copyright © 2019 by IGI Global. All rights reserved. No part of this publication may be reproduced, stored or distributed in any form or by any means, electronic or mechanical, including photocopying, without written permission from the publisher.
Product or company names used in this set are for identification purposes only. Inclusion of the names of the products or companies does not indicate a claim of ownership by IGI Global of the trademark or registered trademark.

Library of Congress Cataloging-in-Publication Data

Names: Srinivasa, K. G., editor. | Lathar, Pankaj, 1974- editor. | Siddesh,
  G. M., 1981- editor.
Title: The rise of fog computing in the digital era / K.G. Srinivasa, Pankaj
  Lathar, and G.M. Siddesh, editors.
Description: Hershey, PA : Engineering Science Reference, [2018]
Identifiers: LCCN 2017061866| ISBN 9781522560708 (h/c) | ISBN 9781522560715
  (eISBN)
Subjects: LCSH: Cloud computing.
Classification: LCC QA76.585 .R57 2018 | DDC 004.67/82--dc23 LC record available at https://
lccn.loc.gov/2017061866

This book is published in the IGI Global book series Advances in Computer and Electrical Engineering (ACEE) (ISSN: 2327-039X; eISSN: 2327-0403)

British Cataloguing in Publication Data
A Cataloguing in Publication record for this book is available from the British Library.

All work contributed to this book is new, previously-unpublished material.
The views expressed in this book are those of the authors, but not necessarily of the publisher.

For electronic access to this publication, please contact: eresources@igi-global.com.

Advances in Computer and Electrical Engineering (ACEE) Book Series

ISSN:2327-039X
EISSN:2327-0403

Editor-in-Chief: Srikanta Patnaik, SOA University, India

MISSION

The fields of computer engineering and electrical engineering encompass a broad range of interdisciplinary topics allowing for expansive research developments across multiple fields. Research in these areas continues to develop and become increasingly important as computer and electrical systems have become an integral part of everyday life.

The **Advances in Computer and Electrical Engineering (ACEE) Book Series** aims to publish research on diverse topics pertaining to computer engineering and electrical engineering. **ACEE** encourages scholarly discourse on the latest applications, tools, and methodologies being implemented in the field for the design and development of computer and electrical systems.

COVERAGE

- Programming
- Sensor Technologies
- VLSI Design
- Optical Electronics
- Computer Hardware
- Computer science
- Power Electronics
- Chip Design
- Algorithms
- Computer Architecture

IGI Global is currently accepting manuscripts for publication within this series. To submit a proposal for a volume in this series, please contact our Acquisition Editors at Acquisitions@igi-global.com or visit: http://www.igi-global.com/publish/.

The Advances in Computer and Electrical Engineering (ACEE) Book Series (ISSN 2327-039X) is published by IGI Global, 701 E. Chocolate Avenue, Hershey, PA 17033-1240, USA, www.igi-global.com. This series is composed of titles available for purchase individually; each title is edited to be contextually exclusive from any other title within the series. For pricing and ordering information please visit http://www.igi-global.com/book-series/advances-computer-electrical-engineering/73675. Postmaster: Send all address changes to above address. ©© 2019 IGI Global. All rights, including translation in other languages reserved by the publisher. No part of this series may be reproduced or used in any form or by any means – graphics, electronic, or mechanical, including photocopying, recording, taping, or information and retrieval systems – without written permission from the publisher, except for non commercial, educational use, including classroom teaching purposes. The views expressed in this series are those of the authors, but not necessarily of IGI Global.

Titles in this Series

For a list of additional titles in this series, please visit:
https://www.igi-global.com/book-series/advances-computer-electrical-engineering/73675

Electronic Nose Technologies and Advances in Machine Ofaction

Yousif Albastaki (University of Bahrain, Bahrain) and Fatema Albalooshi (University of Bahrain, Bahrain)

Engineering Science Reference ● ©2018 ● 318pp ● H/C (ISBN: 9781522538622) ● US $205.00

Quantum-Inspired Intelligent Systems for Multimedia Data Analysis

Siddhartha Bhattacharyya (RCC Institute of Information Technology, India)

Engineering Science Reference ● ©2018 ● 329pp ● H/C (ISBN: 9781522552192) ● US $185.00

Advancements in Computer Vision and Image Processing

Jose Garcia-Rodriguez (University of Alicante, Spain)

Engineering Science Reference ● ©2018 ● 322pp ● H/C (ISBN: 9781522556282) ● US $185.00

Handbook of Research on Power and Energy System Optimization

Pawan Kumar (Thapar University, India) Surjit Singh (National Institute of Technology Kurukshetra, India) Ikbal Ali (Jamia Millia Islamia, India) and Taha Selim Ustun (Carnegie Mellon University, USA)

Engineering Science Reference ● ©2018 ● 500pp ● H/C (ISBN: 9781522539353) ● US $325.00

Big Data Analytics for Satellite Image Processing and Remote Sensing

P. Swarnalatha (VIT University, India) and Prabu Sevugan (VIT University, India)

Engineering Science Reference ● ©2018 ● 253pp ● H/C (ISBN: 9781522536437) ● US $215.00

Modeling and Simulations for Metamaterials Emerging Research and Opportunities

Ammar Armghan (Aljouf University, Saudi Arabia) Xinguang Hu (HuangShan University, China) and Muhammad Younus Javed (HITEC University, Pakistan)

Engineering Science Reference ● ©2018 ● 171pp ● H/C (ISBN: 9781522541806) ● US $155.00

For an entire list of titles in this series, please visit:
https://www.igi-global.com/book-series/advances-computer-electrical-engineering/73675

701 East Chocolate Avenue, Hershey, PA 17033, USA
Tel: 717-533-8845 x100 ● Fax: 717-533-8661
E-Mail: cust@igi-global.com ● www.igi-global.com

Table of Contents

Detailed Table of Contents

Chapter 1

Stojan Kitanov, Mother Teresa University, Macedonia
Toni Janevski, Ss Cyril and Methodius University, Macedonia

Pushing computing, control, data storage, and processing into the cloud has been a key trend in the past decade. However, the cloud alone encounters growing limitations, such as reduced latency, high mobility, high scalability, and real-time execution in order to meet the upcoming computing and intelligent networking demands. A new paradigm called fog computing has emerged to overcome these limits. Fog extends cloud computing and services to the edge of the network. It provides data, computing, storage, and application services to end-users that can be hosted at the network edge. It reduces service latency, and improves QoS/QoE, that results in superior user experience. This chapter is about introduction and overview of fog computing, comparison between fog computing and cloud computing, fog computing and mobile edge computing, possible fog computing architecture, applications of fog computing, and possible research directions.

Chapter 2

Vighnesh Srinivasa Balaji, Ramaiah Institute of Technology, India

In recent times, the number of internet of things (IoT) devices/sensors increased tremendously. To support the computational demand of real-time latency-sensitive applications of largely geo-distributed IoT devices/sensors, a new computing paradigm named fog computing has been introduced. In this chapter, the authors will introduce fog computing, its difference in comparison to cloud computing, and issues related to fog. Among the three issues (i.e. service, structural, and security issues), this chapter scrutinizes and comprehensively discusses the service and structural issues also providing the service level objectives of the fog. They next provide various algorithms for computing in fog, the challenges faced, and future research directions. Among the various uses of fog, two scenarios are put to use.

Chapter 3

Minal Moharir, R. V. College of Engineering, India
Bharat Rahuldhev Patil, R. V. College of Engineering, India

The demerits of cloud computing lie in the velocity, bandwidth, and privacy of data. This chapter focuses on why fog computing presents an effective solution to cloud computing. It first explains the primary motivation behind the use of fog computing. Fog computing, in essence, extends the services of the cloud towards the edge of the network (i.e., towards the devices nearer to the customer or the end user). Doing so offers several advantages. Some of the discussed advantages are scalability, low latency, reducing network traffic, and increasing efficiency. The chapter then explains the architecture to implement a fog network, followed by its applications. Some commercial fog products are also discussed, and a use case for an airport security system is presented.

Chapter 4

Ranjitha G., Ramaiah Institute of Technology, India
Pankaj Lathar, Chaudhary Brahm Prakash Government Engineering
*   College, India*
G. M. Siddesh, Ramaiah Institute of Technology, India

Fog computing enhances cloud computing to be closer to the processes that act on IOT devices. Fogging was introduced to overcome the cloud computing paradigm which was not able to address some services, applications, and other limitations of cloud computing such as security aspects, bandwidth, and latency. Fog computing provides the direct correlation with the internet of things. IBM and CISCO are linking their concepts of internet of things with the help of fog computing. Application services are hosted on the network edge. It improves the efficiency and reduces the amount of data that is transferred to the cloud for analysis, storage, and processing. Developers write the fog application and deploy it to the access points. Several applications like smart cities, healthcare domain, pre-processing, and caching applications have to be deployed and managed properly.

Chapter 5

Nida Kauser Khanum, Ramaiah Institute of Technology, India
Pankaj Lathar, Chaudhary Brahm Prakash Government Engineering
College, India
G. M. Siddesh, Ramaiah Institute of Technology, India

Fog computing is an extension of cloud computing, and it is one of the most important architypes in the current world. Fog computing is like cloud computing as it provides data storage, computation, processing, and application services to end-users. In this chapter, the authors discuss the security and privacy issues concerned with fog computing. The issues present in cloud are also inherited by fog computing, but the same methods available for cloud computing are not applicable to fog computing due to its decentralized nature. The authors also discuss a few real-time applications like healthcare systems, intelligent food traceability, surveillance video stream processing, collection, and pre-processing of speech data. Finally, the concept of decoy technique and intrusion detection and prevention technique is covered.

Chapter 6

Jamuna S. Murthy, Ramaiah Institute of Technology, India

In the recent years, edge/fog computing is gaining greater importance and has led to the deployment of many smart devices and application frameworks which support real-time data processing. Edge computing is an extension to existing cloud computing environment and focuses on improving the reliability, scalability, and resource efficiency of cloud by abolishing the need for processing all the data at one time and thus increasing the bandwidth of a network. Edge computing can complement cloud computing in a way leading to a novel architecture which can benefit from both edge and cloud resources. This kind of resource architecture may require resource continuity provided that the selection of resources for executing a service in cloud is independent of physical location. Hence, this research work proposes a novel architecture called "EdgeCloud," which is a distributed management system for resource continuity in edge to cloud computing environment. The performance of the system is evaluated by considering a traffic management service example mapped into the proposed layered framework.

Chapter 7

S. R. Mani Sekhar, Ramaiah Institute of Technology, India

Sharmitha S. Bysani, Ramaiah Institute of Technology, India

Vasireddy Prabha Kiranmai, Ramaiah Institute of Technology, India

Security and privacy issues are the challenging areas in the field of internet of things (IoT) and fog computing. IoT and fog has become an involving technology allowing major changes in the field of information systems and communication systems. This chapter provides the introduction of IoT and fog technology with a brief explanation of how fog is overcoming the challenges of cloud computing. Thereafter, the authors discuss the different security and privacy issues and its related solutions. Furthermore, they present six different case studies which will help the reader to understand the platform of IoT in fog.

Chapter 8

Naresh E., Ramaiah Institute of Technology, India

Vijaya Kumar B. P., Ramaiah Institute of Technology, India

Aishwarya Hampiholi, Ramaiah Institute of Technology, India

Jeevan B., Ramaiah Institute of Technology, India

This chapter gives an overall role of software engineering in internet of things domain. In this chapter, the following topics are included: glimpse of complete software engineering, main motivation of IoT, how IoT evolved, usage of software engineering concepts in IoT, role of CBSE in IoT, role of aspect-oriented software engineering, heterogeneous boards in designing IoT systems, importance of integration phase in IoT systems, comparison of different IDEs of IoT, testing of IoT systems, and a case study illustrating all the concepts for online blood banking system and forest fire detection.

Chapter 9

Chetan Shetty, Ramaiah Institute of Technology, India

Sowmya B. J., Ramaiah Institute of Technology, India

Anemish S., Ramaiah Institute of Technology, India

Seema S., Ramaiah Institute of Technology, India

The goal of this chapter is to inspect and consider the answer for accidents and reactions to the accidents in the urban zones. Modules have been made to manage the colossal datasets and to bring interesting bits of knowledge into the outcomes. This is done by utilizing decision tree analysis.

Chapter 10

Sowmya B. J., Ramaiah Institute of Technology, India
Chetan Shetty, Ramaiah Institute of Technology, India
Netravati V. Cholappagol, Ramaiah Institute of Technology, India
Seema S., Ramaiah Institute of Technology, India

This chapter gives the real-time solutions to the farmers by providing smart solutions for irrigation, disease monitoring, and decision supporting systems (which involves giving suggestions and solutions to the farmers by monitoring soil conditions, rain, weather, and overall quality of crop growth and the effect on the growth of the crop due to infertile soil or bad climatic conditions). These solutions are provided using the IOT and data analytics technology.

Foreword

The Internet of Things and current-state cloud computing have created a situation where billions of remote sensory devices work perpetually to transmit raw data to centralized cloud data centers for storage and eventual retrieval and analysis. This has caused some concern over whether enterprises, developers and cloud solution designers can build appropriate and secure systems to store the growing surplus of data while allowing quick accessibility to recover the data for useful analytics.

Pushing computing, control, data storage and processing into the cloud has been a key trend in the past decade. However, the cloud alone encounters growing limitations, such as reduced latency, high mobility, high scalability and real-time execution in order to meet the upcoming computing and intelligent networking demands. A new paradigm called Fog Computing has emerged to overcome these limits. Fog extends cloud computing and services to the edge of the network. It provides data, computing, storage, and application services to end-users that can be hosted at the network edge. It reduces service latency, and improves QoS/QoE, that results in superior user experience.

The topics covered in this book are fairly wide and would meet the training requirement for both applied science as well as engineering disciplines. This volume is intended to serve as a general introduction to fog computing for a senior-level student or graduate student. The reader is expected to have a background in basic concepts of IoT and Cloud Computing; only topics specific to the discipline will be discussed herein. It is not intended to be a comprehensive authority on each subject, but rather to serve as a reference and concept review for the upper-level reader.

The authors have endeavored to present a balanced view of issues, diligently avoiding personal biases and fashionable philosophies. It is not the purpose of this textbook to tell you what to think. Rather, our goal is to provide access to information and the conceptual framework needed to understand complex issues so that you can comprehend the nature of problems and formulate your own views. Fog Computing is not only a very important subject, but it is extremely interesting. The extensive use of this book by students, faculty and practicing engineers will bring satisfaction to the authors who have put in a lot of effort in writing this book.

Manohar Lal
IGNOU, India

Preface

With the immense growth of information, we are embracing the prevalence of ubiquitously connected smart devices, which are now becoming the main factor of computing. The information storage, processing and sharing has moved to sophisticated smart gadgets. "Fog Computing" deals with the platforms that provide compute, storage, and networking services between end devices and traditional computing data centre's. The demand for applications for fog computing are foreseen in areas such as manufacturing, smart cities, connected transportation, smart grids, e-health, and oil and gas. Fog computing is considered as a key enabler for, 4G and 5G mobile networks for providing effective ways to address a wide range of challenges that includes securing resource-constrained endpoints or supporting local analytics. Cloud computing and Internet of things(IoT) in the current world of smart devices has changed the way of computing, networking and services provided to the users. Even though cloud computing and IoT can provide a salable solution for deploying and managing applications, it can't meet the stringent requirements of applications with the present generation of computing devices especially in a mobile environment, that includes challenges of latency-sensitive, security/privacy-sensitive, or geographically constrained applications, scheduling and power management, heterogeneity of devices. Fog computing is proposed to enable computing directly at the edge of the network, which can deliver new applications and services especially for the future of Internet.

In recent times, the number of Internet of Things (IoT) devices/sensors increased tremendously. To support the computational demand of real-time latency-sensitive applications of largely geo-distributed IoT devices/sensors, a new computing paradigm named 'Fog computing' has been introduced as the demerits of cloud computing lie in the velocity, bandwidth, and privacy of data. Fog computing is an extension of cloud computing, and it is one of the most important archetype in the current world. Fog computing is like cloud computing as it provides data storage, computation, processing and application services to end-users.

The fog computing enhances the cloud computing to be closer to the process that act on the IOT devices. Fogging was introduced to overcome the cloud computing paradigm which was not able to address some services, applications and other limitations of cloud computing such as security aspects, bandwidth and latency. In the recent years, Edge/Fog Computing is gaining greater importance and has lead to the deployment of many smart devices and application frameworks which supports real-time data processing. But, Security and privacy issues are the challenging areas in the field of Internet of Things (IoT) and Fog computing. In current ages, IoT and Fog has become an involving technology allowing major changes in the field of information systems and communication systems.

The target audience of this book is researchers, graduate students and practitioners in the area of Cloud Computing, Internet of Things, Smart Systems and Fog Computing.

The book contains 10 chapters, which are briefly described as follows:

The first chapter on Introduction to Fog Computing is about introduction and overview of fog computing, comparison between fog computing and cloud computing, fog computing and mobile edge computing, possible fog computing architecture, applications of fog computing and possible research directions.

In Chapter 2, the authors have introduced Fog computing, its difference in comparison to Cloud Computing and issues related to Fog. Among the three issues i.e. service, structural and security issues, this article, scrutinizes and comprehensively discusses the service and structural issues also providing the service level objectives of the Fog. They next provide various algorithms for computing in Fog, the challenges faced and future research directions. Among the various uses of Fog, two scenarios were the advantages of Fog computing are put to use.

Chapter 3 focuses on why fog computing presents an effective solution to cloud computing. It first explains the primary motivation behind the use of Fog computing. Fog computing, in essence, extends the services of the cloud towards the edge of the network, i.e. towards the devices nearer to the customer or the end user. Doing so offers several advantages, some of the discussed advantages are scalability, low latency, reducing network traffic and increasing efficiency. The chapter then explains the architecture to implement a Fog network, followed by its applications. Some commercial Fog products are also discussed and a use case for an airport security system is presented.

Chapter 4 provides a good insight into how fog computing applications are managed and deployed. As Fog computing provides the direct correlation with the internet of things, IBM and CISCO are linking their concepts of internet of things with the help of fog computing. Application services are hosted on the network edge. It improves the efficiency and reduces the amount of the data which is transferred to the cloud for analysis, storage and processing of the data. Developers write the fog application and deploy it to the access points. Several applications like smart cities, healthcare domain, pre-processing and caching applications has to be deployed and managed properly.

In Chapter 5, authors discuss the security and privacy issues concerned with fog computing. The issues present in cloud are also inherited by fog computing, but same methods available for cloud computing are not applicable to fog computing due to its decentralized nature. We also discuss few real-time applications like healthcare systems, Intelligent food trace-ability, Surveillance video stream processing, Collection and pre-processing of speech data. Finally, the concept of decoy technique and intrusion detection and prevention technique is covered.

Edge Computing which is an extension to existing Cloud Computing environment and focus on improving the reliability, scalability and resource efficiency of cloud by abolishing the need for processing all the data at one time and thus increasing the bandwidth of a network is elaborately discussed in Chapter 6. Edge Computing can complement Cloud Computing in a way leading to a novel architecture which can benefit from both edge and cloud resources. This kind of resource architecture may require resource continuity provided that the selection of resources for executing a service in cloud is independent of physical location. Hence this research work proposes a novel architecture called "EdgeCloud" which is a distributed management system for resource continuity in edge to cloud computing environment. The performance of the system is evaluated by considering a traffic management service example mapped into the proposed layered framework.

Chapter 7 provides the introduction of IoT and Fog Technology with a brief explanation of how Fog is overcoming the challenges of cloud computing. Thereafter authors discuss the different security & privacy issues and its related solutions. Furthermore we present six different case studies which will help the reader to understand the platform of IoT in Fog.

Chapter 8 gives an overall role of software engineering in internet of things domain. In this chapter, the following topics are included: Glimpse of complete software engineering, Main motivation of IoT, How IoT evolved, Usage of Software Engineering concepts in IoT, Role of CBSE in IoT, Role of Aspect-oriented software engineering, Heterogeneous boards in designing IoT systems, Importance of integration phase in IoT systems, Comparison of different IDEs of IoT, Testing of IoT systems and a case study illustrating all the concepts for on-line blood banking system and Forest Fire Detection.

The International Traffic Safety Data & Analysis Group (IRTAD) produces enormous amount of accident and mishap datasets. These datasets consists of detailed information of accidents data, for example, the city names, the type of accidents, and amount of light at the accident site, seriousness of mischance, fatality rate, speed zone, Risk factor due to utilization of liquor and so on. The emphasis is laid on the use of information examination to anticipate and reduce the effect of the mishaps and reveal the significant patterns via preparing the framework with the past information utilizing Data Analytics approach. The real causes for the mischance's are recognized and studied by utilizing a portion of the applicable situations like, liquor utilization, attempt of manslaughter cases and so forth. Chapter 9 discusses how IoT and Data analytics in this case study helps to provide a feasible solution.

Finally, Chapter 10 provides a case study on how Fog Computing can be effectively used in Smart agriculture. IoT investigation applications can enable organizations to comprehend the Internet of Things information available to them, with an eye toward diminishing upkeep costs, evading hardware disappointments and enhancing business operations. Internet of Things gadgets can open a radical new universe of information for associations - for instance, sensors can be utilized to proactively screen and keep up pipelines and system loads, which can help maintain a strategic distance from mishaps and blackouts. Understanding IoT-delivered information requires something beyond propelling a Hadoop information lake and retiring until tomorrow, notwithstanding. Here, when we are concerning about the health care we are mainly dealing with Activity trackers during cancer treatment. We analyze the cancer data and give solutions in terms of its symptoms its solution and monitoring the patients using IOT and Data analytics.

The book is a good collection of articles which provide a basic insight into Fog Computing, its applications and different deployment scenario. We would like to express our sincere appreciation to each contributor for his/her work and for their patience and attention to detail during the entire production process. We sincerely hope these eminent contributors will encourage us in the future as well, in the greatest interest of academia. The book will be of interest to a broad audience of Fog Computing, IoT, Cloud Computing and Analytics, or newcomers who want to learn more about the topic.

Acknowledgment

We attribute our efforts for completing this book to all the people who have inspired us and shaped our careers. We thank our college administration, colleagues and students who encouraged us to work on this book.

Srinivasa would like to thank Prof. K C Tiwari, Principal of CBP Government Engineering College, New Delhi who encouraged working on this book. His special thanks to his esteemed colleagues Prof. Harne, Dr. Athar Hussain, and Seema Rani for their valuable suggestions and continuous encouragement.

Both Siddesh and Srinivasa would like to thank Dr. NVR Naidu, Principal, Ramaiah Institute of Technology for his valuable guidance and support. Special thanks to Dr. T V Suresh Kumar, Dr. B P Vijay Kumar and Mr. Ramesh Naik for their continuous encouragement. The authors would like to acknowledge valuable inputs and suggestions by Dr. Anita K, Dr. Seema S, and Mr. Srinidhi H.

Pankaj would like to thank Prof. Manohar Lal, Former Director, SOCIS, IGNOU, New Delhi for his matchless mentorship and also for writing forward for the book. His special thanks to his esteemed senior colleague Prof. Girish Kumar Sharma, BPIBS, Delhi who has always been a source of inspiration. He is grateful to Prof. Yudhvir Singh, Dean Colleges, MDU for his incredible guidance and suggestions.

We are extremely grateful to our families, who graciously accepted our inability to attend to family chores during the course of writing this book, and especially for their extended warmth and encouragement. Without their support, we would not have been able to venture into writing this book.

Chapter 1
Introduction to Fog Computing

Stojan Kitanov
Mother Teresa University, Macedonia

Toni Janevski
Ss Cyril and Methodius University, Macedonia

ABSTRACT

Pushing computing, control, data storage, and processing into the cloud has been a key trend in the past decade. However, the cloud alone encounters growing limitations, such as reduced latency, high mobility, high scalability, and real-time execution in order to meet the upcoming computing and intelligent networking demands. A new paradigm called fog computing has emerged to overcome these limits. Fog extends cloud computing and services to the edge of the network. It provides data, computing, storage, and application services to end-users that can be hosted at the network edge. It reduces service latency, and improves QoS/QoE, that results in superior user experience. This chapter is about introduction and overview of fog computing, comparison between fog computing and cloud computing, fog computing and mobile edge computing, possible fog computing architecture, applications of fog computing, and possible research directions.

INTRODUCTION

The future Internet of Everything (IoE) would become the linkage between extremely complex networked organizations (e.g. telecoms, transportation, financial, health and government services, commodities, etc.), which would provide the basic ICT infrastructure that supports the business processes and the activities of the whole society in general (Brech, Jamison, Shao, & Wightwick, 2013.), (Mitchell, Villa,

DOI: 10.4018/978-1-5225-6070-8.ch001

Copyright © 2019, IGI Global. Copying or distributing in print or electronic forms without written permission of IGI Global is prohibited.

Stewart-Weeks, & Lange, 2013). Frequently, these processes and activities should be supported by orchestrated cloud services, where a number of services work together to achieve a business objective (Zhang, Zhang, Chen, & Huo, 2010).

However, these demands can only be partially fulfilled by existing mobile cloud computing solutions. This is because the future Internet would exacerbate the need for improved QoS/QoE, supported by services that are orchestrated on-demand and are capable to adapt at runtime, depending on the contextual conditions, to allow reduced latency, high mobility, high scalability, and real-time execution. In addition, the emerging wave of Internet of Things (IoTs) would require seamless mobility support and geo-distribution in addition to location awareness and low latency. Also, the existing cloud computing security mechanisms such as sophisticated access control and encryption have not been able to prevent unauthorized and illegitimate access to data.

A new paradigm called Fog Computing, has emerged to meet these requirements (Bonomi, Milito, Zhu, & Addepalli, 2012; Mouradian, Naboulsi, Yangui, Glitho, Morrow, & Polakos, 2017). Fog Computing extends cloud computing and services to the edge of the network. Fog computing would combine the study of mobile communications, micro-clouds, distributed systems, and consumer big data. It is a scenario where a huge number of heterogeneous (wireless and sometimes autonomous) ubiquitous and decentralized devices communicate, and potentially cooperate among them and with the network to perform storage and processing tasks without the intervention of third parties (Vaquero & Rodero-Merino, 2014; Liu, Fieldsend, & Min, 2017). These tasks support basic network functions, or new services and applications that run in a sand-boxed environment. Users leasing part of their devices to host these services get incentives for doing so. The distinguishing fog characteristics are its proximity to end-users, its dense geographical distribution, and its support for mobility. Therefore, fog paradigm is well positioned for real-time big data analytics. Services are hosted at the network edge or even end devices such as set-top-boxes, or access points (Gao, Luan, Liu, & Yu, 2017). By doing so, fog reduces service latency, and improves QoS, resulting in superior user-experience. It supports emerging IoE applications that demand real-time/predictable latency (industrial automation, transportation, networks of sensors and actuators).

This chapter provides an introduction and overview of fog computing. Initially it provides an overview of cloud computing, mobile edge computing, and fog computing. Then it makes a comparison between fog computing and cloud computing, as well as fog computing and mobile edge computing. After that fog computing features are discussed. Finally, at the end fog computing open research directions and conclusion of the chapter are provided.

CLOUD COMPUTING

The idea of cloud computing is based on a very fundamental principal of reusability of IT capabilities (Zhang, Zhang, Chen, & Huo, 2010). Cloud computing is a computing paradigm, where a large pool of systems is connected in private or public networks, in order to provide dynamically scalable infrastructure for application, data and file storage (Dialogic Corporation, 2010). At the same time, the shared cloud resources (networks, servers, data warehouses, applications and services) can be rapidly provisioned and managed with minimal interaction by service providers.

The cloud computing users may use these resources for development, hosting and running of services and applications on demand in a flexible way at any device, at any time and at any place in the cloud. With the advent of this technology, the cost of computation, application hosting, content storage and delivery is reduced significantly.

The framework for cloud computing is defined in the recommendations ITU Y.3501 (ITU-T, Cloud Computing Framework and High Level Requirements, 2013) and Y.3510 (ITU-T, Cloud Computing Infrastructure Requirements, 2013) as well as the NIST standards for cloud computing (NIST, 2013).

Mobile Cloud Computing

Today the mobile devices (smartphones, tablets, etc.) became essential part of the life, as well as, the most effective and convenient tools for communication without any limitations for time and space. The mobile user device accumulates rich experience of the mobile applications (iPhone applications, Google applications etc.), that are executed either on the mobile devices, or on the distant servers through the wireless networks. The fast development of the Mobile Computing (MC) resulted to become a powerful trend in the information technology. However, the mobile devices face with many challenges with their resources (battery life, memory, storage, bandwidth, processing power), environment (heterogeneity, availability and scalability) and security (reliability and privacy). The constrained resources additionally worsen the improvement of the quality of the services.

With the rapid increase of the mobile applications and the support of the cloud computing for different types of services for the mobile device users is introduced the Mobile Cloud Computing (MCC) as an integration of the cloud computing in the mobile environment (Dihn, Lee, Niyato, & Wang, 2011; Khan, Othman, Madani, & Khan, 2014; Fowler, 2013). The mobile cloud computing brings new types of services for the mobile device that would use the benefits of the cloud computing.

MCC is an infrastructure used by mobile applications where both the data storage and data processing are moved away from the mobile device to powerful and centralized computing platforms located in the clouds (Kitanov & Janevski, 2014). The access to this platform is enabled through the wireless network by using a thin web client, or browser. Mobile cloud computing is usually referred to the following two perspectives (Khan, Othman, Madani, & Khan, 2014):

- **Infrastructure Based:** Where the hardware infrastructure is static and provides cloud services to mobile users; and
- **Ad-Hoc Mobile Cloud**: Where a group of mobile devices acts as a cloud and provides cloud services to other mobile devices.

Cloud Computing Model and Architecture

(Mobile) cloud computing is made up of complex network and relationships of and in between infrastructure Providers, Application/Services Providers, End-Users and Developers, all producing and/or consuming applications and/or services on web (Qureshi, Ahmad, & Shuja-ul-islam, 2011). Such MCC model is given on Figure 1.

Figure 1. (Mobile) Cloud Computing Model
Source: Qureshi, Ahmad, and Shuja-ul-islam, 2011

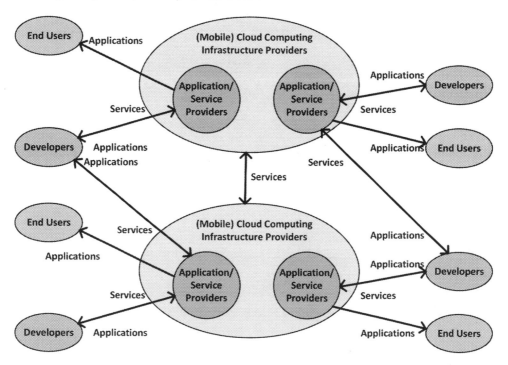

The Infrastructure Providers provide hardware and software infrastructure, or services and applications, and/or all the above. The Application/Services Providers are 1st tier consumer of Cloud Computing. They are typically business consumers of cloud computing infrastructure and providers of applications and/or services. The Developers are 2nd tier consumer of Cloud Computing, and they develop applications and services that are typically hosted on the Cloud. The End Users also known as 3rd tier consumer of Cloud Computing, are typical end users of applications. They consume applications that in turn consume services on the cloud, and they care whether the application works well when needed with the necessary availability level and the security.

A general mobile cloud computing architecture (Dihn, Lee, Niyato, & Wang, 2011) is given on Figure 2. Mobile devices are connected to the mobile, or wireless network (GSM, GPRS, UMTS, HSPA, LTE, LTE-Advanced, LTE-A Pro, etc.) through a base station (BTS, UTRAN, nodeB, enodeB), satellite link or access point (WiFi or WiMAX). The mobile, or wireless network provides internet connectivity to the users. Therefore, the users can access cloud-based services by Internet, if they have mobile devices that support network connectivity.

Mobile users' requests and users' profiles are transmitted to the central processors that are connected to servers providing mobile and wireless network services. Mobile and wireless network operators can provide services Authentication, Authorization and Accounting (AAA) for mobile users based on the Home Agent (HA) and subscribers' data stored in databases. After that, the subscribers' requests are delivered to cloud through Internet. In the cloud, the cloud controllers process the users' requests and provide the corresponding services from the Cloud Computing Service Provider to mobile users.

Recently mobile applications have begun to adapt to cloud computing environment. However, these applications are often linked with server instances running in the

Figure 2. Mobile Cloud Computing Architecture
Source: Dihn, Lee, Niyato, and Wang, 2011

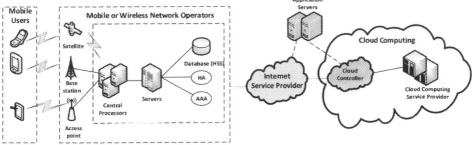

cloud. Because of this, the MCC users may face some problems such as congestion due to the limited bandwidth, network disconnection, and the signal attenuation caused by mobile users' mobility. This would cause delays when MCC users want to communicate with the cloud, so QoS and QoE are significantly reduced.

CloneClouds and Cloudlets are some of the possible solutions which would reduce the network delay (Dihn, Lee, Niyato, & Wang, 2011). *CloneCloud* uses nearby computers, or data centers to increase the speed of running smart phone applications, by cloning the entire set of data and applications from the smartphone onto the cloud and selectively executing some operations on the clones, reintegrating the results back into the smartphone. *Cloudlet* is a trusted, resource-rich computer, or cluster of computers that has good Internet connection and it is available for use by nearby mobile devices. The MCC users may use a cloudlet if it is available, and if they do not want to offload the content and the request to the cloud (maybe due to the delay, cost, etc.).

Cloud Computing Service Oriented Architecture

Once a cloud is established, how its cloud computing services are deployed in terms of business models can differ depending on requirements (Dihn, Lee, Niyato, & Wang, 2011; Goyal, 2014). A layered architecture of cloud computing that demonstrates the effectiveness in terms of meeting the user's requirements is given on Figure 3.

The layer of Data Centers provides the hardware facility and infrastructure for clouds. A number of servers are linked with high-speed networks to provide services for customers. Usually, data centers are built in less populated places, with high power supply stability, and a low risk of disaster.

The Infrastructure as a Service (IaaS) layer is built on top of Data centers layer. The consumer is not able to manage the underlying cloud infrastructure. However, IaaS provides provision processing, storage, networks, and other fundamental computing resources where the consumer is able to deploy and run arbitrary software, which can include operating systems and applications.

The Platform as a Service (PaaS) layer provides an advanced integrated environment for building, testing and deploying custom applications. The consumer

Figure 3. Cloud Computing Service Oriented Architecture

| Software as a Service (SaaS) |
| Platform as a Service (PaaS) |
| Infrastructure as a Service (IaaS) |
| Data Centers |

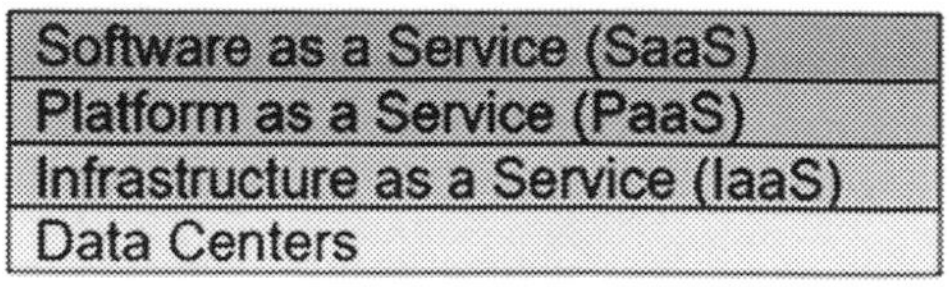

does not control the underlying cloud infrastructure such as network, servers, operating systems, or storage, but has control over the deployed applications and possibly application hosting environment configurations.

The Software as a Service (SaaS) layer provides applications running on a cloud infrastructure. These applications can be accessed by various client devices by using a thin client interface such as a web browser. The consumer is not able to manage, or control the underlying cloud infrastructure including network, servers, operating systems, storage, or even individual application capabilities. However, the consumer may control and manage only limited user-specific application configuration settings.

Also, there are subsets of these service layers that relate to a particular industry or market. Such models are for example Network as a Service and Communication as a Service (Dialogic Corporation, 2010).

Network as a Service (NaaS) is a category of the cloud computing services where the user has an opportunity to use the transport connection services, and/or network connection services between the clouds. NaaS services include flexible and extended VPN, bandwidth on demand, etc.

Communications as a Service (CaaS) is a category of cloud computing services where the user has an opportunity to use real time communication and collaborative services. CaaS services include VoIP, instant messaging service and video conference.

Cloud Computing Deployment Models

Depending on the requirements different deployment models for (mobile) cloud computing exist. The deployment models can be: private cloud, community cloud, public cloud, hybrid cloud and inter-cloud computing (Goyal, 2014; Sqalli, Al-saeedi, Binbeshr, & Siddiqui, 2012).

The Private Cloud, also known as Corporate Cloud, or Internal Cloud is a proprietary computing architecture for an organization that provides hosted services on private networks. The deployment, the maintenance, and the operations of the cloud infrastructure are performed by the organization itself. The operation may be in-house, or with a third party on the premises. However, this model has its own disadvantages, since the organizations still need to purchase, set up, and manage their own clouds.

The Community Cloud is a private cloud infrastructure that is shared among a number of organizations with similar interests and requirements. This may help limit the capital expenditure costs for its establishment as the costs are shared among the organizations. The operation may be in-house, or with a third party on the premises.

The Public Cloud, or External Cloud infrastructure is available to the public on a commercial basis by a cloud service provider. This enables a consumer to develop and deploy a service in the cloud with very little financial outlay compared to the capital expenditure requirements normally associated with other deployment options. The users are connected to the cloud data centers that provide the cloud services via the public Internet.

The Hybrid Cloud can be a combination of private and public clouds that support the requirement to retain some data within the organization, and also the need to offer services in the cloud. The clouds in this model have the ability through their interfaces to allow data, and/or applications to be moved from one cloud to another. The hybrid cloud offers a suitable environment for the needs of the enterprises, but it also introduces the complexity of determining which services and applications should be distributed across the private, public, or both clouds. In this model the Cloud Management System (CMS) is responsible for the administration of hybrid clouds. The CMS should contain some functionality such as security management, resource scheduling (e.g., immediate, on-demand, or for later use), resource allocator, and monitoring the university activities and performance. This information can be used to determine the required resources that need to be allocated in the future. An overview of hybrid cloud computing model is given in Figure 4.

The Inter-cloud computing is a model that provides on demand cloud computing resources, such as processing, storage and network, as well as, a distribution of the workload through the internetworking of the clouds.

Cloud Computing Benefits

Cloud computing and mobile cloud computing would provide many benefits and advantages for cloud computing providers, mobile network operators, and cloud computing consumers such as:

Figure 4. Hybrid Cloud Computing Model
Source: Sqalli, Al-saeedi, Binbeshr, and Siddiqui, 2012

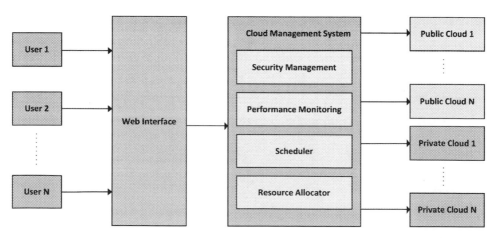

- Sharing information and applications without the need of complex and costly hardware and software since data processing is running on the cloud;
- Enhanced features and functionalities of mobile devices through new cloud applications;
- Easy access to mobile cloud computing through a browser with the mobile devices;
- Possibility of one application to be shared and accessed by many mobile device users;
- Broader reach and dissemination of mobile cloud computing applications;
- Increased battery power for mobile devices;
- Improved data storage capacity and processing power since cloud computing will enable the users to store/access and to process the big data such as modeling of 3D graphics visualization and animation in ecology, global climate solutions, financial risks, healthcare and medical learning,
- Decoding genome projects, etc. through the wireless and mobile networks on the cloud where High Performance Computing (HPC) system resides;
- Higher level of availability of the cloud computing;
- Improved reliability since data and computer applications are stored and backed up on a number of computers; and
- Possibility for Distance Learning system.

Cloud Computing Services

Cloud computing and mobile cloud computing would provide to the consumers the following basic services: platform services, application services and context-rich support services (Bahl, Han, Li, & Satyanarayanan, 2012). Platform services include the following: storage, database, memory caching, content distribution, processing and computing. Cloud computing provider may also offer the following application services: presence service for location-based applications, video transcoding and streaming proxy for video streaming applications, push notifications, and speech and image recognition.

In the near future, many applications would become more personalized, and more context-aware. They will be able to recognize user's identity, user's location, and user's preferences. To support these applications Cloud Computing providers should support context-rich support services such as context extraction service, recommendation service and group privacy service. Of particular importance is the context extraction service that performs data mining analysis of mobile data combined with other forms of data such as social networking data, and sensor network data in order to extract contextual clues relevant to the user. Data mining services should be able to scale and analyze large group of people and large quantities of data (big data) that that they generate in order to extract collective trends among the population of users in real time.

Additionally, crowd actuation services, such as recommendation services based on collective group context rather than individual context need to be created and scaled. By using these clues, a layer of cloud recommendation services can be built that creates output that is adjusted to a user, or set of users with those contextual characteristics.

CLOUD COMPUTING AND TELECOM OPERATORS

In general, the big Over The Top (OTT) players have a leading role in the cloud computing market. Dropbox, Apple, and Google are the main personal cloud providers, while Salesforce.com, Google, and Microsoft are the leaders in SaaS market. Amazon is mostly used for the PaaS and IaaS services.

One part of the cloud computing market would also belong to the Telecom operators. Compared to OTT players, the telco operators have recently entered in the cloud computing market (Brown, 2013).

Why Telecom Operators Should Use the Cloud

There are two main reasons why telecom operators should include the cloud computing. The first reason is to use the benefits of cloud computing for IT optimization (lower costs, bigger elasticity and speed). The second reason is to use the new business opportunities.

The telco operators have a competitive advantage on a local level, where they can benefit from the local commercial presence, compared to many OTT players. Due to their relative close proximity to the users, the telecom operators may offer cloud services with very low latency. Additionally, they can offer services to the users that are flexible and elastic in terms of the frequency bandwidth. Finally, the users have more trust and confidence in telco operators rather than in many Internet brands, or OTT players.

The Cloud in Telecom Operators

Telecom operators are investigating how they can make the best use of their assets, and how future network investment can be aligned with a cloud model (Brown, 2013). One option is to make use of network equipment to host server modules to create telecom-grade clouds. This could include a mix of centralized cloud and a distributed cloud using access network and RAN elements known as Cloud RAN or CRAN, as it is shown on Figure 5.

Cloud Radio Access Network (CRAN)

Since the smart mobile devices have limited capabilities for storing and processing of data, mobile cloud computing solves this issue by moving the storing and processing of data from the smart mobile device to the cloud computing centers. However, this requires high bandwidth and low latency.

In order to solve this issue, the CRAN moves the cloud computing functionalities to the radio access network (Brown, 2013; Peng, Li, Jiang, Li, & Wang, 2014).

Currently hosting content and applications in the CRAN has become popular. By placing storage and computing resources at, or close to, the cell site, operators can improve response times for the services requested by the users in the prevailing radio conditions. This might be useful for congestion control, or rate adaptation for video streams. On the network side, cell site caching can reduce demand on the backhaul network, and potentially play a role in limiting signaling to the core network. The two primary advantages of placing content close to the radio and close to the user are application performance and network efficiency. One emerging application

Figure 5. Cloud Integration with Telecommunication Network
Source: Kitanov, & Janevski, 2014

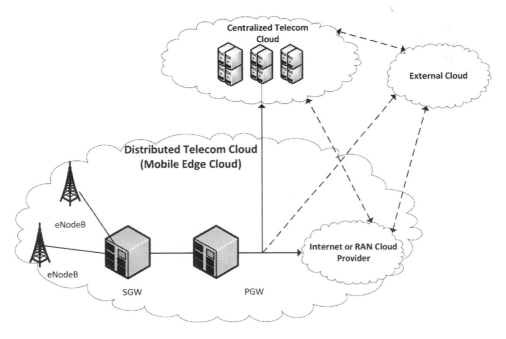

where both application performance and network efficiency could work together in a distributed cloud model is LTE Broadcast that uses evolved Multimedia Broadcast Multicast (eMBMS) technology (Brown, 2013).

However, the application storing and all radio signal processing functions are still centralized at the cloud computing server in the core part of the network. Because billions of smart user devices need to transmit and exchange their data fast enough with the Base Band Unit (BBU) pool, there is a requirement for high bandwidth and low latency.

To overcome this, Heterogeneous Cloud Radio Access Networks (H-CRANs) have been proposed in which the user and control planes are decoupled (Peng, Li, Jiang, Li, & Wang, 2014; Peng, Li, Zhao, & Wang, 2015). as it is shown in Figure 6. The centralized control function is shifted from the BBU pool in CRANs to the High-Power Nodes (HPNs) in HCRANs. HPNs are also used to provide seamless coverage and execute the functions of control plane. The high-speed data packet transmission in the user plane is enabled with the radio heads (RRHs). HPNs are connected to the BBU pool via the backhaul links for interference coordination.

Figure 6. Mobile Network with CRAN and HCRAN

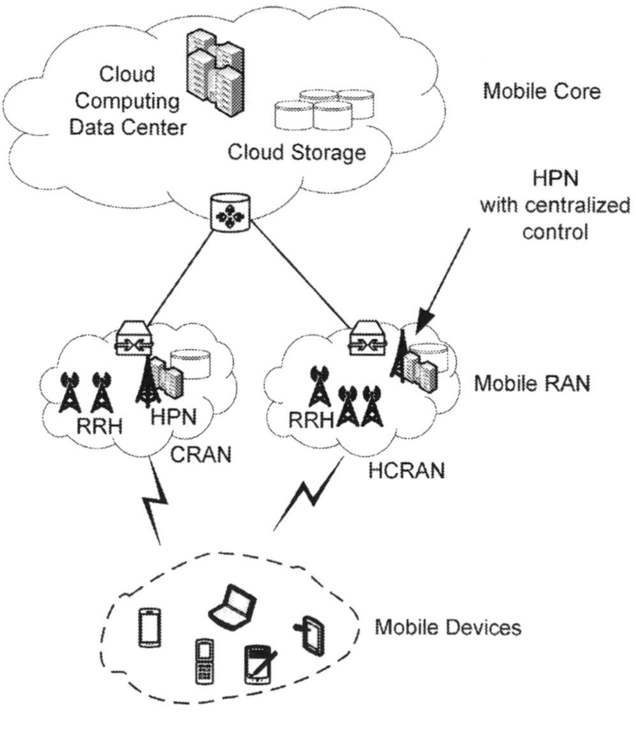

However, HCRANs still have its own drawbacks. The data traffic data over the fronthaul between RRHs and the centralized BBU pool surges a lot of redundant information, which worsens the fronthaul constraints. In addition, HCRANs do not take fully utilize the processing and storage capabilities in edge devices, such as RRHs and smart user devices, which is a promising approach to successfully alleviate the burden of the fronthaul and BBU pool. Finally, operators must deploy a huge number of fixed RRHs and HPNs in H-CRANs in order to meet the requirements of peak capacity, which makes a serious waste when the volume of delivery traffic is not sufficiently large.

MOBILE EDGE COMPUTING

Recently the mobile devices became an important tool for learning, entertainment, social networking, and acquiring new information from the news and the business (Ahmed, Gani, Sookhak, Hamid, & Xia, 2015). However, due to the constrained resources of the mobile devices (the processing power, battery life, and the capacity for data storing) the mobile users do not receive the same quality as the conventional desktop users (Dihn, Lee, Niyato, & Wang, 2011). When the mobile cloud computing appeared, the limited resources in the mobile devices of data storage and data processing was resolved with the transfer of these resources to the cloud. Many cloud computing services such as m-health-care (Hoang, & Chen, 2010), (Adibi, 2014), mobile learning, or m-learning (Sun, & Shen, 2014), mobile video games (m-gaming) (Wu, Yuen, Cheung, Chen, & Chen, 2015) and m-governance (Sabarish, & Shaji, 2014). are already directly available from the mobile devices.

However, because the data need to be transferred from the mobile devise to the cloud computing centers, there is a need for increased bandwidth, and lower latency, which causes a network overload to occur. It is expected the need for the frequency bandwidth to be doubled every year (Ericsson, 2016), (Atzori, Iera, & Morabito, 2010). Moreover, the Internet of Things and the future Internet of Everything, would provide the devices with constrained resources to be connected on Internet (Brech, Jamison, Shao, & Wightwick, 2013.), (Atzori, Iera, & Morabito, 2010).

In order to resolve this issue, one possible proposed solution is the Cloudlet, where the mobile devices transmit data via a WiFi network for further processing to a server with less resources than the cloud, but is nearby to the mobile devices (Satyanarayanan, Bahl, Caceres, & Davies, 2009). However, this approach is less effective due to the following two reasons. Firstly, the access to the Cloudlet is only possible through a WiFi access point. And secondly the Cloudlet possess less resources than the cloud, which means it is not scalable in resource and service provisioning.

Therefore, a better proposed solution is the Mobile Edge Computing (MEC) (Ahmed, & Ahmed, 2016; Beck, Werner, Feld, & Schimper, 2014). MEC is a model that enables business-oriented cloud platform to be implemented within the radio access network, close the mobile users in order to serve applications that are delay sensitive and context aware.

This approach is initiated by ETSI, where data processing and storage happens at the edge in the radio access network in the base station, rather than in cloud computing centers, in order to create new application and service possibilities and opportunities. In this way, the mobile edge computing manages to reduce latency, alleviates the network congestion in the core, enables efficient traffic management, and opens possibility other industrial services to be delivered for the critical applications through the mobile network. This approach provides innovative network architecture where the possibilities for cloud computing and IT services are converged with the mobile network.

The MEC architecture is given on Figure 7. The mobile edge computing entity is positioned next to the radio access network. This entity works with downlink bitstreams from the cloud computing servers to the mobile device and uplink bitstreams from the mobile device to the cloud computing servers. The MEC platform contains standard IT servers and network devices inside, or outside of the base station (Yu, 2016). The external applications are executed in the Virtual Machines (VMs) (Buyya, Broberg, & Goscinski, 2011), connected with network devices. Also, there is a possibility the MEC platform to be implemented with standard IT servers, where the network device is implemented as a software entity, such as Open Virtual Switch, or Open vSwitch (OVS) (Pfaff, Pettit, & Koponen, 2015).

The MEC platform contains the following fundamental modular functionalities: routing, exposure of network capabilities and management. The routing module is responsible for forwarding the packets between the MEC platform and the radio access network and the core part of the mobile network, as well as within the MEC platform itself. The module network exposure provides authorized information to the Radio Network Information Service (RNIS) and the Radio Resource Management (RRM). The management module supports the AAA security function, as well as the management of the external applications within the MEC platform itself. Here is included the orchestration of setting up the application and the authorization for the exposure of the network capabilities station (Yu, 2016).

MEC enables the mobile network to evolve in an innovative way to handle the increased traffic volume, that arise from various domains in the next 5G mobile and wireless network, which are grouped into enhanced Mobile BroadBand - eMBB (Liu, Hou, & Jin, 2017), massive Machine Type Communication - mMTC (Jovović, & Forenbacher, 2015), and Ultra-Reliable and Low Latency Communication – URLLC (Yilmaz, Wang, & Johansson, 2015).

Figure 7. Mobile Edge Computing Architecture

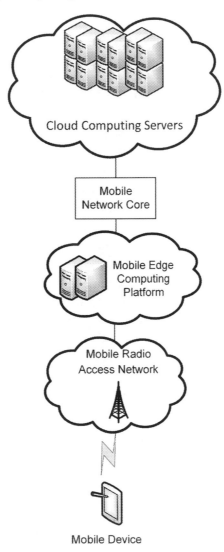

However, mobile edge computing devices and entities within the domain are standalone, or interconnected through proprietary networks with custom security and little interoperability. Although the modern Mobile Edge Computing attempts to include some functions of Cloud Computing like interoperability, local security etc., however, it does not extend to the cloud or across domains.

FOG COMPUTING

In order to resolve the limitations of (mobile) cloud computing and mobile edge computing, a new paradigm known as fog computing arose. Fog Computing extends cloud computing and services to the edge of the network. Fog computing would combine the study of mobile communications, micro-clouds, distributed systems, and consumer big data. It is a horizontal, system-level architecture that distributes computing, storage, control and networking functions closer to the users along a cloud-to-thing continuum (OpenFog Consortium, 2017).

The fog computing architecture uses one, or a collaborative multitude of end-user clients, or near-user edge devices to carry out a substantial amount of storage, communication and management (Chiang, 2015). It carries out a substantial amount of storage, communication and management such as network measurement, control and configuration, at or near the end-user (rather than stored primarily in large-scale data centers).

Rather than concentrating data and computation in a small number of large clouds, many fog systems will be deployed close to the end users or where computing and intelligent networking can best meet user needs. The core idea is to take full advantages of local radio signal processing, cooperative radio resource management, and distributed storing capabilities in edge devices, which can decrease the heavy burden on front haul and avoid large-scale radio signal processing in the centralized baseband unit pool (Peng, Yan, Zhang, & Wang, 2016).

Reasons for the Rise of Fog Computing

There are four main reasons for the rise of fog computing (Chiang, 2015):

1. **Real Time Processing and Cyber-Physical System Control**: Edge data analytics, as well as the actions it enables through control loops, often have stringent time requirement in the order of few milliseconds that can be carried out only at the edge of the network. This is particularly essential for Tactile Internet, that enables virtual-reality-type interfaces between humans and devices.

2. **Cognition or Awareness of Client-Centric Objectives**: The applications can be enabled by knowing the requirements and the preferences of the clients. This is particularly true when privacy and reliability cannot be trusted in the Cloud, or when security is enhanced by shortening the extent over which the communication is carried out.

3. **Increased Efficiency by Pooling of Idle and Unused Local Resources**: The idle and unused gigabytes on many devices, the idle processing power, the sensing ability and the wireless connectivity within the edge may be pooled within a fog network.

4. **Agility, or Rapid Innovation and Affordable Scaling**: It is usually much faster and cheaper to experiment with client and edge devices. Rather than waiting for vendors of large boxes inside the network to adopt an innovation, in the fog computing world a small team may take advantages of smart phone Application Programming Interface (API) and Software Development Kit (SDK), proliferation of mobile applications, and offer a networking service through its own API.

Fog Computing Applications

Fog computing was proposed to support applications whose requirements don't quite match the QoS and QoE guarantees provided by the cloud computing, such as (Gupta, Chakraborty, Ghosh, & Buyya, 2017):

- Applications having stringent latency requirements, such as mobile gaming, video conferencing, etc.;
- Geo-distributed applications where the data collection points are distributed over a wide area, for instance, pipeline monitoring, or sensor networks to monitor the environment;
- Fast mobile applications involving highly mobile users (smart connected vehicle, connected rail); and
- Large-scale distributed control systems consisting of a vast number of sensors and actuators, such as smart grid, connected rail, smart traffic light systems, etc., working in a coordinated manner to improve user experience.

Fog Computing Architecture

An overview of Fog Computing architecture is given in Figure 8 (Kitanov, Monteiro, & Janevski, 2016). It consists of centralized cloud computing center, IP/MPLS core network, RAN network with distributed fog computing intelligence and smart things network. Each smart thing device is attached to one of fog devices in the RAN network. The fog devices could be interconnected to each other, and each of them is linked to the centralized cloud computing center via the IP/MPLS core the network.

The RAN network is actually an intermediate fog layer that consists of geo-distributed intelligent fog computing servers which are deployed at the edge of networks, e.g., parks, bus terminals, shopping centers, etc. Each fog server is a

Figure 8. Cloud Integration with Telecommunication Network
Source: Kitanov, Monteiro, & Janevski, 2016

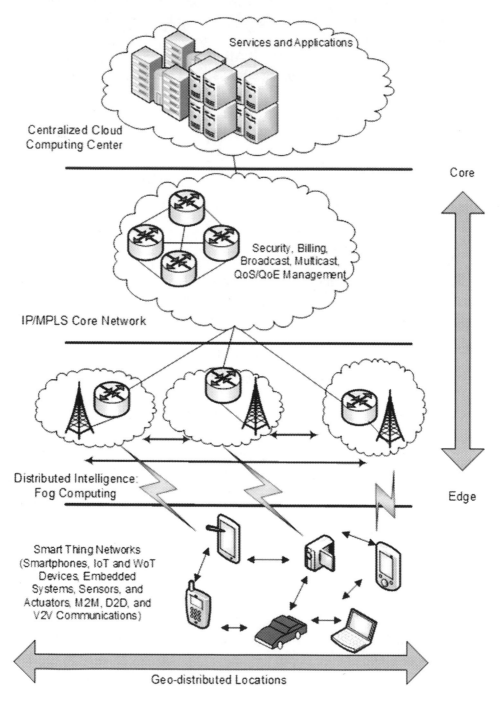

highly virtualized computing system and is equipped with the on-board large volume data storage, computing, and wireless communication facility (Gao, Luan, Liu, & Yu, 2017).

The role of fog servers is to bridge the smart mobile device things and the cloud (Vaquero & Rodero-Merino, 2014). The geo-distributed intelligent fog servers directly communicate with the mobile users through single-hop wireless connections using the off-the-shelf wireless interfaces, such as, LTE, WiFi, Bluetooth, etc. They can independently provide pre-defined service applications to mobile users without assistances from cloud, or Internet. In addition, the fog servers are connected to the cloud in order to leverage the rich functions and application tools of the cloud.

Fog computing and networking contains both data plane and control plane that enable different applications with different communication protocols over all layers in the OSI system (Chiang, 2015). This is illustrated in Figure 9. Fog data plane is focused on 5G mobile network, IoT, and the future IoE. Fog control plane is mainly about cyber physical system control and real-time data analytics.

A Comparison Between Cloud and Fog Computing

A comparison between Fog Computing and Cloud Computing is given in (Gao, Luan, Liu, & Yu, 2017), which is summarized in Table 1.

Fog Computing is targeted for mobile users, while cloud computing is targeted for general internet users. Cloud Computing provides global information collected from worldwide, while fog computing provides limited localized information services related to specific deployment locations. Cloud services are located within the Internet, while fog services are located at the edge of the network. There is a single hop between the smart user devices and the fog computing server, and multiple hops between the user devices and the cloud computing centers. Fog computing contains very large number of server nodes, while cloud computing contains few server nodes. The latency and the delay jitter are very low in fog computing environment, while

Figure 9. Data and Control Plane of Fog Computing
Source: Chiang, 2015

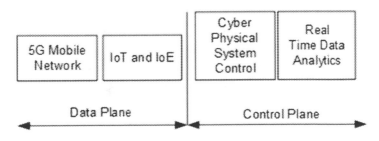

Table 1. A Comparison between Cloud and Fog Computing

	Cloud Computing	Fog Computing
Target Type	General Internet Users	Mobile Users
Service Type	Global Information Collected from Worldwide	Limited localized information services related to specific deployment locations
Service Location	Within the Internet	At the edge of the local network
Distance between client and server	Multiple hops	Single hop
Number of server nodes	Few	Very large
Latency	High	Low
Delay jitter	High	Very low
Geo-distribution	Centralized	Distributed
Security	Undefined	Can be defined
Hardware	Ample and scalable storage, processing and computing power	Limited storage, processing and computing power, wireless interface
Deployment	Centralized and maintained by OTT service providers	Distributed in regional areas and maintained by local businesses

Source: (Gao, Luan, Liu, & Yu, 2017)

in cloud computing provides there are very high latency and delay jitter. The cloud computing centers are centralized, while the fog computing nodes are densely geo-distributed. The security in cloud computing is undefined, while in fog computing it can be defined. The hardware in cloud contains ample and scalable storage, and very high processing and computing power. On the other hand, the hardware in the fog contains limited storage and limited processing and computing power, and wireless interface. Finally, the cloud computing deployment is centralized and maintained by OTT service providers, while the fog computing is distributed in regional areas and maintained by local business, which are close to the end users and therefore they have bigger trust in them.

In addition, the cloud computing represents an efficient and scalable centralized solution for information management and distribution, for the traditional desktop users that request global information from the remote central server such as world news, stock market in different countries, etc. However, nowadays there are mobile Internet users using smartphones and tablets, which massively demand local information around them (Gao, Luan, Liu, & Yu, 2017). For example, a mobile user in a shopping center is interested about the sales, open hour, restaurants and events inside the attended shopping center; while such information becomes useless once he/she leaves the shopping center.

The conventional cloud-based Internet is inefficient in serving the local information desired by mobile users, since the local stores need first to upload their information to a remote cloud server over Internet, and then the mobile users to obtain the desired information from the remote cloud server. Although the physical distance between the mobile user and the stores is short, by using the remote cloud to provide the necessary information, the actual communication distance, from the mobile user to the cloud server to can be far, which may result with increased latency, and high congestion.

Fog Computing, on the other side represents a practical and efficient solution to resolve the mismatch between physical and communication distances. A Fog server can be deployed inside the shopping center or store that will distribute the local store flyers to mobile users. As such, the physical distance is equal to the communication distance and users can acquire low-latency desirable services (Gao, Luan, Liu, & Yu, 2017).

Cloud and fog form a mutually beneficial, inter-dependent continuum (Chiang, 2015). They are inter-dependent, e.g., coordination among devices in a Fog may rely on the Cloud. They are also mutually beneficial: certain functions are naturally more advantageous to carry out in Fog while others in Cloud.

A Comparison Between Mobile Edge Computing and Fog Computing

Although the Mobile Edge Computing provides many benefits, still it has certain constraints and limits compared to the fog computing. In order to see these constraints and limits it is necessary to make a comparison between these two approaches.

Table 2 summarizes the main characteristics and features of mobile edge computing and fog computing (Nebbiolo Technologies, 2015). MEC provides limited application hosting, while fog computing fully supports it. Data service at edge and device and application management are provided by both MEC and Fog Computing. The security and safety are partially solved with Virtual Private Network (VPN) or Firmware (FW) at MEC. On the other side, Fog Computing provides a complete E2E solution for data protection on session level and hardware. Fog computing also provides support of elastic compute and resource pooling, modular hardware, real time control high level availability and virtualization with windows support.

The MEC is developed by ETSI and the vendors for telecommunication equipment in order to deliver standardized MEC architecture and industrial standardized application programming interface for external applications. This concept represents a control and management of independent end user device individually, or through a set of software functions in a cloud domain in the radio access network. The devices

Table 2. Main Features of Mobile Edge Computing and Fog Computing

	Mobile Edge Computing	Fog Computing
Application hosting	Limited	Yes
Data Service at Edge	Yes	Yes
Device and Application Management	Yes	Yes
Security and Safety	Partially solved with VPN or FW	A Complete E2E solution, data protection, on session level and hardware
Elastic compute / resource pooling	No	Yes
Modular Hardware	No	Yes
Virtualization with Windows support	To be defined	Yes
Real time control high level availability	No	Yes

Source: (Nebbiolo Technologies, 2015)

and the entities that perform computing at the edge of the network in the cloud domain are either independent, or mutually connected through proprietary networks with usual security and low degree of interoperability. Recently this approach attempts to redefine the data computing range at the edge by including some functionalities for fog computing, such as interoperability, local security and safety, etc. However, this is not extended to the cloud or through the domains (Nebbiolo Technologies, 2015).

On the other hand fog computing is a concept proposed by CISCO and other manufacturers for Internet equipment and it represents a completely distributed network, multi-layered cloud computing architecture for data processing, where exists billions of devices as part of IoT, multiple local clouds at the edge of the network – fog and main central hyper scalable cloud computing data center. A single application in the fog is distributed through the devices through the cloud components embedded in the nodes in the different network levels, for example in the radio access network, multi-service edge, the core of the network (in the IP/MPLS routers and switches, the gateways of the mobile packet core, etc.). In this way the cloud is closer to the users of mobile devices and is capable to offer ultra-low latency, quicker response, high bandwidth, as well as real time access to the radio information that will be used by the applications in order to offer context related services.

Compared to Mobile Edge Computing, the edge devices in the Fog Computing may independently self-optimize among themselves and collectively to perform measurement and management to the remaining of the network. The fog computing moves the operational functions of the digital objects in Information Centric Networks (ICNs) and virtualized functions in the Software Defined Networks (SDNs) at the edge of the network (Chiang, 2015). Table 3 summarizes the main differences between mobile edge computing and fog computing.

Table 3. Differences between Mobile Edge Computing and Fog Computing

No	Mobile Edge Computing	Fog Computing
1	Device aware and few services aware, unaware of the entire domain	Device independent, intelligent, and aware of the entire fog domain
2	Limited control in the edge domain	Controls all devices in the domain
3	Not aware for the cloud	Extends the cloud to a fog level in a continuum
4	Limited network scope	Complete network scope
5	No IoT vertical awareness	Support and enabler for multiple IoT verticals
6	No IoT vertical integration	Integrates multiple verticals
7	Uses Edge Controllers that are focused on edge device command and control	Uses fog nodes that are very versatile and capable of performing a variety of functions like Real time Control, application hosting and management.
8	Security scope is limited to devices	End-to-End security through data ownership
9	Not designed with virtualization	Enables rich virtualization
10	Analytics scoped to a single device	Fog Analytics enables collection, processing and analysis of data from multiple devices in the edge for analysis, machine learning, anomaly detection and system optimization.
11	Edge Computing typically is embedded in and controls the edge. Certain devices require hard real time control and others require non real time control, and the Edge Computing performs these functions.	Fog Computing uses the devices and the embedded edge control. However, Fog Computing also enables virtual machines that host soft PLC used in real time control.

Source: (Nebbiolo Technologies, 2015)

Although these two concepts are different from each other, still they share a similar vision, which is guided by the future predictions that will be characterized with the Internet of Things, Internet of Everything, Tactile Internet and the existence of appropriate mobile and wireless connectivity. It can be concluded that fog computing is a better solution than MEC and cloud computing. However, better results can be achieved if both concepts are combined (Singh, Chiu, & Yang, 2016).

FOG COMPUTING FEATURES

The following subsections describe some of the main Fog Computing Features.

Ubiquity and Heterogeneity of Fog Nodes and Devices

The main factor which would bring fog into reality is the ubiquity of the devices, whose increase is driven by the user devices and sensors/actuators, and enabled by the presence and usage of devices everywhere around us for different services and applications. By decreasing the size of the device, the device portability is increased. However, the power consumption is also reduced, which may be crucial in some context application. This can be solved with packaging and power management technologies such as System on Chip and System in Package Technologies, 3D Micro batteries, RF powered Computing, etc. that aim to create smaller and more autonomous mobile devices which would run longer at a minimum price (Vaquero & Rodero-Merino, 2014).

Fog nodes come range from high performance servers, edge routers, gateways, access points, base stations, etc. These hardware platforms have varying levels of computation and storage capabilities, run various kinds of operating system (OS), and load different software applications. (Aazam, & Huh, 2016). Therefore, fog nodes are heterogeneous.

Heterogeneity of Fog Computing Network Infrastructure

The network infrastructure of fog computing is also heterogeneous, which includes high-speed links connecting to data center, as well as wireless access technologies (for example, WLAN, WiFi, 3G, 4G, ZigBee, etc.) connecting to the edge devices (Bonomi, Milito, Natarajan, & Zhu, 2014).

Support for Seamless Mobility

In fog computing scenarios, there are various mobile devices such as smart phones, vehicles, and smart watch, as well as there are also static end devices, such as traffic cameras. In addition, fog computing nodes in the radio access network can also be a mobile or static computing resource platform. (Varshney & Simmhan, 2017; Hossain & Atiquzzaman, 2013).

Therefore, it is essential for fog computing to communicate directly with mobile devices. Moreover, various mobile devices can also communicate directly to each other. The data does not have to be transmitted to the cloud or even the base station. The end device itself or intermediate devices process the massive data generated by the Internet of things, and truly realizing mobile data analysis. So, it can provide services for more extensive nodes.

Low Latency and Real Time Interactions

Fog nodes are capable to process and store data generated by sensors and devices, by network edge devices in local area network. This significantly reduces data movement across the Internet and provides speedy high-quality localized services supported by endpoints. Therefore, it provides low latency and meets the demand of real time interactions, especially for latency-sensitive or time sensitive applications (Bonomi, Milito, Zhu, & Addepalli, 2012), Tactile Internet, etc.

Effective Bandwidth Saving

Fog computing extends the computation and storage capabilities to the network edge to perform data processing and storing between the end nodes and traditional cloud. Some computation tasks, such as, data preprocessing, redundancy removing, data cleaning and filtering, valuable information extraction, are performed locally. Only part of useful data is transmitted to the cloud, and most of the data don't need to be transmitted over the Internet. In this way, fog computing saves the bandwidth effectively, especially for big data processing.

Geographical Distribution and Decentralized Data Analytic

In IoT and ubiquitous computing environment, the purpose is to achieve the interconnection and interworking among ubiquitous things, which are huge in number, and widely distributed. The characteristic of geographical distribution and decentralized data analytics can effectively meet the above demands.

The fog computing architecture consists of large number of widely geographically distributed nodes, that have the ability to track and derive the locations of end devices in order to support the mobility. Instead to process and store information in centralized cloud computing data centers far away from end-user, the decentralized architecture of fog computing ensures the proximity of data analytics to the customer. This characteristic can support faster analysis of big data, better location-based services, and more powerful capabilities of real-time decision making.

For example, fog computing can provide a wealth of Internet of Vehicles (IoV) services (including traffic security and data analysis, urban and road conditions, entertainment information, etc.) based on the connection and interaction of vehicle to vehicle, vehicle to access points (Kang, Wang, & Luo, 2016).

Interoperability

Due to their heterogeneous nature, fog nodes and end devices come from different providers and are usually deployed in the various environments. Therefore, fog computing nodes and devices must be able to interoperate and cooperate from different providers in order to cope with wide range of services and seamlessly support certain services (Kang, Wang, & Luo, 2016).

Network Management

The configuration and the maintenance of many different types of services running on many heterogeneous devices would only exacerbate the current management problems. Therefore, in fog computing environment heterogeneous devices and their running services need to be managed in a more homogeneous manner with the following technologies: Network Function Virtualization (NFV); small edge clouds to host services close to, or at the endpoints; and peer-to-peer (P2P)- and sensor network-like approaches for auto-coordination of applications (Vaquero & Rodero-Merino, 2014).

NFV is the reaction of telecom operators to their lack of agility and constant need for reliable infrastructures. It is capable of dynamically deployment for on-demand network services, or user-services. Software Defined Networks (SDNs) are one of the main enablers for NFV. For example, the router can be seen as an SDN-enabled virtual infrastructure where NFV and application services are deployed close to the place where they are actually going to be used, which would result in cheaper and more agile operations. However, NFV capabilities still do not reach end user devices and sensors.

Telecom operators had already started to deploy clouds in their Long-Term Evolution (LTE) Networks closer to the edge (to the user), because the Evolved Packet Core (EPC) more efficiently delivers services close to users (at the edge) and confines traffic there while reducing the traffic overload with the help of SDNs. The fog would enable the devices to become virtual platform, that can lease some computing/storage capacity for applications to run on them.

The peer-to-peer (P2P) and sensor network-like approaches exploit the locality and allow endpoints to cooperate in order to achieve similar results, but can scale better, and can be implemented in a fog. A fog application can be seen as a Content Distribution Network (CDN) where a data is exchanged between peers. As a result, the applications and data are no longer required to stay in centralized data centers.

A part of a network and some user devices/sensor can act as mini-clouds in a fog computing environment. The mini clouds can be implemented by using droplets, or small pieces of code that run in a secured manner in devices at the edge with minimum interaction with central coordinating elements, and thus reducing the unnecessary and undesired uploads of data to central servers in corporate data centers. The users are able to retain control and ownership of their own data and applications, and the scalability is improved.

Fog Connectivity

The presence of many mobile devices that consume and produce big data at the edge of the network may cause a huge bottleneck in the fog (Vaquero & Rodero-Merino, 2014). On physical level the following technologies can cope with this: LTE-Advanced, WiFi ac, Bluetooth Low Energy, ZigBee, etc.

On the network level, each node must be able to act as a router for its neighbors and must be resilient to node churn (nodes entering and leaving the network) and mobility. Mobile Ad-hoc Networks (MANETs) and Wireless Mesh Networks (WMNs) can provide these functionalities (Vaquero & Rodero-Merino, 2014). MANET would enable the formation of densely populated networks without requiring fixed and costly infrastructures to be available beforehand.

WMNs on the other side use mesh routers at its core. Nodes can use the mesh routers to get connectivity, or other nodes if no direct link with the routers can be established. Routers would grant access to other networks such as cellular, Wi-Fi, etc.

On higher levels some protocols already exist for IoT, such as Message Queue Telemetry Transport (MQTT) and Constrained Application Protocol (CoAP), that provide low resource consumption and resilience to failure (Vaquero & Rodero-Merino, 2014). The network and IoT protocols can benefit from data locality, since they no longer need to send all the data around the world all the time, except for potential congestion problems at the edge of the network. Data locality has also a very positive impact on privacy.

Fog Privacy and Security

The greatest concern of fog users is data ownership, i.e. data security and privacy (Stojmenovic & Wen, 2014; Stolfo, Salem, & Keromytis, 2012). One method to maintain the privacy is by storing encrypted sensitive data in traditional clouds. However, the existing cloud computing data protection mechanisms such as encryption have failed in preventing data theft attacks, especially those perpetrated by a malicious insider.

However, the value of stolen information can be decreased. This can be achieved through a preventive disinformation attack, by using the following additional security features: user behavior profiling, decoys and combination of both (Stolfo, Salem, & Keromytis, 2012).

User behavior profiling is used to model the normal user behavior, i.e. how, when, and how much a user accesses his/her information in the cloud (Stolfo, Salem, &

Keromytis, 2012). Such profiles contain volumetric information, i.e. how many files are accessed and how often. The occurrence of abnormal access to a user information in the cloud can be determined by monitoring this normal user behavior, based partially upon the scale and the scope of data being transferred.

Decoys are any bogus information that can be generated on demand. They are used to:

- Validate whether data access is authorized when abnormal information access is detected, and;
- Confuse the attacker with bogus information (Stolfo, Salem, & Keromytis, 2012).

The serving decoys would confuse the malicious attacker into believing that he/she has ex-filtrated useful information, but he/she has not. The attacks can be prevented by deploying decoys within the fog by the service customer and within personal on-line social networking profiles by the individual users.

A combination of decoys with user behavior profiling would provide unprecedented levels of security for the fog, and would improve detection accuracy. When the access to user information is correctly identified as an unauthorized access, the fog security system would deliver unbounded amounts of decoy information to the attacker. Thus, the true user data is protected from unauthorized disclosure. When abnormal access to the fog service is not recognized, decoy information may be returned by the fog and delivered in such a way as to appear completely legitimate and normal. The true owner of the information, would identify when decoys are returned by the fog. Hence the legitimate user could alter the fog responses through a variety of means, such as challenge questions, to inform the fog security system that has inaccurately detected an unauthorized access. At the moment the existing security mechanisms do not provide this level of security (Stolfo, Salem, & Keromytis, 2012).

Low Energy Consumption

Since the fog computing nodes are widely dispersed geographically, it will not generate a lot of heat due to concentration, and need not additional cooling system. In addition, short range communication mode and some optimal energy Management Policies of mobile nodes evidently reduce communication energy consumption (Zhang, Niyato, Wang, & Dong, 2016). This would lead to reduce power consumption, save energy and decrease the cost. Therefore, fog computing would provide a greener computing paradigm.

FOG COMPUTING RESEARCH DIRECTIONS

Many of the ideas in Fog Computing have evolved from Peer-To-Peer (P2P) networks, Mobile Ad Hoc Network (MANET) and edge computing (Chiang, 2015). Compared to P2P networks, fog is not just about content sharing (or data plane as a whole), but also network measurement, control and configuration, and service definition. Compared to MANET, today there are much more powerful and diverse off-the-shelf edge devices and applications, together with the broadband mobile and wireless networks. Compared to edge computing, in the edge devices in fog computing environment may optimize among themselves, and they collectively measure and control the rest of the network.

Fog computing also relocates the operating functions on digital objects of Information Centric Networks and the virtualized functions in Software Defined Networks at the network edge (Chiang, 2015). Because fog computing is recently new emerged paradigm there are many challenging questions that need to be resolved, such as:

- **Cloud-Fog Interface and Fog-Fog Interface**: Cloud would remain useful as Fog arises. The tasks that require real-time processing, end user objectives or low-cost leverage of idle resources should go to Fog, while the tasks that require massive storage, heavy-duty computation, or wide area connectivity. Therefore, the cloud-fog interface and fog-fog interface need clearly to defined in order to make the transfer of information much easier.
- **Interactions between Smart User Device Hardware and Operating Systems:** Once the operating functions are moved on smart user devices, the interface with their OS and hardware becomes essential, particularly for pooling idle edge resources.
- **Trustworthiness and Security (Vaquero & Rodero-Merino, 2014):** Because of the proximity to end users and locality on the edge, fog computing nodes can act as the first node of access control and encryption, provide contextual integrity and isolation, and enable the control of aggregating privacy-sensitive data before it leaves the edge.
- **Convergence and Consistency Arising Out of Local Interactions:** Typical concerns of distributed control, divergence/oscillation and inconsistency of global states, become more acute in a massive, under-organized, possibly mobile crowd with diverse capabilities and virtualized pool of resources shared unpredictably. Use cases in edge analytics and stream mining provide additional challenges on this recurrent challenge in distributed systems.

- **A Decision of What Kind of Information to Keep Between Distributed (Local) and Centralized (Global) Architectures**: While maintaining resilience through redundancy.
- **Distributed P2P Mobile Cloud Computing Among the Smart User Devices**: In order to guarantee certain QoS/QoE level.

CONCLUSION

This chapter provided an introduction and overview of fog computing. Initially it provided an overview of cloud computing, mobile edge computing, and fog computing. Then was made a comparison between fog computing and cloud computing, as well as fog computing and mobile edge computing. After that fog computing features were discussed. Finally, at the end fog computing open research directions and were provided.

Fog computing is an extension of the traditional cloud-based computing model where implementations of the architecture can reside in multiple layers of a network's topology. Due to its proximity to end-users, its dense geographical distribution, and its support for mobility, fog computing reduces service latency, and improves QoS, resulting in superior user-experience. It is well positioned for real-time big data analytics, emerging IoE applications, 5G, Tactile Internet, etc.

However, all the benefits of cloud should be preserved with these extensions to fog, including containerization, virtualization, orchestration, manageability, and efficiency. Therefore, many challenging questions such as cloud-fog interface, and fog-fog interface, security, etc. need to be resolved in order fog computing together with cloud computing to be fully operational.

In the future, more and more virtual network functionality would be executed in a fog computing environment, which would provide mobiquitous service to the users. This should enable new services paradigms such as Anything as a Service (AaaS) where devices, terminals, machines, and also smart things and robots would become innovative tools that would produce and use applications, services and data.

REFERENCES

Aazam, M., & Huh, E. N. (2016). Fog computing: The cloud-iot/ioe middleware paradigm. *IEEE Potentials*, *35*(3), 40–44. doi:10.1109/MPOT.2015.2456213

Adibi, S. (2014). Biomedical Sensing Analyzer (BSA) for Mobile-Health (m-Health) – LTE. *IEEE Journal of Biomedical and Health Informatics*, *18*(1), 345–351. doi:10.1109/JBHI.2013.2262076 PMID:24403433

Ahmed, A., & Ahmed, E. (2016). A Survey on Mobile Edge Computing. *IEEE International Conference on Itelligent System and Control (ISCO 2016)*. 10.1109/ISCO.2016.7727082

Ahmed, E., Gani, A., Sookhak, M., Hamid, S. H., & Xia, F. (2015). Application Optimization in Mobile Cloud Computing: Motivation, Taxonomies, and Open Challenges. *Journal of Network and Computer Applications*, *2*, 52–68. doi:10.1016/j.jnca.2015.02.003

Atzori, L., Iera, A., & Morabito, G. (2010). The internet of things: A survey. *Computer Networks*, *54*(15), 2787–2805. doi:10.1016/j.comnet.2010.05.010

Bahl, P., Han, Y. R., Li, E. L., & Satyanarayanan, M. (2012). Advancing the State of Mobile Cloud Computing. *Proceedings of the 3rd ACM workshop on Mobile cloud computing and services (MCS 2012)*, 21 – 28. 10.1145/2307849.2307856

Beck, M., Werner, M., Feld, S., & Schimper, S. (2014). Mobile edge computing: A taxonomy. *Sixth International Conference on Advances in Future Internet*.

Bonomi, F., Milito, R., Natarajan, P., & Zhu, J. (2014). *Fog Computing: A Platform for Internet of Things and Analytics*. Springer International Publishing.

Bonomi, F., Milito, R., Zhu, J., & Addepalli, S. (2012). Fog Computing and its Role in the Internet of Things. *Proceedings of the First Edition of the ACM SIGCOMM Workshop on Mobile Cloud Computing (MCC 2012)*. 10.1145/2342509.2342513

Brech, B., Jamison, J., Shao, L., & Wightwick, G. (2013). *The Interconnecting of Everything*. IBM Corp.

Brown, G. (2013). *Converging Telecom and IT in the LTE RAN*. White paper at Heavy Reading on behalf on Samsung Cloud Computing Principles and Paradigms.

Chiang, M. (2015). *Fog Networking: An Overview on Research Opportunities*. White Paper.

Dialogic Corporation. (2010). *Introduction to Cloud Computing*. Dialogic Corporation White Paper.

Dihn, T. H., Lee, C., Niyato, D., & Wang, P. (2011). A Survey of Mobile Cloud Computing: Architecture, Applications, and Approaches. *Wireless Communications and Mobile Computing, Wiley*, *13*(18), 1587–1611.

Ericsson. (2016). *Ericsson Mobility Report on the Pulse of the Networked Society.* Stockholm, Sweden: Ericsson.

Fowler, S. (2013). Survey on Mobile Cloud Computing Challenges Ahead. *IEEE CommSoft E-Letters*, 2(1), 13–17.

Gao, L., Luan, T. H., Liu, B. W. Z., & Yu, S. (2017). Fog Computing and Its Applications in 5G. In 5G Mobile Communications (pp. 571-593). Springer International Publishing Switzerland.

Goyal, S. (2014). Public vs Private vs Hybrid vs Community – Cloud Computing: A Critial Review. *International Journal of Computer Network and Information Security*, 6(3), 20–29. doi:10.5815/ijcnis.2014.03.03

Gupta, H., Chakraborty, S., Ghosh, K. S., & Buyya, R. (2017). Fog Computing in 5G Networks: An Application Perspective. In Cloud and Fog Computing in 5G Mobile Networks: Emerging advances and applications (pp. 23-54). The Institute of Engineering and Technology (IET), IET Telecommunications Series 70.

Hoang, D. B., & Chen, L. (2010). Mobile cloud for assistive healthcare (mocash). *Services Computing Conference (APSCC).*

Hossain, M. S., & Atiquzzaman, M. (2013). Cost analysis of mobility protocols. *Telecommunication Systems*, 52(4), 2271–2285. doi:10.100711235-011-9532-2

ITU-T. (2013). *Cloud Computing Framework and High Level Requirements.* ITU-T Recommendation Y.3501.

ITU-T. (2013). *Cloud Computing Infrastructure Requirements.* ITU-T Recommendation Y.3510.

Jovović, I., & Forenbacher, I. M. P. (2015). Massive Machine-Type Communications: An Overview and Perspectives Towards 5G. *The 3rd International Virtual Research Conference In Technical Disciplines.*

Kang, K., Wang, C., & Luo, T. (2016). Fog computing for vehicular ad-hoc networks: Paradigms, scenarios, and issues. *Journal of China Universities of Posts and Telecommunications*, 23(2), 56–96. doi:10.1016/S1005-8885(16)60021-3

Khan, A. R., Othman, M., Madani, S. A., & Khan, S. U. (2014). *Survey of Mobile Cloud Computing Application Models. IEEE.*

Kitanov, S., & Janevski, T. (2014). State of the Art: Mobile Cloud Computing. *Proceedings of the Sixth IEEE International Conference on Computational Intelligence, Communication Systems and Networks 2014 (CICSYN 2014)*, 153-158. 10.1109/CICSyN.2014.41

Kitanov, S., Monteiro, E., & Janevski, T. (2016). 5G and the Fog – Survey of Related Technologies and Research Directions. *Proceedings of the 18th Mediterranean IEEE Electrotechnical Conference MELECON 2016*. 10.1109/MELCON.2016.7495388

Liu, G., Hou, X., Jin, J., Wang, F., Wang, Q., Hao, Y., ... Deng, A. (2017). 3-D-MIMO With Massive Antennas Paves the Way to 5G Enhanced Mobile Broadband: From System Design to Field Trials. *IEEE Journal on Selected Areas in Communications*, *35*(6), 1222–1233. doi:10.1109/JSAC.2017.2687998

Liu, Y. J. E., Fieldsend, E. J., & Min, G. (2017). A Framework of Fog Computing: Architecture, Challenges and Optimization. *IEEE Access: Practical Innovations, Open Solutions*, *5*, 25445–25454. doi:10.1109/ACCESS.2017.2766923

Mitchell, S., Villa, N., Stewart-Weeks, M., & Lange, A. (2013). *The Internet of Everything for Cities Connecting People, Process, Data, and Things to Improve the 'Livability' of Cities and Communities*. CISCO, white paper.

Mouradian C., Naboulsi D., Yangui S., Glitho H. R., Morrow J. M., & Polakos A. P. (2017). A Comprehensive Survey on Fog Computing: State-of-the-art and Research Challenges. *IEEE Communications Surveys and Tutorials*, 1 – 51.

NebbioloTechnologies. (2015). *Fog vs Edge Computing v1.1*. Milpitas, CA: Nebbiolo Technologies Inc.

NIST. (2013). *NIST Cloud Computing Standards Roadmap*. NIST Special Publication 500-291, Version 2.

OpenFog Consortium. (2017). *OpenFog Reference Architecture for Fog Computing*. OpenFog Consortium Architecture Working Group.

Peng, M., Li, Y., Jiang, J., Li, J., & Wang, C. (2014). Heterogeneous cloud radio access networks: A new perspective for enhancing spectral and energy efficiencies. *IEEE Wireless Communications*, *21*(6), 126–135. doi:10.1109/MWC.2014.7000980

Peng, M., Li, Y., Zhao, Z., & Wang, C. (2015). System architecture and key technologies for 5G heterogeneous cloud radio access networks. *IEEE Network*, *29*(2), 6–14. doi:10.1109/MNET.2015.7064897 PMID:26504265

Peng, M., Yan, S., Zhang, K., & Wang, C. (2016). Fog Computing based Radio Access Networks: Issues and Challenges. *IEEE Network*, *30*(4), 46–53. doi:10.1109/MNET.2016.7513863

Pfaff, B. J., Pettit, J., & Koponen, T. (2015). *The design and implementation of open vSwitch*. Networked Systems Design and Implementation.

Qureshi, S. S., Ahmad, T., & Shuja-ul-islam, K. R. (2011). Mobile Cloud Computing as Future for Mobile Applications – Implementation Methods and Challenging Issues. *Proceedings of IEEE Conference on Cloud Computing and Intelligence Systems (CCIS)*.

Sabarish, K., & Shaji, R. (2014). A Scalable Cloud Enabled Mobile Governance Framework. *Global Humanitarian Technology Conference - South Asia Satellite (GHTC-SAS)*. 10.1109/GHTC-SAS.2014.6967554

Satyanarayanan, M., Bahl, P., Caceres, R., & Davies, N. (2009). The Case for VM-based Cloudlets in Mobile Computing. *IEEE Pervasive Computing*, *8*(4), 14–23. doi:10.1109/MPRV.2009.82

Singh, S., Chiu, Y., & Yang, Y. T. (2016). Mobile Edge Fog Computing in 5G Era: Architecture and Implementation. *2016 International Computer Symposium*.

Sqalli, H. M., Al-saeedi, M., Binbeshr, F., & Siddiqui, M. (2012). UCloud: Simulated Hybrid Cloud for a University Environment. *IEEE 1st International Conf. on Cloud Networking (CLOUDNET)*.

Stojmenovic, I., & Wen, S. (2014). The Fog Computing Paradigm: Scenarios and Security Issues. *Federated Conference on Computer Science and Information Systems, 2*(5).

Stolfo, S. J., Salem, M. B., & Keromytis, A. D. (2012). Fog Computing: Mitigating Insider Data Theft Attacks in the Cloud. *Proceeding of IEEE Symposium on Security and Privacy Workshops (SPW)*. 10.1109/SPW.2012.19

Sun, G., & Shen, J. (2014). Facilitating Social Collaboration in Mobile Cloud-based learning: A Teamwork as a Service (TaaS) Approach. *IEEE Transactions on Learning Technologies*, *7*(3), 207–220. doi:10.1109/TLT.2014.2340402

Vaquero, L. M., & Rodero-Merino, L. (2014). Finding your Way in the Fog: Towards a Comprehensive Definition of Fog Computing. *ACM SIGCOMM Computer Communication Review Newsletter*, *44*(5), 27–32. doi:10.1145/2677046.2677052

Varshney, P., & Simmhan, Y. (2017). *Demystifying Fog Computing: Characterizing Architectures, Applications and Abstractions*. arXiv:1702.06331

Wu, J., Yuen, C., Cheung, N.-M., Chen, J., & Chen, C. (2015). Enabling Adaptive High-frame-rate Video Streaming in Mobile Cloud Gaming Applications. *IEEE Transactions on Circuits and Systems for Video Technology, 1-1.*

Yilmaz, O. N., Wang, Y.-P. E., & Johansson, N. A. (2015). Analysis of ultra-reliable and low-latency 5G communication for a factory automation use case. *IEEE International Conference on Communication Workshop (ICCW).* 10.1109/ICCW.2015.7247339

Yu, Y. (2016). Mobile Edge Computing Towards 5G: Vision, Recent Progress, and Open Challenges. *China Communications, 13*(Supplement No. 2), 89–99. doi:10.1109/CC.2016.7833463

Zhang, S., Zhang, S., Chen, X., & Huo, X. (2010). Cloud Computing, Research and Development Trend. *Proceedings of the 2nd IEEE International Conference on Future Networks.*

Zhang, Y., Niyato, D., Wang, P., & Dong, I. K. (2016). Optimal energy management policy of mobile energy gateway. *IEEE Transactions on Vehicular Technology, 65*(5), 3685–3699. doi:10.1109/TVT.2015.2445833

Zhang, Z., Zhang, J., & Ying, L. (n.d.). *Multimedia streaming in cooperative mobile social networks.* Academic Press.

Chapter 2
Fog Computing and Its Challenges

Vighnesh Srinivasa Balaji
Ramaiah Institute of Technology, India

ABSTRACT

In recent times, the number of internet of things (IoT) devices/sensors increased tremendously. To support the computational demand of real-time latency-sensitive applications of largely geo-distributed IoT devices/sensors, a new computing paradigm named fog computing has been introduced. In this chapter, the authors will introduce fog computing, its difference in comparison to cloud computing, and issues related to fog. Among the three issues (i.e. service, structural, and security issues), this chapter scrutinizes and comprehensively discusses the service and structural issues also providing the service level objectives of the fog. They next provide various algorithms for computing in fog, the challenges faced, and future research directions. Among the various uses of fog, two scenarios are put to use.

INTRODUCTION

In recent times the number of internet of things has increased rapidly in such a way the use of "Cloud Computing" is not sufficient. Due to the increasing need for real-time latency-sensitive applications of geo-distributed devises a new computing paradigm called "Fog Computing" has been introduced. Generally, Fog extends the services of the cloud-based computing, storage and networking facilities as the fog resides closer to the Internet of Things (IOT) devices. Fog computing is a distributed computing paradigm that acts as an intermediate layer in between Cloud data centres and IoT devices/sensors. Fog computing was introduced by Cisco in

DOI: 10.4018/978-1-5225-6070-8.ch002

Copyright © 2019, IGI Global. Copying or distributing in print or electronic forms without written permission of IGI Global is prohibited.

2012 to resolve the challenges faced by cloud computing. Since cloud computing is geo-centric, it often fails to deal with storage and processing demands of billions of geo-centered IoT devices. Fog datacentres are distributed at the edge of the network along with latency-sensitive requirements. However, fog computing does not substitute cloud computing, rather these two complement each other which allows the users to experience a new breed of computing technology that provides the advantages of both the paradigms (Haruna, Abdu, Manis, Francisca, Oladipo, Ezendu, & Ariwa, 2017).

In simple words, computation done at the network's edge is referred to as fog computing, with its purpose to provide computing, storage and connectivity services to the users at the network edge. It's a supporting computer paradigm for the internet of things and will also boost the development of IOT applications (Makwana, 2017). This paper scrutinizes the challenges related to Fog computing, ways to overcome them and future research directions.

DIFFERENCE BETWEEN FOG AND CLOUD

Cloud computing is usually a model for enabling convenient, on-demand network use of a shared pool of configurable computing resources (e.g., networks, servers, storage, applications, and services) that may be rapidly provisioned and released with minimal management effort or vendor interaction. Cloud is located within the network with various topologies, speeds and no central control due to which there are a few qualities of service factors unresolved. One such issue is latency, as many applications require real time data processing, and services provided by the cloud cannot satisfy these requirements. Another such a problem is security and privacy. In the internet today, the applications are located far off from the service providers and so depending on the number of intermediate nodes the data moves through public cloud thus compromising confidentiality and integrity of the data as specified in Figure 1.

Fog computing was introduced by CiscoSystems as new a model to ease wireless data transfer to distributed devices in the Internet of Things (IoT) network paradigm. Fog Computing acts as a paradigm that extends Cloud computing and brings its related services to the network edge. Fog, similar to Cloud, provides data, compute, storage, and application services to end-users. The characteristics distinguishing Fog are its dense geographical distribution, its proximity to end-users, and its support for mobility. By doing so, it improves QoS and also reduces latency, increases its mobility which supports the internet of everything (IoE). Thanks to its wide geographical distribution the Fog paradigm is well positioned for real time big data and real time analytics. Fog supports densely distributed data collection points,

Figure 1. Confidentiality and integrity of the data

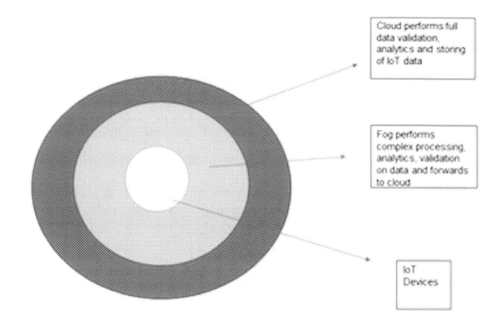

Table 1. Differences between Fog and Cloud Computing (Maher, 2015)

Cloud Computing	Fog Computing
Requires more time as it involves processing of data and applications in a cloud	Requires less time as processing of data and application is done at network edge rather than working on a centralized cloud
Sending every bit of data over a cloud channel results in a bandwidth problem	Instead of sending every bit of data over cloud channel, they were aggregated at certain points which reduces the demand for bandwidth
Depending on remote servers, results in slow response time and scalability problems	It is possible to remove the problem of response time and scalability problems by placing small edge servers in the visibility of the users

hence adding a fourth axis to the often-mentioned Big Data dimensions (volume, variety, and velocity).

Fog

• Fog nodes are geographically distributed over the edge each network and are logically decentralized as different nodes are owned by different organizations which makes them unreliable.

- Provide transient storage, often 1–2 hours.
- Send periodic data summaries to the cloud.

Cloud

- Cloud servers are centralized and situated in large warehouse like datacentres. This allows for recovery, load balancing and failure recovery which makes them more reliable.
- Receives and aggregates data summaries from many fog nodes.
- Stores large amounts data and performs analysis on IOT data. (CISCO, 2015).

SERVICE LEVEL OBJECTIVES

The fog has various services at different stages and each service pertains to a particular functionality, each crucial and different in its own way. However, each service needs to performed with certain objectives kept in mind. E.g. the services must ensure there is no latency in their execution.

Here are a few objectives of the services provided by the Fog.

1. Latency Management

The most severe dis-advantage of cloud is the time latency, this has to be overcome using Fog computing. Each service will have a maximum tolerable threshold for service delivery which gives us the maximum tolerance of a service or a QoS requirement and we must ensure that the service needed is given with this threshold. This is done using Latency Management. This can be done in various ways one such was where nodal collaboration is emphasized, so that any service can be distributed among all the nodes so that the service is provided within the threshold (Oueis, Strinati, Sardellitti, & Barbarossa, 2015).

Another way is to distribute tasks equally between the client and fog nodes so as to improve the latency problem (Zeng, Gu, Guo, Cheng, & Yu, 2016). Yet another solution is to use a low latency fog network. The main objective here is to select a fog node among the entire network that provides the least latency.

2. Cost Management

Cost management in Fog computing is related to Capital Expenses(CAPEX) and Operating Expenses(OPEX). The main contributor of CAPEX is the deployment cost of the fog nodes and the network. One way to reduce to this to optimize the number of nodes based on their functionality and also to optimize the places where the nodes have to be placed (Zhang, Lin, Yin, & Zhao, 2016). Fog nodes have been considered a platform to launch VMs. One way to reduce OPEX is to find a suitable set of fog nodes to host the VM so as to reduce total overdue cost (Gu, Zeng, Guo, Barnawi, & Xiang, 2015).

3. Network Management

Network management in Fog computing includes core-network congestion control, support for Software Define Network (SDN)/ Network Function Virtualization (NFV), assurance of seamless connectivity, etc.
    This can be done in three ways:

1. **Network Management:** The overhead of fog nodes which includes interaction with cloud and also with various IOT end devices and sensors greatly decrease efficiency. This burden of overhead can be solved using a layered architecture of fog nodes so that the computational tasks and overhead is distributed among the various layers (Aazam, & Huh, 2014).
2. **Virtualization:** Virtualization is one of the best ways to improve network management. This is done by virtualizing the conventional networking system. One of the key enablers of virtualized network is SDN. SDN networking technique that decouples the control plane from networking equipment and implements in software on separate servers. An important aspect of SDN is its support for NFV. NFV is a brilliant architectural concept that virtualizes traditional networking functions like Network Address Translation (NAT), Domain Name Service(DNS), caching etc.
3. **Connectivity:** This ensures seamless communication of end devices with other entitieslike Cloud, Fog, Desktop computers, Mobile devices, end devices, etc. despiteof their physical diversity. As a consequence, resource discovery, maintenance of communication and computation capacity become easier within the network. Several works in Fog computing have already targeted this issue and proposed new architecture of Fog nodes e.g. IoT Hub (Cirani, Ferrari, Iotti, & Picone, 2015) and Fog networking, Vehicular Fog Computing (Hou, Li, Chen, Wu, Jin, & Chen, 2016) for connectivity management and resource discovery.

4. Computational Management

In all the Fog nodes there is a lot of data needed to be processed and with the growth of IoT, computation on data is required every second.

Computation, again can vary among nodes depending in the applications and the services required. Computational management ensures all the computation of all the nodes have to equally distributed.

The most crucial Service Level Objective is proper Computational Management. This is done in three ways.

1. **Resource Estimation:** Knowing the exact resources required the resources can be allocated according to certain policies so that certain QoS could be achieved by which accurate service price can be imposed. Resource estimation policies are based on user characteristics, experienced QoE, features of service accessing devices etc. (Aazam, & Huh, 2016).
2. **Workload Allocation:** Ensures that there is maximum allocation of resources and minimum delay in the provision of services. The main reason for this introduction is to balance computation load on Fog nodes and client devices. As a consequence, overhead on both will be reduced (Zeng, Gu, Guo, Cheng, & Yu, 2016).
3. **Coordination:** Due to the distribution of fog nodes among various organizations, the deployment of large scale applications is done in various nodes. In such cases proper coordination among fog nodes is vital (Giang, Blackstock, Lea, & Leung, 2015).

5. Application Management

Programming platforms are essential for efficient application management. Besides, scalability and offloading techniques contribute to application management.

1. **Programming Platforms Provide Run Time Environment, Libraries and Packages to the Fog Nodes:** Due to the dynamic nature of the fog nodes assurance of proper programming platforms is challenging. To solve this challenge, a new programming platform called Mobile fog is introduced (Hong, Lillethun, Ramachandran, Ottenẅalder, & Koldehofe, 2013). This provides simplified abstraction of programming models to develop large scale applications.
2. **Scaling:** Refers to the adaption capability of applications even after unexpected events. Scaling techniques also be applied inusers service access and application scheduling. To support scalable scheduling of data stream applications, architecture of a QoS-aware self-adaptive scheduler has been recently proposed in Fog computing.
3. **Offloading:** Refers to techniques to send tasks from resource constrained nodes to resource enriched nodes for computation (Carla, Mouradian, Diala, Naboulsi, Sami, Yangui... Polakos, 2017).

ISSUES RELATED TO FOG COMPUTING

The three main issues are discussed as follows:

1. Structural Issues
    a. Identification of techniques and metrics for inter nodal collaboration and resource sharing are vital and equally difficult as in Fog computing the nodes are distributed across the edge of the network and maybe shared or virtualized.
    b. The components used in Fog computing usually both edge and core network components have various kinds of processors but not usually equipped with general purpose computing. To provide general purpose computing to them might be difficult.
    c. Although the structural orientation is compatible with IOT, competency assurance in other networks like CDN, vehicular network is a real challenge.
    d. The selection of nodes, corresponding resource allocation is also crucial in Fog computing.
2. Service Oriented Issues
    a. Some fog nodes are resource enriched while others are resource constrained. Large scale applications when developed in resource constrained nodes makes it difficult for computations to continue. So, programming platforms are required.
    b. There must be specific policies to distribute computational tasks are resource among Fog nodes.
    c. There are many factors that affect the Service Level Agreement(SLA) e.g. service cost, energy usage, application characteristics, data flow etc.
3. Security Oriented Issues
    a. As fog nodes are distributed among various organizations, security concerns are rising. Authentication is required for services.
    b. The design of Fog nodes is based on networking, fog nodes are vulnerable to security attacks.
    c. Malicious users might also be present among the normal users, which may cause additional threats.

ALGORITHMS FOR COMPUTING IN THE FOGSYSTEM

Here we list a few existing algorithms for each sub-heading and their associated drawbacks. Like for any large-scale computing system, application-agnostic and application-specific algorithms have been proposed for fog. Furthermore, the application-agnostic algorithms cover the computing, storage/distribution, and energy consumption, like in most large-scale distributed computing systems. This section discusses the application- agnostic algorithms and the application-specific algorithms for fog systems.

Many algorithms have been proposed for computing in the fog systems. In the following, we review them. We first present compute resource sharing algorithms. We then cover task scheduling algorithms and present after that offloading and load redistribution algorithms. In each we suggest the best algorithms available.

Resource Sharing

In computing, resource sharing refers to one host making available computer resources to other hosts on the same network. It refers to a piece of information that can be remotely accessed for various reasons on any other computer. Inter process communication makes resource sharing possible.

When it comes to computing in the fog systems, a first aspect that has been investigated is the compute resource sharing and cooperation among the nodes. These aspects have been tackled so far in the fog stratum, with the objective of executing compute demands.

1. One way is to provide resource sharing among the fog nodes in the same fog domain. Fog nodes involve themselves in a one-to-one paring in such a way that the required task can be fulfilled. This algorithm defines a utility metric for a couple of nodes that account for communication costs. Using this metric, a node first finds a preference list of pairing nodes. The target node based on its previous level of pairing decides whether or not to make connection with this new node. This pairing continues to happen across the fog domain. The evaluation of this strategy shows that it outperforms a greedy approach when it comes to total utility. In this strategy Quality of Service criterion is not met and the evaluation is based on a small section of nodes and scalability and mobility of nodes criterions are also not met.

2. Another algorithm forms small cluster of nodes containing a small number of nodes that share resources for offloading. It aims at simultaneously forming clusters and respecting each node's latency constraint keeping the main objective to minimize power consumption. Even in this algorithm the mobility and scalability criterions are not met.

Task Scheduling

In computing, scheduling refers to the method in which work by some means is allocated to resources. The way in which task is scheduled by the fog nodes among the billions of tasks available to them is task scheduling.

As the fog systems provide additional computing capabilities at the edge of the network, a major question that they raise is how to manage task execution. More precisely, how to decide which tasks to execute in the IoT/end-user's stratum, the fog stratum, and the cloud stratum? On a finer level, to which nodes a particular task should be assigned? What metrics to consider in deriving decisions?

1. First algorithm's task scheduling operates in two major steps. First step allocates computational resources to each node based on a specific objective and at the end of this step some request may not be processed due to lack of resources and this carried out in the next step again based on a particular order and objective. However, this algorithm fails to meet the scalability and mobility of nodes criterion.

2. A second algorithm proposes a proactive resource sharing algorithm to all users based on their historical data and allocates resources to users that are loyal to the services requested. By doing this the QoS has greatly improved. In addition to this the algorithm also has a pricing strategy that accounts for user's loyalty.

3. A third algorithm considers that in a fog domain in the fog stratum, a *fog server manager* receives the user's requests and is responsible for matching the fog resources and the user demands. Upon the receipt of a request, the *fog server manager* verifies whether enough computational resources are available in the fog domain. Depending on the available resources, either it executes all tasks, executes part of them and postpones the execution of others, or it transfers the demand to nodes in cloud stratum, in order to run tasks over the cloud nodes. Simulation results show that the proposed algorithm is more efficient than other existing strategies aiming at optimizing the response time or enabling load-balancing. It leads to a lower maximum response time and lower maximum processing time values, at lower costs. Even this like the previous algorithms fails to meet the scalability and mobility criterions.

Offloading and Load Redistribution

Among the various Fog nodes available the tasks that are allocated to each node may vary for various reasons. Each task requires resources to complete and if a node has too many tasks then its resources may get depleted, so load among the various nodes have to redistributed properly.

As discussed in the previous section, several task-scheduling algorithms have been proposed. While they allow distributing compute tasks over compute nodes across the three strata of the system, the possibility of unbalance in terms of workload has not been discussed. Thus, the need for the algorithms that perform offloading and load redistribution in the system has increased.

One of the algorithms start with an atomization step that maps physical resources into virtual resources. A graph representing the system is then built. In this graph, a node represents a virtual resource with a certain capacity and a couple of these nodes are linked through edges, weighted by the bandwidth of communication link between them. Upon the arrival of new fog nodes, in order to balance the loads, redistribution of loads in its neighbourhood is done by the algorithm while accounting for the task distribution degree and the links among the nodes. In case of node removal, a reverse strategy is adopted. The evaluation of the algorithm is done against a static one from the literature. The results show the proposed strategy has led to a lower number of moves in the graph, which implies a lower migration cost. Additionally, it requires less time to derive results with respect to the static strategy.

ALGORITHMIC CHALLENGES AND RESEARCH DIRECTIONS

In this section, the most important algorithms to fog computing are discussed along with the challenges faced and their future research directions.

Heterogeneity

By heterogeneity, we mean the level of difference of computational facilities and storage capabilities of the systems, this degree of heterogeneity has huge impact on performance. In this respect, two complementary challenges are addressed:

1.   First challenge concerns existing computing and storage devices around us, e.g., end-user mobile devices that can serve as fog nodes. These end devices which act as fog nodes apart from their own functionality need to allocate memory and resources to serve the requests from other fog nodes. The question is how much of their resources can they spare to serve as fog nodes, capable of processing other devices requests and storing their content? Actual usage patterns are concluded from deriving the actual usages of the storage resources

and computing of the existing devices. When conducted over a large variety of potential devices, assessing the capabilities that these devices can offer are analysed. As a result, the degree of heterogeneity in terms of computing and storage capabilities that these devices impose on the system is determined. Adequate prediction models can then be derived accordingly to enable decision-making over the future. Such models can be inspired from those proposed in the context of volunteer computing systems (Sekma, Dridi, & Elleuch, 2015).

2. Second, apart from existing devices around us that can serve as fog nodes additional computing and storage nodes can be added in the system. These devices in turn participate in defining the heterogeneity degree of the system. Here, the question is how to decide the dimensioning and placement of these additional nodes. One research direction is to study the corresponding optimization problem. It aims to full-fill the demand of IoT/end-user devices in the fog system considered as an input. After consideration of a number of aspects the algorithm, which include power consumption and resource costs, would then optimize the dimensioning of nodes. (Farahani & Hekmatfar, 2009).

QoS Management

The incorporation of latency constraint addresses this problem. Along with the latency, other crucial performance metrics such as uplink and downlink bandwidth or resource usage costs on the user's side are generally not taken into account – which have to be addressed as a different challenge. Other algorithms, targeting resource utilization or particular applications, need in turn to account for different performance metrics and relevant costs. Instead of having these metrics as part of constraints, they should form the algorithm's objective. This can improve QoS, rather than imposing a limit on a certain QoS metric.

One big challenge is that QoS metrics are covered as individual objectives, instead of considering them together with other objectives, has not received significant attention so far. However, in reality, several objectives that can even be contradictory may need to be covered at the same time. One example is to minimize completion time and minimize power consumption costs in the fog system when managing compute resources. In this case, the need for more resources minimizing completion time in the system, in contrast to minimizing power consumption. Thus, there is always a trade-off to consider. Due to the complexity of such problems, so far, only has addressed such contradictive objectives. However, the study remains limited to a video streaming application in content delivery networks and only targets the distribution of content from the data centres to the fog nodes.

Scalability

Operation of an algorithm in the fog system over a large scale is very important. Validating an algorithm in a small-scale environment, with a few devices and nodes does not guarantee it performs well over a large scale. Despite the importance of this criterion, most of the proposed algorithms have been evaluated over small-scale scenarios.

Besides the considered scale, proposed algorithms need to operate in real-world conditions. Consider the case where a task scheduling algorithm needs to be operational for real-world traffic patterns. Most of the proposed algorithms except for a few experimental evaluations, have not been tested in real-world environment but only validated in simplistic simulation environments, with no clear motivation for system parameters. As a result, some other problems may arise when these algorithms are tested in a real-world environment, diverging from the expected performance. To handle these challenges, a possible research direction is to run real-world experimental evaluations over a large scale. However, due to high costs this may not be possible. Large-scale realistic evaluations remain the best option to compare the different algorithms. However, to do so, two major aspects are to be highlighted. First, as of now, we still unfortunately lack a clear knowledge of real-world system deployments. Second, we do not yet acquire a clear understanding of the real-world evolution of application and services consumption on the side of IoT/end-user devices. Only through machine learning techniques, characterization can only be achieved through thorough analysis of corresponding real-world traces. When acquired, proper models need to be derived based on it to enable proper evaluations through realistic simulations.

Mobility

Mobility poses significant challenges in fog systems when IoT devices are considered. The services provided by a Fog domain must be valid even if it crossed the domain of that fog through various other fog domains which needs proper strategies that allow handling the mobility however, efforts in this direction still remain limited. A migration strategy that allows moving components across fog domains according to the movement of devices. A research direction here is to derive realistic mobility models, to do so, real-world mobility traces need to be integrated into the analysis, as done in the case of VM migration in mobile cloud systems. Moreover, accurate mobility prediction methods are needed to complement algorithms operating in real-time. Depending on the context, these schemes would either target individual or group mobility and can be built based on collected traces of IoT/end-user devices.

Similarly, to manage the mobility of a fog node, we also need to ensure the offered services are not interrupted. In fact, the fog nodes' mobility is even more complex to handle, as it involves the serving resources availability. For instance, as a fog node leaves a fog domain, it implies the need to offload tasks assigned to it to other fog nodes in the system. Instead, as a fog node joins/creates a fog domain, additional/novel resources would be available for IoT/end-user devices that can be connected to it.

Federation

Among all the algorithms it is seen that that the federation has been mostly ignored. Resource sharing algorithms is considered among only among one distributor and not among various distributors. Indeed, federation among the distributors greatly improves the efficiency and functionality of the system. Indeed, the federation among providers extends the capabilities of the system and has not received so far, any attention from an algorithmic perspective.

USE CASES

A Fog System Use Case for CDN

To deliver Quality of Experience and delivering of video at a cost-efficient rate CDN is used. It uses two types of servers i.e. origin servers and surrogate servers. The content of the origin server is duplicated to the surrogate servers based on conditions like physical distance, network conditions, content availability. Cloud based CDN are recently developing, called CCDN. Some servers while providing a video game to an end user may be located at a greater physical distance and might therefore reduce the QoE. A potential solution is to introduce a fog stratum between the cloud and the end users.

In Figure 2, use-case suppose Jason wants to stream some video on his phone, the surrogate server replicates this data to access point A (action 1) and Jason can access (Action 2) it with lesser delay as compared to when it is given directly by the surrogate server. Now suppose Jessica also wants to access the same video can do some with increased QoE (Action 3). And now Jason moves to a different point further from A then point A distributes its content to Point B (Action 5) so that it can be accessed by Jason (Action 6) with a better QoE as when compared to the surrogate server replicating the data.

Figure 2. A Fog System Use Case for CDN

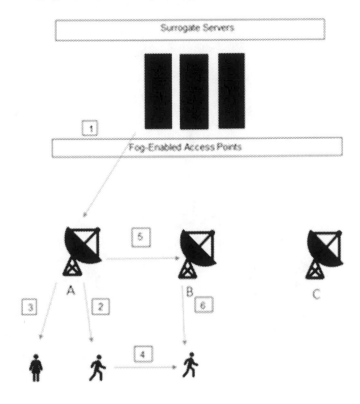

A Fog System Use Case for Fire Detection and Fighting

A Fire-detecting and Fire-fighting use case is provided. It dispatches firefighting robots based on the intensity of the fire, contour, wind intensity. It is made up of three components: *Fire Detector (A)*, *Firefighting Strategies (B)*, and *Robots Dispatcher (C)*. Usually these are located in the cloud far from the IoT devices but placing them in Fog stratum increases the QoE and reduces latency and chances to detect and fight fire are increased.

First the fire-detector or robot dispatcher are moved to the fog from the cloud (Action 1) and detecting of fire can be made with very low latency (Action 2). In case of fire the fire-detector notifies the fire-fighting strategies (Action 3) which communicates with the robot-dispatcher (Action 4) which fights the fire and extinguishes it (Action 5). Figure 3 shows the sample diagram of fire-fighting and detection algorithm (Carla, Mouradian, Diala, Naboulsi, Sami, Yangui... Polakos, 2017).

Figure 3. A Fog System Use Case for Fire Detection and Fighting

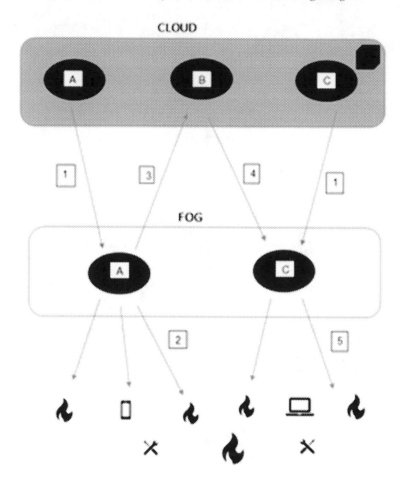

CONCLUSION

In this chapter we have learnt the basics of Fog computing and its fundamental difference to Cloud computing. In order to improve the QoS of Fog there are a few service level objectives which have to be met such as latency, cost, network, computational and application management. Although Fog computing has various advantages over Cloud computing, this too has certain issues to it which are classified as service, structural and service related issues. We have surveyed the various algorithms to compute in the Fog and the corresponding challenges faced in each. Moreover, based on these challenges the future research directions have been mentioned along with the use cases of Fog computing in day-to-day activities.

REFERENCES

Aazam, M., & Huh, E. N. (2014). *Fog computing and smart gateway based communication for cloud of things. In Future Internet of Things and Cloud (FiCloud).* IEEE.

Aazam, M., St-Hilaire, M., & Lung, C. H. (2016). Mefore: Qoe based resource estimation at fog to enhance qos in iot. *23rd International Conference on Telecommunications (ICT).* 10.1109/ICT.2016.7500362

Carla, Diala, & Sami, Roch, Glitho, Morrow, & Polakos. (2017). A Comprehensive Survey on Fog Computing: State-of-the-art and Research Challenges. *IEEE Communications Surveys and Tutorials.*

Cirani, S., Ferrari, G., Iotti, N., & Picone, M. (2015). The IoT hub: a fog node for seamless management of heterogeneous connected smart objects. *Sensing, Communication, and Networking-Workshops (SECONWorkshops). 12th Annual IEEE International Conference on IEEE.* 10.1109/SECONW.2015.7328145

CISCO. (2015). *Fog computing & the internet of things: extend the cloud to where the things are.* Retrieved from https://www.cisco.com/c/dam/en_us/solutions/trends/iot/docs /computing-overview.pdf

Farahani, R. Z., & Hekmatfar, M. (2009). *Facility Location, Concepts, Models, Algorithms and Case Studies. Contributions to management science.* Heidelberg, Germany: Physica-Verlag.

Giang, N. K., Blackstock, M., Lea, R., & Leung, V. C. M. (2015). Developing iot applications in the fog: A distributed dataflow approach. *5th International Conference on the Internet of Things (IOT).* 10.1109/IOT.2015.7356560

Gu, L., Zeng, D., Guo, S., Barnawi, A., Xiang, Y. (2015). Cost-efficient resource management in fog computing supported medical cps. *IEEE Transactions on Emerging Topics in Computing.*

Haruna, Manis, Oladipo, & Ariwa. (2017). *User Mobility and Resource Scheduling and Management in Fog Computing to Support IoT Devices.* IEEE.

Hong, K., Lillethun, D., Ramachandran, U., Ottenẅalder, B., & Koldehofe, B. (2013). Mobile fog: A programming model for large-scale applications on the internet of things. In *Proceedings of the second ACM SIGCOMM workshop on Mobile cloud computing.* ACM. 10.1145/2491266.2491270

Hou, X., Li, Y., Chen, M., Wu, D., Jin, D., & Chen, S. (2016). Vehicular fog computing: A viewpoint of vehicles as the infrastructures. *IEEE Transactions on Vehicular Technology, 65*(6), 3860–3873. doi:10.1109/TVT.2016.2532863

Intharawijitr, K., Iida, K., & Koga, H. (2016). *Analysis of fog model considering computing and communication latency in 5G cellular networks.* IEEE. doi:10.1109/ PERCOMW.2016.7457059

Maher. (2015). *IoT, from Cloud to Fog Computing.* Retrieved from https://blogs. cisco.com/ perspectives/iot-from-cloud-to-fog-computing

Mahmud, R., Kotagiri, R., & Buyya, R. (2018). Fog Computing: A Taxonomy, Survey and Future Directions. In B. Di Martino, K. C. Li, L. Yang, & A. Esposito (Eds.), *Internet of Everything. Internet of Things (Technology, Communications and Computing).* Singapore: Springer. doi:10.1007/978-981-10-5861-5_5

Makwana. (2016). *Introduction to Fog Computing.* AI-eHive.

Oueis, J., Strinati, E. C., Sardellitti, S., & Barbarossa, S. (2015). Small cell clustering for efficient distributed fog computing: A multi-user case. In Vehicular Technology Conference (VTC Fall). IEEE. doi:10.1109/VTCFall.2015.7391144

Sekma, N. C., Dridi, N., & Elleuch, A. (2015). Analyses toward a prediction system for a large-scale volunteer computing system. *2015 World Congress on Information Technology and Computer Applications (WCITCA).* 10.1109/WCITCA.2015.7367017

Zeng, D., Gu, L., Guo, S., Cheng, Z., & Yu, S. (2016). Joint optimization of task scheduling and image placement in fog computing supported software-defined embedded system. *IEEE Transactions on Computers, 65*(12), 3702–3712. doi:10.1109/TC.2016.2536019

Zeng, D., Gu, L., Guo, S., Cheng, Z., & Yu, S. (2016). Joint optimization of task scheduling and image placement in fog computing supported software-defined embedded system. *IEEE Transactions on Computers, 65*(12), 3702–3712. doi:10.1109/TC.2016.2536019

Zhang, W., Lin, B., Yin, Q., & Zhao, T. (2016). *Infrastructure deployment and optimization of fog network based on microdc and lrpon integration.* Peer-to-Peer Networking and Applications Springer.

Chapter 3
Fog Computing and Networking Architectures

Minal Moharir
R. V. College of Engineering, India

Bharat Rahuldhev Patil
R. V. College of Engineering, India

ABSTRACT

The demerits of cloud computing lie in the velocity, bandwidth, and privacy of data. This chapter focuses on why fog computing presents an effective solution to cloud computing. It first explains the primary motivation behind the use of fog computing. Fog computing, in essence, extends the services of the cloud towards the edge of the network (i.e., towards the devices nearer to the customer or the end user). Doing so offers several advantages. Some of the discussed advantages are scalability, low latency, reducing network traffic, and increasing efficiency. The chapter then explains the architecture to implement a fog network, followed by its applications. Some commercial fog products are also discussed, and a use case for an airport security system is presented.

INTRODUCTION

With continuous innovations in the fields of Internet of Things(IoT), Artificial Intelligence and Virtual Reality, there is an increase in the abundance of data. These technologies are changing the way people live, commute and work. With future 5G applications, data from homes, communities, hospitals, factories and other sources

DOI: 10.4018/978-1-5225-6070-8.ch003

Copyright © 2019, IGI Global. Copying or distributing in print or electronic forms without written permission of IGI Global is prohibited.

is expected to grow from 89 exabytes per year in 2016 to 194 exabytes per year by 2020. Current Cloud-only architectures cannot keep up with this increase in data.

Fog computing poses a promising solution to this problem. In order to enable data-dense use cases, Fog architectures selectively move compute, communication, storage and decision-making choices nearer to the network edge, where the source of the data lies. In this way, Fog computing establishes the missing link in the cloud-to-thing continuum. Is it frequently mistaken with edge computing, but it differs from edge computing in that fact that Fog works in tandem with Cloud, whereas edge computing excludes the Cloud. Also, Fog has a hierarchical structure whereas edge computing is defined by a limited number of layers.

Fog computing can be defined as *a horizontal, system-level architecture that distributes computing, storage, control and networking functions closer to the users along a cloud-to-thing continuum*. It is an extension of the Cloud-based computing model and hence, all the benefits of Cloud are preserved in these extensions including containerization, virtualization, orchestration, manageability, and efficiency.

A Fog network can be defined as *an architecture that uses one or a collaborative multitude of end-user clients or near-user edge devices to carry out a substantial amount of storage, communication and management*. Fog architectures can be centralized, distributed or a mixture of both. They are established using software, hardware or both. Fog architectures differ from Cloud architectures primarily in the following aspects:

- Fog employs a considerable amount of storage near or at the end-user whereas Cloud uses distributed large-scale data centers.
- Fog carries out significant quantity of communication near or at the end-user whereas Cloud communicates through a backbone network.
- Fog establishes a substantial amount of management near or at the end-user whereas Cloud is controlled mainly by gateways.

Cloud and Fog are not two independent choices rather they are interdependent, for example, coordination among devices in the Fog may partly depend upon the Cloud. In this manner, they also form a mutually beneficial continuum. Fog provides a strategic option to certain functions while others do well in the Cloud. In fact, the interface between Fog and Cloud is a major aspect of Fog research.

MOTIVATION

Fog computing has emerged due to two main factors - abundance of data and privacy. To explain the factor of ever growing data, consider Endomondo, a fitness and health tracking application with over thirty million users. Endomondo has released certain data statistics of their application. The statistics show that an average workout of a user generates 170 GPS tuples, and in a month's time this number can easily reach to around 6.3 million tuples. This in turn calculates to around 25,000 tuples per second. Within a single application, there is a considerable amount of data with high velocity. Consider then the real-time data sources in a typical city - data from health care chips, sensors in connected cars, sensors in pollution monitoring systems and many more. It is estimated that an average person creates around 650MB of data every day, and this amount is to double by the year 2020. Also, autonomous driving cars will generate terabytes of data every day. Cloud architectures do not have the capability to deal with such large amounts of data and velocity in real time. The second factor that cannot be dealt with by Cloud servers is the privacy of data. Many users are not comfortable releasing their data onto the Cloud even if it provides for detailed analysis and reports. Therefore the need arose to design computational and storage devices nearer to the source of the data and at the same time require connectivity to the Internet. Such devices are called edge devices and can collect and work on local data streams. On this note, Fog architectures have the capability to work on large amounts of data with confidentiality.

CHARACTERISTICS

As discussed, Fog computing extends the services of the Cloud to the edge devices as shown in Figure 1. It provides for distribution of computing power, networking and storage devices between the Cloud computing resources and the edge devices. Therefore Fog computing involves components of an application running concurrently both in the Cloud as well as between the sensors and the Cloud as shown in Figure 1.

Following are several advantages of Fog computing:

1. **Reduction of Network Traffic:** Day by day there is an increase in the number of smart devices being used by the people and in the industry. Cisco estimates that the number of devices worldwide could go up to 50 million in 2020. The increased number of sensors used in these devices demand that the computational capabilities be closer to the edge devices near the user rather than sending the data over networks to the Cloud. These sensors, depending on their configuration could send data every few seconds to every few hours. Therefore, it is necessary to filter out the useful information before sending a bulk of data to the Cloud. Hence, a Fog network acts as an analyzer of data and filters the data generated by these sensors to generate local views. This in turn decreases the volume of network traffic to be sent to the Cloud.

Figure 1. Cloud to the Edge of the Network

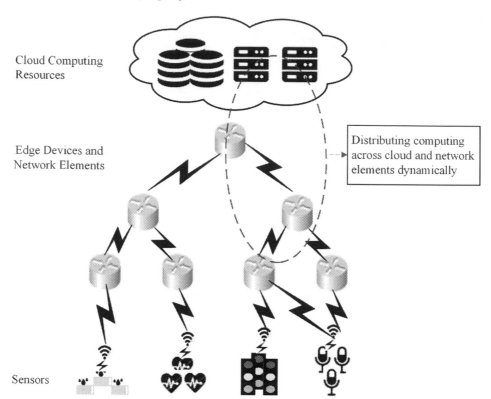

Cloud Computing
Resources

Edge Devices and
Network Elements

Distributing computing
across cloud and network
elements dynamically

Sensors

2. **Suitability for IoT Applications:** Certain applications do not necessarily need to connect to the Cloud every now and then in order to function efficiently. Instead, they need data from their immediate surroundings. Take for example, the Endomondo application which helps users track their health care data and provide statistics based on the data. If an Endomondo user wishes to find company for a particular activity, the applications can locate users who have similar interests in sports in his local area and suggest them. For this need, it makes logical sense to use local data in a Fog infrastructure rather than a Cloud. Another logical example would be that of a smart connected car. Self-driving cars such as the Tesla need to capture events that in the range of a few hundred metres ahead of it with extreme precision. Hence, here too by bringing processing power closer to the edge, Fog computing presents a compelling case.

3. **Low Latency:** Real-time data processing is needed by various mission critical systems. Some examples include robots, drones and braking systems in vehicles. In robots and drones, data is collected from their sensors and processed by a

control system. If these control systems were on the Cloud, this could lead to communication failures and slower reaction times. Hence by bringing computing power closer to the control system, Fog computing provides low latency reaction times to real-time applications.

4. **Scalability:** The Cloud is said to have virtually infinite resources, but the caveat here is that the Cloud might get congested if data is continuously being sent from a number of sources. Hence, this results in loss of data and produces a burden on the processing power of the Cloud. However, Fog computing processes the data near the source itself, thereby reducing the burden of processing on the Cloud. In this manner, Fog produces a solution to the increasing number of sources in a network and addresses the scalability issue.

5. **Efficiency:** An important characteristic of Fog networks is pooling of resources. For example, hundreds of gigabytes that sit idle among various household devices such as tablets, laptops and so on can be pooled. Similar pooling of resources can be done in a company or even a public area. Therefore, efficiency in Fog networks is increased in this manner. Resources that can be pooled extend to idle processing power, wireless connectivity and shared sensors.

ARCHITECTURE

A reference architecture for Fog computing is shown in Figure 2. The first layer (bottom layer) consists of the sensors, edge devices, gateways and user applications. This second layer provides network capabilities for communication among the components of the first layer as well as with the Cloud. The third layer consists of the Cloud services and resources. This layer provides processing power for compute intensive tasks such as IoT. It also has resources that support resource management. The next layer contains a software-defined resource management system that ensures quality of service in Fog applications and manages the infrastructure of the Fog network. The last layer consists of various applications and software that leverage the Fog network to provide service to the end users. The various elements described as present in Figure 2 are for reference only, all these elements need not be employed to build a Fog application.

The software-defined resource management layer in Figure 3 provides a number of services to ensure low latency, cost optimization and increase performance of applications. Hence, it acts as a middleware to optimize Cloud and Fog services. These services include:

1. **Flow and Task Placement:** This service constantly communicates with the monitoring service from which it receives task and flow information and keeps

Figure 2. Reference Architecture for Fog Computing

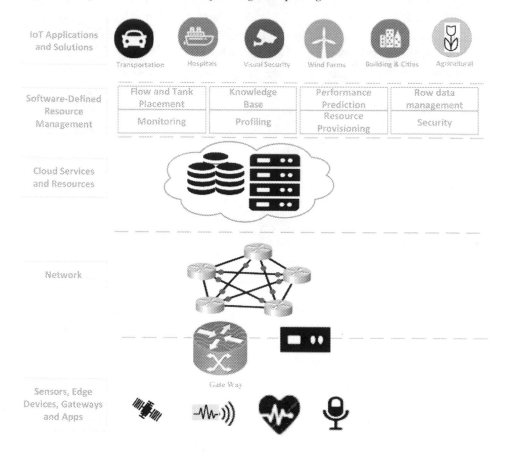

track of free Fog and network resources. It provides the gathered information to the Resource Provisioning service which carries out the dynamic allocation of resources.

2. **Knowledge Base:** Statistics are needed on past application transactions and demands in order to predict future needs beforehand. The knowledge base stores past data so that it can be used by other services in their decision-making processes.

3. **Performance Prediction:** This service uses the information gathered in the Knowledge Base to predict the performance of current Cloud resources. These predictions are used by the Resource Provisioning service to estimate the volume of extra resources that are needed when the performance of the Fog network is not as expected.

4. **Raw Data Management:** A service is required that can perform queries on the data sources. This service provides this functionality by providing views (result of a query) based on simple (SQL) or complex (MapReduce) queries.

5. **Monitoring:** This service continuously monitors the status of various applications and services as well as the performance of the Fog network that is in turn used by the other services.

6. **Profiling:** From the data provided by the Knowledge Base and Monitoring services, the Profiling service builds resource and application profiles that are used by other services.

7. **Resource Provisioning:** This service ensures dynamic allocation of resources to the Fog applications. It uses the information obtained from the other services as mentioned and also the user's requirements to decide the volume of resources to be provided to the particular application. For example, this service immediately provides resources to low latency mission-critical tasks.

8. **Security:** This service is responsible for providing authorization, cryptography and authentication as needed by the applications and services.

APPLICATIONS

Figure 3 shows a number of Fog computing applications that range from a small scale to a global scale.

Some important applications are as follows:

- Healthcare
    - There have been many recent advances in Fog assisted healthcare applications. One such application is FAST, an analytics system to monitor fall for stroke patients. The creators of the system have been successful in developing a fall detection algorithm based on acceleration measurements and time series analysis methods. Moreover, the fall detection task is split between edge devices and the Cloud, thereby keeping response time and energy efficiency to the current standards.
    - There has also been development in the field of smart-healthcare infrastructure. It involves adding a Fog layer to improve the existing architecture. The proposed architecture consists of a role model, layered Cloud architecture and a Fog computing layer. This Fog layer provides low latency, mobility support and security measures. This model can be used as a template for future sensor-based smart healthcare infrastructure.

Figure 3. Applications of Fog computing

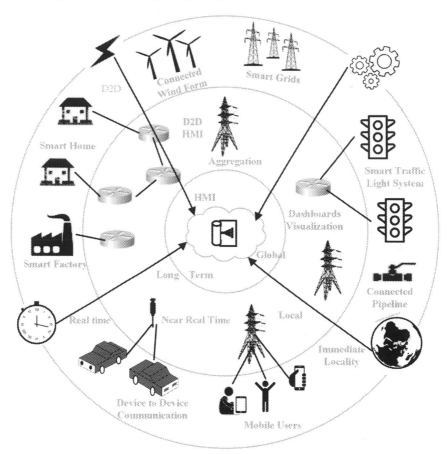

- Augmented Reality
  - As augmented reality applications are highly latency intolerant, Fog computing has the potential to contribute in this field. Zoe et al have built an Augmented Brain Computer Game based on Fog computing. The game employs the use of Electroencephalography (EEG) sensors to obtain information on the state of the brain. This process involves heavy signal processing tasks to be carried out in real-time. Therefore a combination of Fog and Cloud servers enables continuous real-time brain state classification based on EEG readings collected by the sensors. In this way, Fog computing helps in compute intensive augmented reality applications.

- Manufacturing
  - Fog computing can enhance manufacturing processes in small and large scale industries. With Fog computing it is possible to provide real-time monitoring and diagnostics and predictive maintenance to increase the uptime and lifespan of equipment. Using Fog computing, factories can predict unexpected failures and malfunctions of machines in real-time. It can also help improve product quality by analyzing sensor readings and identifying the root cause for defective parts. Semiconductor companies, for example, are continuously trying to increase their yield rate and maximize their profits. These companies can use Fog computing to identify false positives and false negatives in real-time. Moreover, data generated in the fabrication process are subject to confidentiality and cannot be moved to the Cloud. Hence, Fog computing solves this issue by bringing analytics close to the source of the data rather than moving the data to the Cloud.
- Oil and Gas
  - Oil and gas extraction operations are extremely high-stake operations involving real-time on site intelligence processing. This is needed in order to ensure monitoring and protection to reduce equipment failure and environmental damage. This scenario presents a perfect stage to employ Fog computing to ensure maximum production and safety. An application of Fog computing in the oil and gas industry is the use of proactive pipeline optimization systems. There are more than 2.5 million miles of oil and gas pipelines in the United States. Many sensors have been installed in these pipelines to monitor flow, pressure and compressor conditions. These sensors generate enormous volumes of data. An average 100-mile long pipeline itself produces 50 gigabytes of data, then the total data across the country would be unmanageable. Therefore, Fog computing relieves this data problem by analyzing on the data by the sensors at the source itself and reporting any issue and acting automatically. For example, a valve can be closed automatically in case of a leak and a report be sent via an alert to a mobile phone. With Fog computing, pipeline operators can lower risk and costs which is not possible with a Cloud only solution. Fog computing also helps in anticipating machine failures. The Electric Submersible Pump (ESP) extracts oil from the bottom of the well to pump it to the surface. Failure of this machine could result in loss of huge amounts of money and

hobble the entire operation. Therefore a Fog based predictive system can monitor the data provided by the ESP and automatically shut down the process if it predicts a malfunction. In this way Fog computing analyses the real-time data with low latency and at the same time sends only relevant information to the Cloud for future analyzing purposes. This solution also reduces the cost of data transfer to the Cloud.

- Mining
  - The primary motivation to employ Fog computing in mining industry is that mining faces extreme environmental conditions in remote locations that do not have access to the Internet. Fog computing can be employed in this case since it does not need frequent access to the Cloud.
  - The mining industry faces several challenges due to shortage of skilled labor and falling commodity prices. Hence, mining companies are moving towards the use of automated trucks, tunneling and boring machine to increase productivity and worker safety. Sensors are installed on these vehicles to enable real-time asset monitoring and to gather data for predictive maintenance. In addition, health monitoring devices and sensors can monitor the physical health of mine workers and send alerts in case of any accidents. Therefore, a Fog computing system can provide resources for real-time responses with low latency.
  - In addition, mining machines also generate terabytes of data everyday which the mining companies use to optimize processes, reduce energy consumption and increase production. Since mining occurs in remote locations, data cannot be uploaded to a Cloud network as the connectivity is too low for such a large volume of data. Hence, Fog computing solves this issue as it analyzes the data and provides real-time insight to the mining companies and therefore reducing the bandwidth required as it sends only a subset of the data to the Cloud which is needed for future analysis.

FOG PRODUCTS

CISCO IOx

Cisco was in fact the first to introduce the term Fog computing. Cisco IOx is a product that aims to integrate essential IoT elements and Fog computing. It provides for distributed computing within the Fog, secure communications and rapid system integration and application management. Cisco IOx has four components - Cisco IOx, Fog Director, SDK and development tools and Fog applications. Cisco IOx brings together Cisco IOS software, the industry-leading networking operating system, and Linux, the leading open-source platform. The Cisco Fog Director establishes a managing system to monitor and troubleshoot Fog applications running in the IOx environment. Cisco's SDK allows the users to develop applications in a programming language of their choice, it supports Java and Python as well. Finally, the Fog applications ready for execution are deployed onto the IOx infrastructure.

Some features of Cisco IOx include:

- Flexible application development and deployment approaches.
- Ability to process high volumes of data and deliver closed loop system control in real time
- Built-in security for application deployment and management.
- Integration with PaaS (Platform as a Service) capabilities associated with application programming environments.

LocalGrid Fog Computing Platform

LocalGrid Fog Computing Platform is a framework that enables users to build Fog applications without worrying much about the complexity of the Fog network. Therefore it allows for quick development of products with reduced costs. Some of its features include:

- **Rapid Onboarding of Heterogeneous Edge Devices**: This allows sensors and devices of different protocols to interact with each other with minimum effort by the application developer.
- **Peer to Peer Communication**: Direct communication allows for real time control and coordination without having to rely on a centralized server.
- **Supports Development:** In many programming languages on most platforms (C, C++, C#, Java, Python and Labview).
- **It Enables the Use of the Field Message Bus**: Thereby eliminating any dependency on a central command and thus there is no single point of failure.
- **Reduced Bandwidth**: Allows for faster real-time decisions
- **Security**: Data is stored locally on each device and not sent to the Cloud, and accessed by devices when needed only with successful authentication.

Vortex Fog by Adlink Technologies IST

Vortex Fog is a platform that allows for secure forwarding of data between Fog subsystems in a Vortex Cloud. These Fog subsystems contain edge node applications communicating with each other on a Local Area Network (LAN) or other subsystems over a Wide Area Network (WAN). Similar to the property of a Fog network, Vortex Fog allows only selected data to be forwarded to the WAN. It supports secure data sharing between the subsystems via encrypted communications and authentication mechanisms. The Intelligent Vortex Data Sharing Platform supports automatic discovery independent of underlying topology. In order to provide low latency, quality of service Vortex provides implementations that are optimized for various device platforms. Some features of Vortex Fog include:

- Plug and play integration and data sharing between different parts of a Vortex system deployed on either a LAN or a WAN.
- Boundary Security with TLS based encryption, certificate–based authentication and access control rules between subsystems.
- Uses UDP multicast to enable efficient, low latency device-to-device data sharing.
- Adaptation to underlying network - for example it will dynamically switch to TCP if UDP is not available.

USE CASE FOR FOG COMPUTING

Fog computing presents a solution for many compute intensive applications, one such use case is security at airports. Security at airports still involves some manual tasks which have the potential to be automated. Cameras at the airport play the most significant role in providing security. The videos from these cameras are processed to determine a possible threat. Each camera can generate up to 1TB of video data in a day, which make it a suitable candidate for Fog computing. Several applications of these cameras connected to computational units (or Fog nodes) are discussed next.

First and foremost, cameras are used to capture license plate numbers as they enter and leave the airport, Fog nodes employed here can be used for optical character recognition. Similarly, Fog nodes can be deployed for other visual analytics purposes such as screening, observing parking lots, monitoring arrival and departure areas and terminals. A convolutional neural network can be employed in the Fog node in these cases as they achieve excellent image classification.

From the time a passenger enters the airport, up until he reaches his destination, Fog computing can be employed in various scenarios to ensure monitoring a person for security purposes. When the passenger enters the airport, the car he arrives in is monitored by Fog nodes scanning the license number plates. The Fog node also helps the airport authorities to scan the RFIDs if the vehicle is equipped with one and also check if a suspicious car enters the airport.

Next, when the passenger makes his way to the screening area and checks in his luggage, by this time the Fog nodes would have acquired the passenger's information. This includes the information including the car he arrived in, his destination and flight information. The information about a particular passenger is aggregated by using a Fog network among the Fog nodes. Then the passenger is monitored up until he leaves the destination airport. With machine learning techniques, this acquired information can be used to detect suspicious behavior. The several components that are essential to the functioning of this procedure are as follows:

- **Vehicle Capture:** As discussed, this converts the images or video to gain information on the car, such as the license plate, car model and other vital data.
- **Facial Capture:** This component is used to track the passenger throughout the entire process. It uses the appropriate API to tag a person's face and track his movements.
- **Data Fusion:** This component ensures that that all the gathered data is matched accurately. For example, the passenger to his car number, the passenger to his ticket number and so on.
- **Behavior Monitor:** This component uses the video feed to suspect abnormal behavior. The Fog node associated with this component can use data from previous cases and machine learning techniques to learn and detect anomalies.
- **Baggage Capture:** This component contains the API needed to detect luggage, identify its owner and continuously track it.
- **Alerter:** This component sends out an alert to the respective authorities in case of abnormal behavior so that immediate action can be taken.

Using these components, results have to be computed in real time within milliseconds which is possible only with Fog nodes. A similar Cloud model would not be able to achieve the same results with this large amount of data and requirements of fast processing speed with low latency. In this way, a Fog network forms an efficient airport security system.

REFERENCES

Bonomi, F. (2014). Fog Computing: A Platform for Internet of Things and Analytics. In N. Bessis & C. Dobre (Eds.), *Big Data and Internet of Things: A Roadmap for Smart Environments* (pp. 169–186). Springer. doi:10.1007/978-3-319-05029-4_7

Bonomi, F., Milito, R., Natarajan, P., & Zhu, J. (2014). Fog Computing: A Platform for Internet of Things and Analytics. In N. Bessis & C. Dobre (Eds.), *Big Data and Internet of Things: A Roadmap for Smart Environments. Studies in Computational Intelligence* (Vol. 546, pp. 169–186). Springer. doi:10.1007/978-3-319-05029-4_7

Cao, Y. (2015). FAST: A Fog Computing Assisted Distributed Analytics System to Monitor Fall for Stroke Mitigation. *Proc. 10th IEEE Int'l Conf. Networking, Architecture and Storage (NAS 15)*, 2–11. 10.1109/NAS.2015.7255196

Chiang, M. (2015, December). *White Paper on Fog Networking: An Overview on Research Opportunities*. Academic Press.

Cisco IOx and Fog Applications. (2017). Retrieved from https://www.cisco.com/c/en_in/ solutions/internet-of-things/iot-fog-applications.html

Cristea, V., Dobre, C., & Pop, F. (2013). Context-aware Environments for the Internet of Things. *Internet of Things and Inter-cooperative Computational Technologies for Collective Intelligence Studies in Computational Intelligence, 460*, 25–49.

Dastjerdi, Gupta, Calheiros, Ghosh, & Buyya. (2016). Fog Computing: Principles, Architectures, and Applications. Internet of Things Principles and Paradigms, 61–75.

Gia, T. N., Jiang, M., Rahmani, A.-M., Westerlund, T., Liljeberg, P., & Tenhunen, H. (2015). Fog Computing in Healthcare Internet of Things: A Case Study on ECG Feature Extraction. In Computer and Information Technology; Ubiquitous Computing and Communications; Dependable, Autonomic and Secure Computing; Pervasive Intelligence and Computing. CIT/IUCC/DASC/PICOM.

Li, J. (2015) EHOPES: Data-Centered Fog Platform for Smart Living. *Int'l Telecommunication Networks and Applications Conf. (ITNAC 15)*, 308–313. 10.1109/ATNAC.2015.7366831

OpenFog Reference Architecture for Fog Computing, Produced by the OpenFog Consortium Architecture Working Group. (2017, February). Retrieved from http://www.OpenFogConsortium.org

Stantchev, V. (2015). Smart Items, Fog and Cloud Computing as Enablers of Servitization in Healthcare. *J. Sensors & Transducers*, *185*(2), 121–128.

Zao, J. (2014) Augmented Brain Computer Interaction Based on Fog Computing and Linked Data. *Proc. 10th IEEE Int'l Conf. Intelligent Environments (IE 14)*, 374–377. 10.1109/IE.2014.54

Chapter 4

Fog Computing Application Deployment and Management

Ranjitha G.
Ramaiah Institute of Technology, India

Pankaj Lathar
Chaudhary Brahm Prakash Government Engineering College, India

G. M. Siddesh
Ramaiah Institute of Technology, India

ABSTRACT

Fog computing enhances cloud computing to be closer to the processes that act on IOT devices. Fogging was introduced to overcome the cloud computing paradigm which was not able to address some services, applications, and other limitations of cloud computing such as security aspects, bandwidth, and latency. Fog computing provides the direct correlation with the internet of things. IBM and CISCO are linking their concepts of internet of things with the help of fog computing. Application services are hosted on the network edge. It improves the efficiency and reduces the amount of data that is transferred to the cloud for analysis, storage, and processing. Developers write the fog application and deploy it to the access points. Several applications like smart cities, healthcare domain, pre-processing, and caching applications have to be deployed and managed properly.

DOI: 10.4018/978-1-5225-6070-8.ch004

Copyright © 2019, IGI Global. Copying or distributing in print or electronic forms without written permission of IGI Global is prohibited.

INTRODUCTION

The fog computing enhances the cloud computing to be closer to the process that act on the IOT devices. It is also known as fogging. Fog computing is invented by CISCO. Fog computing provides services and storage to the client. Fog computing also provides the services between the cloud data centers and enterprise end devices. It is wireless information transferring across the distributed devices in the Internet of things (IOT) network. Fogging was introduced to overcome the cloud computing paradigm which was not able to address some services, applications and other limitations of cloud computing such as security aspects, bandwidth and latency. The protection mechanism which was used in cloud for encryption was failed in providing the security for the data from the attackers. Fog computing address these type of issues.

Fog computing applications are considered as the edge network computing. Edge network devices provide an entry point to the provider's network. In fog computing communication takes place as peer to peer. In Internet of thing the sensor will generate extremely large amount of data. With the network connection the fog devices which are known as fog nodes can be deployed anywhere. It can be deployed on power pool, floor or the factory, vehicle, side of a railway track, etc. The fog nodes are routers, switches, controllers in industries, surveillance camera's etc. This type of communication is used to provide storage and efficient sharing and to take the decisions. FC is a novel idea which is expected to solve problems and provides solution for the latency, sensitive information computing problems. The local computing resources are used by the fog computing instead of real cloud for processing data. The transmission latency is reduced because of the proximity between the processors and data sources.

Figure 1. Fog computing

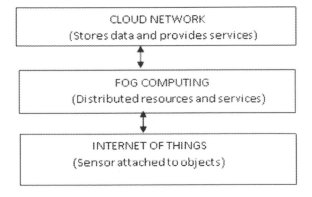

FEATURES OF FOG COMPUTING APPLICATIONS

1. **Local Data Processing:** It is implemented in a way that provides intelligence at the gateway which helps to analyze the streaming of data locally (Bonomi, Milito, Zhu, & Addepalli, 2012). It helps in handling large amount of data in less time span. It responses to the various conditions.
2. **Adaptive Applications:** The fog layer data transmission need to be adaptive. It includes data request and also transmission rate from fog to cloud layer.
3. **Local Storage:** Gateways process the incoming data locally. It contains an operating system that handles the repository. In non-volatile memory it stores the data. It compresses and encrypts the data and stores it locally.
4. **Security:** Security is the most major requirements of application. If the system is not secured it leads to serious vulnerabilities. Iptables are used for configuring the IP packets and it also contains set of rules.
5. **Interoperability:** It plays an important role for the success of an application. IOT based system contains the mixture of protocols, technologies and platforms. Integrating these application is major challenge. Fog computing provides easy integration of these network and technologies.
6. **Sensor Node Energy Efficiency:** Sensor nodes has to be processed properly. Fog computing provides a signal processing tasks from the nodes to gateways. It uses low power transmission protocol to save the energy during transmission.

Figure 2. Features of fog computing applications

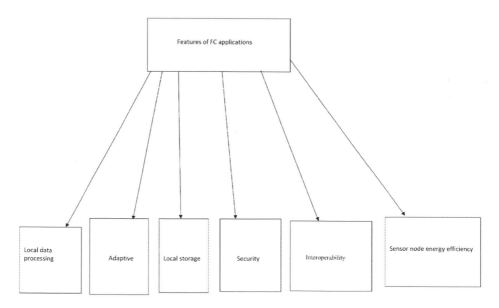

APPLICATIONS OF FOG COMPUTING

Fog computing provides the direct correlation with the internet of things. IBM and CISCO are linking their concepts of internet of things with the help of fog computing. The important area where the fog computing plays an important role are shown in Figure 3.

Application services are hosted on the network edge. It improves the efficiency and reduces the amount of the data which is transferred to the cloud for analysis, storage and processing of the data. IOT is system of interconnected computing devices, machine to machine interaction takes place. The amount of IOT devices estimation is billions with the growing number of sensors, storage and computing is difficult. In traditional data is just pushed into the cloud. Filtering and analysis has to be computed properly.

Figure 3. Applications of Fog computing

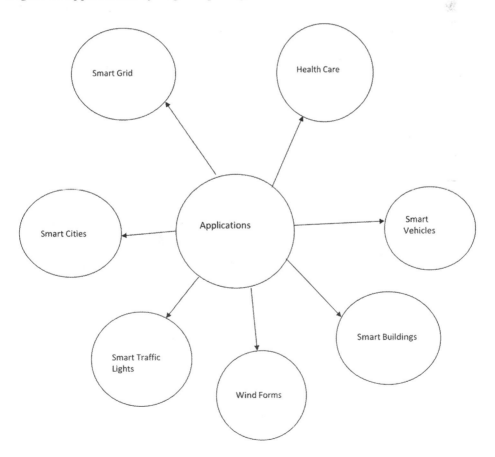

Developers write the fog application and deploy it to the access points (Bonomi, Milito, Zhu, & Addepalli, 2012). Then fog nodes will receive the data from IOT. Then the data is distributed on basis of how soon the action is required. Fog nodes will receive the data from IOT devices in real time and it will process the data that the IOT device can make decision.

DIFFERENT TYPES OF DEPLOYMENT MODELS:

Indie fog infrastructure makes use of the customer network devices such as router to provide fog computing environment (Chang & Satish Narayana Srirama, n.d.). Mainly it reduces the IOT service providers to deploy devices throughout a fogging system. It is more flexible and cost effective.

The two types of Indie fog deployment models are:

1. Integrated form.
2. Collaborative form.

1. **Integrated Form**: The gateway is responsible for providing functionality of integrating it into indie server which in turn connected to user devices and different data sources. The router itself provides virtual server which intern acts as fog node.
2. **Collaborative Form:** The workstation are responsible for providing the functionality in the subnet as the source devices through the internet gateway. It connects through the internet gateway. Cloud service providers provides equipment which is designed for the particular application.

Indie fog provides facilities for deploying four types of models:

1. **Indie Fog Cluster:** The group of fog nodes in a close proximity within a subnet or which resides in the same building are responsible for establishing the software defined cluster (Chang & Satish Narayana Srirama, n.d.). It helps in performing the preprocessing of the information which is collected by the sensors device and sources. It will reduce the time and bandwidth which are required to send data to cloud.
2. **Infrastructural Indie Fog:** The deployment of fog devices in cameras provide a ubiquitous application infrastructure. It requires temporary storage of data which has to be processed in short time. Example: The scientist invest for indie fog server with the sensor functions which are pre- installed to collect the data which are required for research.

Figure 4. Integrated form

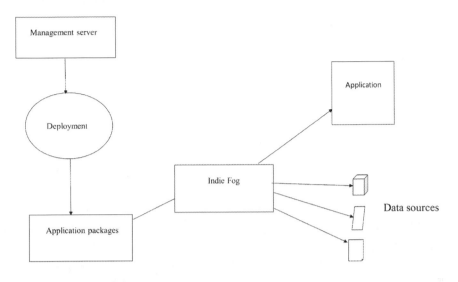

Figure 5. Collaborative form

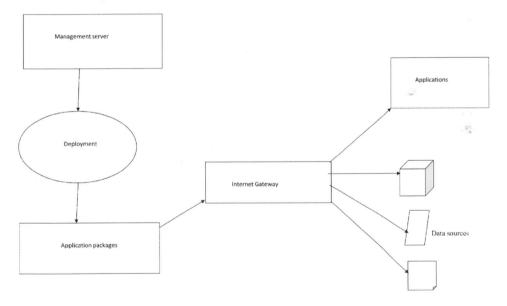

3.   **Vehicular Indie Fog:** Vehicles can also host their nodes. The system can dynamically deploy vehicular software defined for sensing network which collects the information of traffic, transportation and metropolitan information for public. It enables the sequential data streams and data on the changing environment.

4. **Smart Phone Indie Fog:** The smart phone users move regularly devices will not be able to form stable cluster environment. The deployment of fog will help in these areas. The server nodes collect the information of sensor data. The phone will be able to process.

MANAGING THE FOG APPLICATION

1. **Dashboard:** Dashboard is the first page which is presented to the user after the login. It gives an overview to the end users what all is happening.
2. **System Overview:** The system overview is the box that contains the current end users, IP, server address and how users have been logged. It also provides the information of how many users logged into the system and how long the system is running.
3. **System Activity:** It contains the unicast queue. It shows the number of unicast deployed and which are in progress. Based on the storage groups the queue would differ. It also provides the information of queued task, running and updates information. It provides bandwidth graph. The editing can also be performed using fog configuration.
4. **Service Management:** It allows to control the client service functions.
5. **User Management:** This information is provided by menu bar. It contains the information of administrators of individual fog resources.
6. **Monitoring:** It provides functionality of operational locally. It allows to save the data and processed results in local and synchronizes it with cloud.
7. **Host Management:** It gives the information of host which are imaged and to extract images.
8. **Disk Information:** Disk information displays the storage services. It also provides the information of the available storage on the storage server. The user is provided by drop-down box to change to storage nodes for monitoring the disk information.
9. **Image Management:** It allows to manage the image files stored on the fog servers.
10. **Snap-in Management:** It provides the imaging of the post tasks.
11. **Printer Management:** Allows the user to manage the printers to create printer objects which can be assigned later to the hosts or group.
12. **Fog Used Task:** It provides the task id and type. It provides an information of deploy, captured, debug and test disk depending on the current state. Type ID contains the job.
13. **Report Management:** Are the information from the fog database which can be of pdf, csv or html.

14. **Storage Management:** It allows the customer to add or remove the fogging system.
15. **Host:** It contains the description information, Ip address, operating system, kernel, arguments of kernel and primary disk information.

CASE STUDIES

Smart Cities

The challenges which are faced by large cities are traffic, safety of public, energy usage is high and municipal services. These challenges can be overcome by single IOT network by installing fog nodes. The connectivity and broadband bandwidth is the major problem in establishing the smart cities. Most of the modern cities have one or more cellular network which provides adequate coverage this network will often have bandwidth limitation and capacity issues. The smart cities also face the problem of security and safety where it requires real time performance. The network may carry traffic and sensitive data.

Figure 6. Smart city

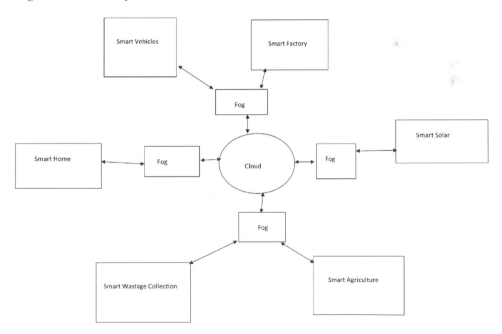

The deploying of fog computing will allow the fog nodes to provide storage and local processing which in turn optimizes the network usage. Fogging will address the issues such as security, encryption of data and distributed analytics.

Health Care Domain

The resource constrained devices are connected to the network. The majority of these devices are not capable of storing data which are generated by large scale (Zhu, & Jiang, 2013). This data was transferred directly to cloud for processing. It provides local data processing which is very important in case of medical field which in turn enables the system to react faster for medical emergencies. It provides local data processing which is very important in cases of medical which in turn enables the system to reach faster for medical emergencies. Fog computing provides greater flexibility in meeting the requirement of healthcare. It filters the data and preserve the privacy in order to reduce load at the network.

Deploying Healthcare Application

The healthcare application includes users, devices and connectivity.

Figure 7. Healthcare application

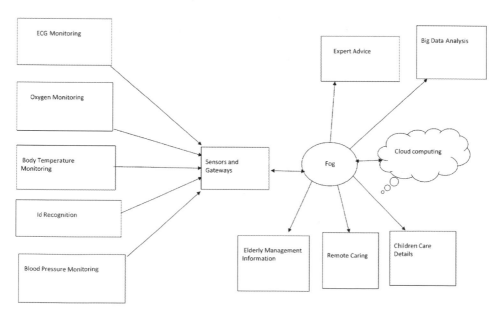

1. **Mobiles:** It acts as a hub between the cloud and the sensor devices. The base unit are mobile phone which collect data from various devices and process the data and returns it back to the back-end servers. The major purpose of fog computing is to provide battery life for the wearable sensor device. *Example:* COPD (chronic obstructive pulmonary disease).

2. **Hospital:** The devices are owned and maintained by the hospital itself. These systems are more complex and requires more qualified professionals. The smart shirts will allow monitoring data and the patient location. The data acquisition and processing board will process, collect and merged. This information are obtained from sensors. The wireless transmission board collects the information from the data acquisition and processing board and sends it to the management subsystem in single packed which is located at LAN level. The subsystem uses this information to monitor the patient medical parameters and it also verifies for alarm is activated or not.

3. **Premises of Non-Hospital:** It includes less staff and infrastructure facility like clinic and nursing homes. The core devices are maintained and owned by the clinic. It reduces the traffic between the detection system which is located at the cloud and LAN (Zhu, & Jiang, 2013).

4. **Transport:** In emergency situation the data is collected from the patients wearing the medial device.

Managing Application

1. **Data Collection:** The data as to be collected properly which is examined by the doctor for reference.

2. **Data Analysis:** The critical analysis has to be taken care properly. The monitoring of cardiac through ECG should alert in case of critical situations. The control of the critical condition as to be detected when the alarm is obtained. Example: Proper oxygen has to be provided to the patients. Fog computing will assist the system for detecting and predicting the emergency situations. Fog computing offers fault detection which allows faster for emergency situation. Fog computing implements real time responses.

3. **Context Management:** The context management helps in taking proper decisions and plans.

4. **Filtering of Data:** Data received from various sensors for pre-processing at the edge and data analysis is performed. The Bio-signals are collected from patient body which are the primary source of information. Information contains

amplitude, frequencies and complex shapes. Noise which is accumulated distorts the quality of signals. Fog computing will address these types of issues at interface sensors. It receives data from sensors by various communication protocols.

5.   **Data Compression:** It is used to reduce latency and energy which is consumed during the transaction. For ECG monitoring of real time application and it provides signal with high precision.

6.   **Fog Computing Data Fusion:** It enables to decrease large volume of data and reduces the energy consumption. The data fusion is categorized into three classes they are: complementary, cooperative and competitive. The complementary contains global knowledge which in turn contains the information of difference in body temperature of patients and environment provided by sensors. Competitive improves accuracy and consistency of the results in case of failure of sensors. Cooperative provides the vital signals.

Figure 8. Smart grid

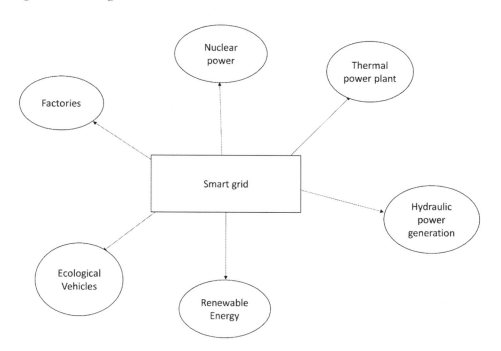

Smart Grid

The major problem in traditional electric generation was fossil fuel. The fuel consumption was threatening the global warming. Smart grid integrates green power resources controlling usage of power and it also helps in balancing the energy load. Smart grid employs meters by which two-way electricity flows information to manage and monitoring the electricity consumption. Smart meters produce huge amount of data which is difficult to process, store and analyze using cloud computing. Fog computing is responsible for processing, storing and collecting information before transmitting it to cloud. It acts as a communicating bridge between smart grid and cloud.

Fog computing for smart grid can be deployed to address the issues of moving the data to the cloud. It enables the user to access the data in secure and faster manner. Advanced metering infrastructure provides secure, reliable and cost-effective services. The data which are collected by meter includes some private data about users. As the size of smart applications increases the data collected by meter also increases.

Deploying Smart Grid Applications

1. The smart meters are used to measure the electricity usage of every applications. To provide data privacy and authentication smart meter encrypts the data using smart keys and shares among different fog server.
2. Upon receiving the encrypted data the fog server will decrypts and store it for a period as required by users.
3. The fog server calculates the total usage of the smart meter and sends it to the cloud. This work would help in reducing the data storage in the cloud centers.
4. Fog computing is responsible for storing private data of the customer locally and sends public information to the cloud. These provides privacy of the information.
5. Using fog computing in smart grid application reduces the access time and searching as data are stored locally.

Managing Smart Grid Application

Smart grid offers users detailed usage information of electricity. The customer can analyze and monitor the electricity consumption of daily, week and monthly. The detailed information may contain some private data of the users. Fog computing will treat it as private data. Customer can charge the device using ID information. The smart meter sends the information to the owners. It enables the active participation of the customers.

The Preprocessing and Cache Application

The edge servers are used for improvement of the website performance. Through the fog boxes users will be able to connect to the internet Fog nodes provides an optimization and reduces the amount of time where the user needs to wait.

Deploying and Managing Preprocessed and Cache Application

Other than the generic optimizations which includes reorganization, caching of the html component, composition reduces the size of the object, fog computing will also perform the optimization of user behavior and the condition of the network.

Example: In network congestion it provides low resolution graphics to the customer to reach out the acceptable time of response. The edge deices is used for monitoring of the client machine performance and it is also depends on the rendering time of the browser.

The major thing which has to be considered is data trimming. It is nothing but pre-processing of the data has to be done before sending it to the cloud. Forwarding this large amount of information is difficult as it leads to data center congestion problem. Fog computing provides gateway based smart communication which is used to integrate cloud with the IOT. Fog computing will handle the pre-processing and trimming of data before sending it to cloud directly. The smart gateway for the operation of the data which is generated by IOT devices in context aware and sensitive data latency manner. This approach will provide greater usage of IOT applications.

Smart Agriculture

Agriculture is most important as it provides food supply chain and provides many ways of communication concentrates in cities. Fog computing helps in collecting various information. The heat event may have an effect on crops. Flowering time is major event for crops. The sensors has to collect the information of crops, climate, weather, water and season information.

Deploying Agriculture Application

1. It contains sensors network to collect various information. The field, crop, climate conditions are collected.
2. The sensor states are used to monitor the crops in the land. Air balloons are used to monitor the crops in the land. Fog computing plays an important role in sensing adaptively and efficiently analyzing the information obtained.

Figure 9. Smart architecture using fog

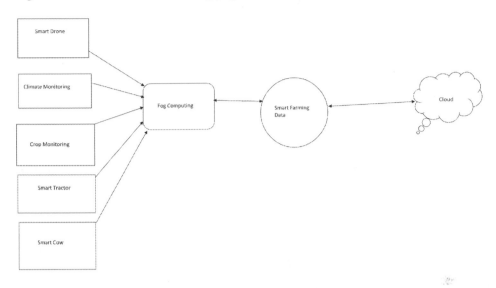

3. Fog gateway devices can be used in three different types according to phenonet project. Phenonet has a group of sensors which helps for sensing devices. The first gateway device is phenomobiles which acts as an edge devices.
4. The blimps will help in combining the sensors and gateway devices. The different data frames help in reducing data storage. Sensor data has to be deployed in such a way that it senses location and time sensitive data.
5. Each sensor has to be deployed by considering the context information. The heat and frost can damage the mechanism of the crop. The sampling rate vary based on the season. *Example:* The high sampling ideal thing may vary for summer season. The lower sampling is required for winter season.
6. The sensor should continuously sense the crop. The frost event cannot be detected without temperature. The configuring of humidity sensor is the ideal idea where the temperature is replaced and starts sensing immediately.
7. These type of reconfiguration will help in eliminating the ineffectual sensing and improves the network communication.

Managing the Smart Agriculture

Monitoring: Plants are monitored using different types of sensing devices and techniques. Context information plays a major role. It provides an efficient sensing technique in smart agriculture related problems.

The main reason for collecting data gives information of plants by applying reasoning and fusing technique.

CONCLUSION

Fog computing is most attribute solution for the problem of IOT and data processing. The devices relies on the network edge and reduces latency of application. The review shows the different deployment scenarios for variety of application with benefits of fog computing. It mainly filters the data to reduce traffic and to provide privacy. Flexibility of fog computing is therefore suitable for meeting the requirement of various application.

REFERENCES

Akella & Xiong. (2014). Quality of service (qos)-guaranteed network resource allocation via software defined networking (sdn). In *Dependable, Autonomic and Secure Computing (DASC), 2014 IEEE 12th International Conference on* (pp. 7–13). IEEE.

Bonomi, F. (2011). Connected vehicles, the internet of things, and fog computing. *The Eighth ACM International Workshop on Vehicular Inter-Networking (VANET)*.

Bonomi, F., Milito, R., Zhu, J., & Addepalli, S. (2012). Fog computing and its role in the internet of things. In *Proceedings of The First Edition of The MCC Workshop on Mobile Cloud Computing* (pp. 13–16). ACM. 10.1145/2342509.2342513

Bonomi, Milito, Zhu, & Addepalli. (2012). Fog computing andits role in the internet of things. In *Proceedings of The First Edition of The Mcc Workshop on Mobile Cloud Computing*. ACM.

Chang & Srirama. (n.d.). *Indie Fog: An Efficient Fog-Computing Infrastructure for the Internet of Things*. University of Melbourne and Manjrasoft Pty Ltd.

Cisco, Tech. Rep. (2014). *Cisco Delivers Vision Of Fog Computing To Accelerate Value From Billions Of Connected Devices*. Cisco.

Cisco. (n.d.). *New cisco internet of things (iot) system provides a foundation for the transformation of industries*. Retrieved from https://newsroom.cisco.com

Rohila & Singla. (2016). An effective review of fog computing using virtualization. *International Journal of Innovation Research of Computer and Communication Engineering, 4*(4).

Zhu, J. (2013). Improving web sites performance using edge servers in fog computing architecture. In *Service Oriented System Engineering (SOSE), 2013 IEEE 7th International Symposium on*. IEEE.

Chapter 5
Confidentiality and Safekeeping Problems and Techniques in Fog Computing

Nida Kauser Khanum
Ramaiah Institute of Technology, India

Pankaj Lathar
Chaudhary Brahm Prakash Government Engineering College, India

G. M. Siddesh
Ramaiah Institute of Technology, India

ABSTRACT

Fog computing is an extension of cloud computing, and it is one of the most important arch015etypes in the current world. Fog computing is like cloud computing as it provides data storage, computation, processing, and application services to end-users. In this chapter, the authors discuss the security and privacy issues concerned with fog computing. The issues present in cloud are also inherited by fog computing, but the same methods available for cloud computing are not applicable to fog computing due to its decentralized nature. The authors also discuss a few real-time applications like healthcare systems, intelligent food traceability, surveillance video stream processing, collection, and pre-processing of speech data. Finally, the concept of decoy technique and intrusion detection and prevention technique is covered.

DOI: 10.4018/978-1-5225-6070-8.ch005

Copyright © 2019, IGI Global. Copying or distributing in print or electronic forms without written permission of IGI Global is prohibited.

INTRODUCTION

The Internet of things (IoT) will be the "Internet of future" due to its growth rate in massive domains like wearable technology, smart city, smart transportation, smart grid. These smart applications require certain amount of resources like storage, battery, computation power and bandwidth. The IoT devices are not configured with so much resources. Therefore, they are generally assisted by robust server ends. Cloud is considered as an auspicious solution to deliver services to end users, and for its adaptable resources at very low cost. The server ends used by IoT are deployed in Cloud for its fair benefits provided to the users.

Even though cloud has several advantages, it cannot solve all problems due to its own drawbacks. Latency is one of the major issue in cloud because the data centers are located near the core network. The real-time applications like gaming, augmented reality and real-time streaming are subtle to latency and cloud is not a feasible choice for the application deployment that require very quick response and avoid round-trip latency during transmission of data from/to terminal nodes to/from cloud servers for processing. The data is sent through multiple gateways during transmission. In addition, there are also unresolved glitches that regularly need agility support, geo-distribution and location-alertness in IoT applications (Shanhe et al., 2015).

However, the state-of-the-art technology in computing standard is to impulse computation and storage resources to the control of networks. This results in growth of an auspicious computing architype called fog computing that provides services to the edge devices instead of relying on cloud services. Fog computing eradicates many issues arising in cloud computing service. It retains computation and data local to end users by providing low latency, location-awareness and high bandwidth. It gets the title as fog because it is a cloud present close to the ground. The devices that provide fog services to the edge devices are named as fog nodes. Fog nodes can not only be resource-rich devices but they can also be resource-poor devices like end devices, smart TVs/set-top-boxes and gateways. Usually cloud computing is collaborated with fog computing by forming a three-layered architecture comprising of end users, fog and cloud service as shown in Figure 1.

Cloud computing and fog computing share many similar characteristics like adaptable resources (computation, storage and networking). There resources are building blocks for both cloud and fog computing, signifying that utmost cloud computing technologies can be pragmatic to fog computing. Nevertheless, the new paradigm fog has quite a few exclusive features that makes it diverse from other present computing architectures. One of the imperative feature is maintaining close distance to end users. To support applications that are latency-sensitive, it is vigorous to preserve computing resources at the core of the network. The other stimulating feature is that the fog nodes which are geographically distributed can infer its own position and keep a track of all the end devices by providing mobility. It also provides reduced delay and bandwidth by dropping data volume to great extent at primary stage by preprocessing the data at fog nodes before sending it to cloud for further analytics. This property yields many benefits for stream mining and edge analytics. This has a significant role in the era of big data (Bonomi et al., 2012).

There are many features that are enhanced in fog computing when compared to cloud. It provides mobility, large IoT device support, extensibility, reduced delay, decentralization and many more. Along with vast benefits, fog computing welcomes many issues in security and privacy of devices and information stored. The main concern of this chapter is understanding the security and privacy issues in fog computing. It also includes the architecture of fog computing and its interaction with other counterparts (cloud and IoT) that gives an overview of differences among the different layers. The present techniques that are employed to make fog secure is also discussed. Real-time applications are discussed that face security and privacy issues. At the end of the chapter an intrusion detection and prevention technique is proposed.

ARCHITECTURE OF FOG COMPUTING

Fog computing has a very basic and simple architecture that consists of three tiers (Sarkar, Chatterjee & Misra, forthcoming). Figure 1 shows the architecture and components included in fog computing. This architecture is widely used and each of the tiers are discussed below:

- **Tier 1 – End Devices:** This tier consists of service patrons and IoT enabled devices. Some of the common end devices that are likely to be a part of fog computing are sensor nodes, Smart hand-held devices like smartphones, smartwatches and tablets and many more. Almost all the devices are fortified with Global Positioning System (GPS) to provide location awareness to fog nodes. These devices are generally termed as Terminal Nodes. These devices request services from cloud or fog nodes. Therefore fog-terminal nodes interface must be designed to enrich secure resource exploitation.
- **Tier 2 – Fog:** This tier consists of devices that has minimal resource availability like storage, computation etc. This rank is also labelled as fog computing layer. Most of the network devices like router, switches, gateways and Access Points (APs) are part of this tier. The devices collaborating their services like storage and computation are often called fog nodes. These fog nodes provide storage and computation facilities to terminal nodes whenever

Figure 1. Architecture of Fog computing with three tiers

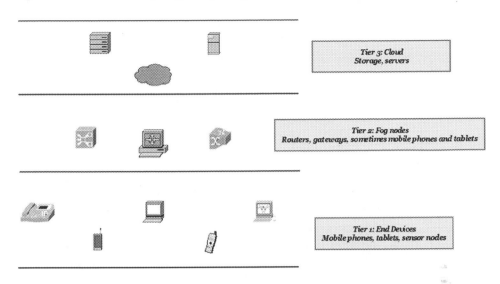

requested. Fog nodes collaborate with each other to provide efficient service by sharing storage and computation tasks. Hence it is one of the important task to design fog-fog interface and protocol that empowers fog nodes to collaborate with each other when required.

- **Tier 3 – Cloud:** The devices with appropriate storage and computing resources are part of this layer. Traditional cloud servers, cloud gateways and Data Centers reside on topmost layer in this architecture. Cloud servers are responsible to distribute the tasks to fog nodes and maintain them. Thus, cloud-fog interface (Chiang & Zhang, 2016) must be able to handle all fog nodes and schedule the tasks among fog computing.

INTERACTION BETWEEN CLOUD, FOG AND INTERNET OF THINGS

The advancement in IoT has led to development in many use cases that produce substantial amount of data (Diaz, Martin & Rubio, 2016). There are huge number of devices that are geographically distributed and capable of producing vast amount of data, dealing with big data is another imperative challenge. Fog computing was proposed to efficiently manage and analyze time sensitive data (Bonomi et al., 2014). As researchers know that cloud computing models are incapable of handling certain services requested by IoT devices that require high speed consciousness and response to events. Fog computing discards this disadvantage from cloud services. Interaction between all the devices must be without any trouble (Cisco, 2017).

The Table 1 summarizes the features of fog computing, cloud computing and Internet of things. It describes the differences in each domain based on those features.

FEATURES OF FOG COMPUTING

Fog computing is distributed in nature where it offers services to IoT application at the edge of the network by utilizing edge resources. One of the major feature provided by fog computing is to confront the IoT applications by exploiting the fog nodes placed near users to deliver convenient services like storage, computation, transmission, control and management of data locally. Cloud computing and fog computing are similar in many ways but they vary in many aspects as listed below and shown in Figure 2. They constitute as features of fog computing that are discussed below.

- **Decentralization:** Unlike cloud computing, fog computing does not have centralized server to manage its resources and services. Fog nodes

Table 1. Features of Fog, clod and IoT and differences among them

Features	Fog Computing	Cloud Computing	Internet of Things
Main Users	Mobile users	General Internet users	Stationery and mobile devices
Node count	Large	Few	Large
Architecture	Distributed	Centralized	Dense and distributed
Working Environment	Outdoors (fields, streets, tracks) or Indoor (home, malls, restaurants)	Indoor with immense planetary and ventilation	Outdoor and indoor
Location alertness	Yes	No	Yes
Real-time connections	Supported	Supported	Supported
Mobility	Supported	Limited Support	Supported
Service type	Localized data service, limited to precise deployment location	Global data collected worldwide	Data precise to end devices
Duration of data storage	Short duration as it transmits big data to cloud	Months and years because it manages big data	Temporary because it is the source of big data
Major service provider	Cisco IOx	Amazon, IBM, Microsoft	Bosch, Atmel, ARM

Figure 2. Features of fog computing

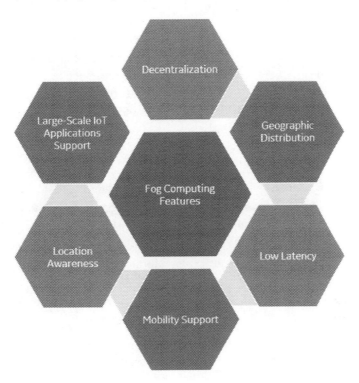

communicate among themselves by self-organizing, scheduling and co-operating among them to form a decentralized system. This enhances the real-times services and IoT requests to users (Vaquero & Rodero-Merino, 2014).

- **Geographic Distribution:** The main purpose of fog computing is providing minimal delay in services and mobility to terminal nodes. For this purpose, the fog nodes are geographically distributed and end users can take benefit of any fog node irrespective of its location. Fog nodes can be located anywhere like highways and roadways, on a museum floor, on cellular base stations and any other place of interest. Fog nodes receive high quality data from the terminal nodes due this feature (Ahmed & Rehmani, 2017).

- **Low Latency:** In this era of real-time application services, there are certain applications and IoT devices that require hasty analysis of data generated by them. This is not feasible with cloud computing as the servers are present at remote location. Fog nodes with resources play a major role by providing services for computation and services for terminal nodes. As these fog nodes are adjacent to terminal nodes the latency to provide amenity is highly reduced when compared to cloud computing. Hence fog nodes can make decisions based on local data without assistance of cloud (Ahmed & Rehmani, 2017).

- **Location Awareness:** Terminal nodes can access the services from fog nodes based on the location of fog node. This requires tracing of devices location actively and passively to provide high quality service to IoT applications. In fog paradigm, the IoT application accesses the fog nodes that are present nearest to end devices. This delivers rich service by providing the information about the location of nodes and hence enabling superior quality of service and resource (Ahmed & Rehmani, 2017).

- **Large-Scale IoT Application Support:** An evolving wave of internet organizations, most particularly Internet of Things that require various necessities like location awareness, mobility support, low latency in addition to geographic distribution. All these assets are provided by fog computing. This enable it to support large scale IoT applications to utilize the resources offered by fog nodes. There are many applications that exploit the services of fog nodes and manages large scale IoT applications like climate change monitoring, smart grid management, environment monitoring etc. (Bonomi et al., 2012).

There are many more features offered by fog computing to enhance the computation power and quality of service to IoT applications. The other features are mobility that enables users to move freely with same benefit of service irrespective of their location. It also provides local preprocessing of data before sending it to the cloud by reducing the strain on cloud servers. It also assists in local real-time online data analytics and interplay with the cloud (Ni, n.d.; Bonomi et al., n.d.).

SECURITY AND PRIVACY ISSUES IN FOG COMPUTING

Cloud computing has huge storage and computing resources, it assists clients in many ways by affording the services. But it also has many drawbacks, one among them is its decentralized architecture to manage and store data. This makes cloud computing vulnerable to external attacks on centralized data storage and computing framework. There are high possibilities of data leakage from cloud servers, cloud computing merchants like Google, Yahoo and Amazon have experienced data leakage due to uncontrolled external attacks. Security is a major concern in cloud computing that restricts its growth in many fields. As fog computing is an extension to cloud computing, many of its drawbacks are withdrawn from fog computing. It is considered that fog computing has more secure architecture than that of cloud computing. Some of the reasons to make fog more securely dependent than cloud are (Roman, Lopez & Manbo, 2018):

- End devices transmit the data to nearest local fog node where data is stored and analyzed transiently, this decreases the dependency of the devices on the Internet connection. As the data is stored locally, it's quite difficult for a hacker to access the data stored on fog nodes. This reduces probability of an unauthorized access of information.
- Cloud and end devices do not exchange information in real-time as fog nodes act as intermediate nodes and provides real-time service to end devices. This makes harder for eavesdropper to discern sensitive data of a precise user.

Nevertheless, fog computing is not considered as completely secure as it inherits many security and privacy issues from cloud computing. Fog and cloud service providers are only concerned with their benefits by providing services to end devices/end users. They may not deviate from the agreement signed between them but they might snoop the content of the data that was entrusted by users to store at their resource premises. They can also acquire any user sensitive data, this might cause privacy leakage for users. There is a possibility where fog and cloud are targets by hackers that can use various methods to reach their goal. There can be many attacks on fog nodes and some of them are mentioned below (Roman, Lopez & Manbo, 2018):

- **Forgery:** Malicious attackers can act as fake fog nodes by forging identities and contours. They can also mislead other nodes and end devices by generating fake information. This might also lead to excess consumption of resources like storage, bandwidth and computation to process unnecessary fake information.
- **Tampering Attack:** The fog nodes and other terminal nodes are connected through wireless channel this may result to tampering attack by dropping, delaying or modifying the information transmitted between the source and fog nodes. This reduces the efficiency of fog computing due to the delay caused to deliver the service. As fog computing provides mobility support to users, it might lead to transmission failure and delay.
- **Spam Attack:** The attackers produce unwanted data, redundant information by some means. This information is spread across different fog nodes misleading other fog nodes and end devices. The attacker can also access user specific information leading privacy leakage. By consuming large amount of unwanted or redundant data will cause needless network resource consumption.

- **Jamming Attack:** As mentioned above, the attackers can generate large amount of unwanted information. Fog nodes get busy to compute this fake information. Processing large amount unnecessary data will block the fog nodes. Other legitimate user cannot communicate with fog node to get serviced. The attacker jams fog nodes and disrupting the normal communication between end devices and fog nodes.

- **Eavesdropping:** Malicious attackers can listen when there is a communication channel established between fog nodes and terminal nodes. They can capture the packet that are being transmitted and read the content in the packet if there is lack of encryption on actual data. This type of attack is difficult to detect. Hence the fog nodes and terminal nodes that are transmitting packets are often unaware of third party reading their information in packets transmitted.

- **Denial-of-Service (DoS):** Fog nodes are quite vulnerable to Denial-of-Service when compared to cloud computing as they have minimal amount of resources for storage, bandwidth and computation. The attacker floods unnecessary requests to fog nodes by disrupting the normal services provided to terminal nodes by making them unavailable to their intended users. This kind of attack consumes network resources to prevent fog nodes serve their legitimate users.

- **Collusion Attack:** In general, collusion attackers are combination two or more parties colluding together to increase the power of an attack. They mislead, deceive or defraud the legal authorities or attain an unfair advantage. In fog computing, many attacking parties can collude to increase their capability to defraud or imbalance the normal communication. Several fake fog nodes or Terminal nodes can lead to this attack. The attack can occur between IoT devices and cloud, or Fog nodes with IoT devices.

- **Man-in-the-Middle Attack:** This type of attack is quite difficult to detect as the users think they are in sync with each other but are unaware of presence of malicious attacker that has an ability to manipulate or relay the information transmitting between two devices. Fog computing has its application many real-time environments like smart power grid, healthcare, transportation. The data transmitting between these nodes in fog environment is critical information, modification of such data can sometimes to lead to accidents or loss of life in case healthcare environment.

- **Impersonation Attack:** A malicious attacker enacts as a legitimate terminal node by spoofing the right identity and enjoying the benefits of services provided by fog nodes. In another case, fog computing nodes can be duplicated. They attackers can provide false data or services to users and misleading other fog nodes as well.

There are twelve more threats that are identified by organization named Cloud Security Alliance (Alliance CS, 2016). The following shows twelve security issues recognized by some researchers (Stojmenovic & Wen, 2014; Stojmenovic et al., 2015; Yi, Qin & Li, 2015) to formulate a systematic review:

- **Advance Persistent Threats (APT):** The main purpose of this attack is to steal data and intellectual property. This can be achieved by compromising the company's infrastructure and devices used in fog computing.
- **Access Control Issues (ACI):** As mentioned above, this attack leads to getting the access to unauthorized data and permissions to install software and change configurations. When the organization has poor management, the tendency of this attack increases gradually.
- **Account Hijacking (AH):** The name describes the purpose of the attack, hijacking one or more fog nodes by any means to fetch the services offered to that account and utilizing the data and permissions available for the hijacked device. The most popular technique for account hijacking is phishing.
- **Denial-of-Service (DoS):** it is an attacking technique where legitimate users are prevented or denied for their services. The attacker overloads fog nodes by fake requests and makes fog node unavailable to other legitimate end users.
- **Data Breaches (DB):** When user specific data, private or confidential data is stolen or released by an attacker it leads to severe sensitive data breaches.
- **Data Loss (DL):** Fog nodes are geographically distributed, this might cause any damage to fog nodes due to natural disaster resulting to data loss stored at fog nodes. This can be accidental or deliberately by an attacker.
- **Insecure APIs (IA):** Many fog service providers utilize Application Programming Interface (APIs) to provide an interfacc for users to contract the services provided by fog nodes. The security of these APIs is an important task before implementation of any application.
- **System and Application Vulnerabilities (SAV):** The attacker can penetrate and compromise any system by exploiting bugs arising in the system.
- **Malicious Insider (MI):** It is an authorized person with an intention of stealing data or performing an attack to mend the architecture or system of an organization. A fog node can become rogue and disrupt the normal communication among other fog nodes and devices.
- **Insufficient Due Diligence (IDD):** This frequently occurs when an organization urges development, design and implementation of any system without considering all the scenarios and exceptions that can arise after implementation.

- **Abuse and Nefarious Use (ANU):** This arises when attackers utilize the fog resources when its freely available, they can misuse the resources and block the fog nodes to only serve them.
- **Shared Technology Issues (STI):** Sharing technology, infrastructure, hardware, applications or platforms might lead to some overload on the system. There might be devices that cannot handle serving too many users.

All the above attacks are shown in Figure 3 along with other privacy issues in fog computing. Users sensitive data is involved in the collection, transmission, processing and sharing. Most of the users would like to keep their information in private, but this is not possible in many cases. Users sensitive data can be leaked by many reasons. Some of the attacks to get the private information are listed below:

- **Identity Privacy:** In most cases users submit their identity information to fog nodes for authentication purpose. A user can have various identity information like name, address, phone number, license number, public-key certificate, visa number. All this information is linked to specific user. Disclosure of such private is vulnerable to user's identity.
- **Data Privacy:** Users data stored on fog nodes is on high risk of privacy leakage to third party. The data can be exposed to an untrusted party when the data is upheld on fog nodes and transmitting the data between two parties. Exposure of this data enables an attacker to analyze this data and obtain user specific details like users address, preferences, location, occupation and political disposition. For example, leaking data related to health status of a user can open the information regarding the health issues with the user.
- **Usage Privacy:** The attackers analyze the usage patterns of users and predict their behavior and information. The pattern of any device using the service of a fog node can be obtained and analysis of this information can constrain usage privacy. For example, examining and analyzing reading of smart meter can disclose the information regarding power consumption of a house and disclose the living habits of a family like the time when family goes to sleep or when they are not at home. This violates residents' privacy and may lead to robbery planning for a house using this information.
- **Location Privacy:** Nowadays enormous applications on mobile devices collect users' location information. To enjoy some online facility, users need to sacrifice our location information. Navigation and location-based service require users' location to provide service to them. Though location data is commonly shared among the application, its preservation is critical indeed. The attacker can traverse the users travelling route by collecting location information from fog nodes. As devices are mobile, they take services from

the nearest for node, hence a conclusion can be drawn that device is present close to this fog node rather than other fog nodes. Moreover, users path trajectory can be disclosed to fog nodes by analyzing the request sequence to different fog nodes at different locations. As users are mobile and accesses services from fog nodes deployed at different locations, this information can violate the location privacy of the user by exposing the users route.

IoT devices in Fog Computing architecture are main sources for information and security threat. With increase in count of linked IoT devices the vulnerability for security and privacy threat also increases. IoT devices are more exposed to hacking, breaking or getting stolen due to its fewer security features. When these devices are hacked they can interrupt normal execution of services and tasks. Due to security and privacy issues shown in Figure 3, it is very critical to plan, design an efficient security and privacy-conserving mechanisms in fog computing. With lack of security

Figure 3. Security and privacy issues in fog computing

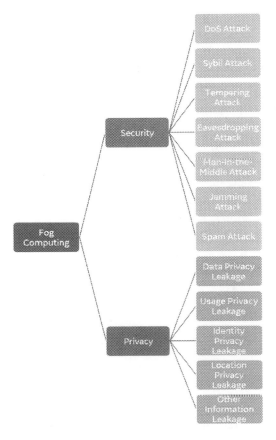

measures, the users might not be willing to participate in IoT applications and impeding the growth of fog computing. The next topic discusses real-time scenarios and security threats that in the applications.

REAL-TIME SCENARIOS OF FOG COMPUTING AND SECURITY ISSUES CONFRONTED

This part of the chapter explains some the application of fog computing. It also explains some of the security issues faced by those applications.

- **Improvising Healthcare Systems and Their Performance:** Healthcare is a vast domain and consists of elderly care systems, where huge number of sensors send large amount data to cloud for processing and storage. Fog computing can be applied to healthcare system, where the sensor nodes send data to fog nodes instead of cloud directly. Using a small organization of healthcare with large number of sensors, the data that is sent to fog nodes is preprocessed by tagging and classification. This reduces load on cloud servers when the data is ready for analysis as it enters the cloud environment. Fog layer delivers sophisticated data to cloud system for further processing and analytics (Prieto Gonzalez et al., 2016). Combining cloud computing and fog computing makes a better infrastructure with better Quality of Service (QoS) and domination (Stantchev et al., 2015). One of the real-time application of the above described methodology is OpSIT Healthcare project in Germany. The healthcare facility takes advantage of fog computing by providing services from nearest located fog nodes, store heterogenous information. The facility consists of smart low power devices and has an ability to shift among different communication protocols by providing flexibility. The entire architecture facilitates distributed computing. The tasks are distributed among cloud and fog nodes efficiently to provide scalable solution allowing the system to swift detection of a patient abnormalities and development (Shi et al., 2015).

Patient health records comprises sensitive data that describes the health conditions of the patient. There is large probability of compromising this sensitive data. The data can be lost or negotiated due to some external attack by an unauthorized entry into the system. It might be also caused by any malicious insider that can leak the sensitive and violate the privacy issues. Sensor terminal nodes keep sending data to fog nodes continuously either through wireless or wired connection. Data can be compromised while transmission by any third party (Li et al., 2010). There are high chances of DoS, description disruption, and forwarding attacks due to the ease-of-access provided by the system. The above security and privacy issues can be managed and prevented by implementing strong policies to maintain high-level control over the system. Unauthorized access can be avoided by implementing multifactor authentication. Private network and strong encryption techniques for communication and transmission of data can avoid privacy issues (Ren, Lou & Zhang, 2008).

- **Intelligent Food Traceability:** Tracing food management can benefit for the stakeholders in multiple ways to maintain food quality and track the transportation of the food items. Fog computing can be applied for food traceability management. This method utilizes value-based processing to remove poor quality products from food chain supply. There are many attributes like location, transportation devices and processing devices that helps in physical tracing of the food item. Fuzzy rules are implemented to make decisions on the quality of food based on distributed food traceability though Cyber Physical System (CPS). Fog nodes maintain and collect information regarding the traceability and quality, where the complete food supply chain is observable. Now, the entire information about all traced food objects is stored at fog nodes and the information about the quality can be sent forward to cloud for analysis. This information from cloud can be viewed by many other stakeholders using internet (Chen, 2017).

The security issues with this application can arise when an attacker can hinder the normal execution of food supply chain processes. Suppose any fog node is compromised by means of hijacking or exploiting systems and application liabilities, this can lead to data falsification or corruption by the attacker. When food quality data is fabricated, which eventually fallouts in the sale of substandard and low-quality food products. Large number of wireless devices in a network and Machine-to-Machine (M2M) communication prompts many security concerns. In one such scenario, a resonance attack can be activated where the sensor devices are forced to function at diverse frequency and causing incorrect data to be transmitted. This attack effects the convenience and operation of network and data transmission. These security concerns can be prevented by implementing integrity check, redundancy to avoid single-point failure and detecting dishonesty attacks (Saqib et al., 2015).

- **Surveillance Video Stream Processing:** In an application where well-organized processing and prompt decision-making is required, fog computing is best solution for the application to adopt. For example, consider tracking of multiple targets in a drone video stream as mentioned in Chen et al. (2016).

To bring about fog computing in this application, live video feeds can be sent to fog nodes instead of cloud-based applications. Fog nodes can be any device with minimal resources like mobile phones, laptops or tablets. These devices can execute tracking algorithms and process raw video stream frames. With this in the system architecture, the latency to deliver raw video stream frames to cloud can be reduced to great extent. The real-time implementation results of fog computing in this scenario reduced total processing time to average of 13%. "Proximal Algorithm" can be implemented in fog nodes to support large-scale video streaming application. It can also provide solution to joint resource allocation issue. The potential in finding missing children or people becomes strong. It can also be used to locate any person with criminal records (Shi & Dustdar, 2016).

Fog nodes store and process the data generated from respective camera sensors. The data can be video and audio that is stored in fog nodes, therefore the stream must be secured and privacy of the data must be maintained as this information will be shared among heterogenous users. All the devices involved in the transmission must be secured. Providing security to fog nodes is not sufficient, terminal nodes and cloud servers should also contain security management strategies especially against APTs. The data can be leaked, tampered or even deleted if the fog platform consists of any bugs due to negligence during design. Fine grained access control, careful encryption mechanism and restrictive number of connections are some of the security measures that can be considered in this real-time application of fog computing (Do et al., 2015; Varalakshmi, Sudha & Jaikishan, 2014).

- **Collection and Pre-Processing of Speech Data:** The next real-time application of fog computing is for patients with Parkinson's disease. This application enables android smart-watches coupled with a smart tablet that has ability to collect, store and process speech information generated by the patients. The fog computing interface (FIT) (Monteiro et al., 2016) reduces the load of data that is supposed to be delivered to cloud. FIT extracts the required information like short-time energy, spectral centroid, volume and zero-crossing rate from the speech data collected by the fog nodes. Bandwidth resource can be minimized by only transmitting only main factors that are extracted by FIT instead of transmitting the complete audio speech data. Preprocessing of data is performed before transmitting data to cloud server.

The security and quality of the service can be compromised due to large amount applications hosted on smartphones and tablets. The data should be accessed by only legitimate applications which is often decided by the user installation. Violating the access control over the speech data can cause many cyber-attacks (Heuser et al., 2016). Usually the fog platforms are constituted and built on mobile phones or tablets as mentioned above. The fog platform must be secured and protected as they are deployed on mobile operating system. When the fog platform is configured to be open-source, there is a high risk of malicious application negotiating fog processes and the connected network. User's personal data is also on jeopardy due to this. These security issues can be resolved by adopting the following methods: anti-virus, software patching, firewall, constant data backups, Intrusion Prevention System, creating system restore points and running behavior analysis methodologies through dynamic monitoring (Wei et al., 2012).

Fog computing delivers and receives high quality data to cloud and from terminal nodes. With many advantageous features provided by fog computing, it also introduces some drawbacks related to security and privacy issues. The security and privacy issues that can arise were discussed in previous section of the chapter, ant this section explains the issues in real-time application. Table 1 summarizes the possible attacks that can occur in fog computing applications.

EXISTING SECURITY SOLUTIONS FOR FOG COMPUTING

Applications that require low-latency services can adopt fog computing to enhance its capability to serve mobile end devices. Many users do not opt for fog computing due the security and privacy issues that come along with its implementation. To increase the acceptance of fog computing paradigm, one must guarantee safe communication and privacy for user's data. Therefore, building real-time applications by considering all the above issues is critical task. Researchers discuss some techniques that are used to enhance privacy preservation and prevent attack on fog applications (Ni, n.d.).

Table 2. Possible security issues that can occur in real-time applications among the twelve categories of security

Application	APT	ACI	AH	DoS	DB	DL	IA	SAV	MI	IDD	ANU	STI
Healthcare System		✓	✓	✓	✓		✓	✓	✓			
Food Traceability			✓			✓		✓				
Surveillance Video Processing	✓				✓					✓		
Speech data						✓			✓			

- **Identity Authentication:** Fog nodes, cloud and terminal nodes must be authenticated to provide authenticity and creditability to access the data and services. Improper authentication system might lead to external attacks on the fog nodes. Providing upright authentication service is critical task.

There many methods employed to provide authentication to all the devices on fog computing. But these mechanisms do not support mobility of devices. In fog computing, the services are delivered to users that are mobile in nature, these devices move out of coverage area from one fog node to another. Providing authentication to all the devices that are in movement can delay the operation of fog nodes when the count of users increases. Hence, authentication service with minimal latency and cooperative authentication schemes must designed and employed for better authentication scheme in fog computing. These schemes must avoid redundant authentication exertions when different set of users are communicating the same message.

In some applications, users are not willing to share their identities to fog nodes during validation. When a user is travelling, he/she might be reluctant to share their identity information to avoid leakage of private data. If an attacker gets hold of such information, then the attacker can track the users' location. Many devices like smart watch, smart glasses and smart jewels like bracelets reveal the location and identity evidence to fog nodes. Researchers can solve this issue by using Anonymous authentication mechanism, where user does not have to reveal its identification or location. There are many anonymous authentication algorithms, some of them are pseudonyms, group signatures and k-anonymity. With these techniques, fog nodes cannot distinguish other users based on the identification key. A hybrid algorithm that can have properties of both mechanism is more suitable.

- **Policy-Driven Secure Management of Resources:** This type of security mechanism enhances safe communication, interoperability and sharing by implementing preliminary policy management agenda for the capitals of fog computing (Ahmed & Rehmani, 2017). As described by the policy there are five major modules:
  a. Policy Decision Engine (PDE) for acting based on pre-defined policy rules.
  b. Application Administrator (AA) to manage fog multi-tenancy.
  c. Policy Resolver (PR) for attribute-based authentication
  d. Policy Repository (Prep) holding rules and policies
  e. Policy Enforcer (PE) to detect any discrepancies in policy implementation.

The responsibility to define rules and policies by considering multi-tenancy, communication services, data sharing and applications is engaged by AA. All the requests that are made from users are forwarded to PR whose responsibility is to identify user based on a detailed set of attributes that were registered by the user during authentication phase. The user attributes and their agreements are stored in a database that is maintained by PR. PR examining the attributes and agreements and then provides access to the user against requested resource. The role of PDE is taking user specific information from the PR, it also extracts rules from Prep. After extraction of rules, PDE analyzes them and enforces them through the PE. The best method to create is "eXtensible Access Control Markup Language (XACML)" and the context for building PDE is OpenAZ framework. This kind of policy management framework is suitable for distributed computing which is enforced in fog computing. It provides strong control for access, resource management and identification in fog computing. Nevertheless, this security mechanism is only suitable for systems that consists of devices which distribute dedicated resources for large number of computations required by different modules to execute the framework within fog platforms. This mechanism might cause some delay to execute the operations for authentication, and hence by causing some latency to time-sensitive applications. This mechanism is also vulnerable for DoS due to compound authentication methods in PR and PDE. The response to devices might slow down when malicious user sends large number of requests, the system repeats validation process for the same connection by delaying other services. Hence a better policy management framework is required to handle large number of requests and efficiently maintain resources of the devices.

- **Encryption and Decryption Mechanisms:** To make secure communication among the fog nodes and terminal nodes or fog nodes and cloud, light weight encryption-decryption mechanism is implemented. The data is encrypted based on private key that is shared by fog nodes and terminal nodes. When data is sent from terminal node, it is encrypted in a specific format. When the fog node receives data from terminal node, the information can be extracted by decrypting in same format based on the encryption key shared with devices. A malicious third party cannot get information about the information that is being transmitted. This method prevents Man-in-Middle attack. There are some drawbacks with this mechanism, terminal nodes lack resources for storage and computation, therefore encrypting data before sending it to fog nodes requires large amount of computation resources. The terminal nodes might not be able handle the load of such heavy computations. This also causes small delay in processing data as it consumes to apply encryption and decryption at both the ends of connection. Applications that are time-sensitive are not favorable for this mechanism. If the encryption is leaked to any other third party then it's no use of this technique as the attacker can get information with key. Therefore, a secure communication protocol must be designed to safeguard the resources and data on fog nodes.

PROPOSED SECURITY TECHNIQUE

The main reasons for an attack is unauthorized access to resources and data, when authorization to legitimate users is given then risk of any data loss or any attack can be reduced. Detection of malicious user is one of the main tasks. Researchers propose an intrusion detection and prevention technique that can handle and avoid different attacks.

If each user is provided with an authentication key, and fog node provides access based on this authentication key. A terminal node must get the authentication key from the cloud service or any fog node before sending the request. Cloud and fog nodes distributes the key based on the user details and policies. The same authentication key can be used every time the user sends a request to fog nodes. A database can be maintained for authentication key provided to users. This database information can be shared by other fog nodes. When the user is mobile and sends a request to fog node, fog node checks its database for the authentication purpose, if the user is an authorized user then service is offered to the user through fog node. The fog node also keeps track of user location, it sends the user authentication details to other fog nodes where the user can request for service. The database is updated by the fog nodes time to time and the information is also maintained at cloud for backup purpose.

When a malicious user is detected that is trying to access some data, then fog node sends a notification to legitimate user about the action. If the legitimate user declines the notification, then user is marked as an attacker and actions can be taken against the malicious user by plotting honeypots. Fog node can send fake data to the malicious user, when the user downloads the data, an .exe file can be run that extracts IP and mac address of the user. By this way the malicious attacker can be identified. The IP address can be changed but mac address remains same for the device, therefore extracting mac address of the attacker device should be focused and this information must be transmitted to the respective fog node. Fog node can send this information to other fog nodes and cloud to prevent other attacks on other fog nodes. Hence each fog node maintains two kinds of information. That is details of authorized users and details of unauthorized malicious users. Before permitting the user for any service or resource, fog node must check both the databases for safe and secure protection. Figure 4 and Figure 5, shows the workflow of the proposed mechanism to tackle security and privacy issues in fog computing.

Figure 4. Proposed Intrusion Detection and Prevention Technique

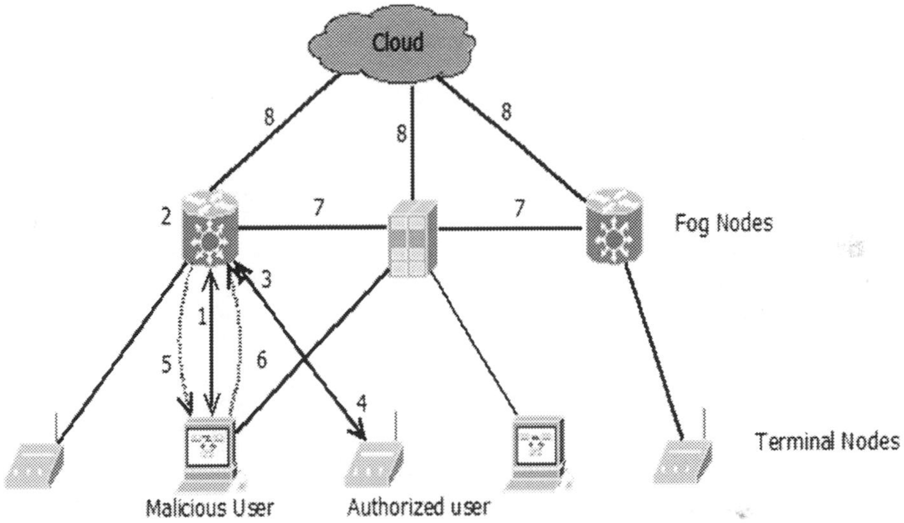

Figure 5. Proposed Intrusion Detection and Prevention Algorithm

Intrusion detection and prevention in fog computing

1. Malicious attacker sends a request to access some data to fog node.
2. Fog nodes checks its database for authorization. node is not updated in the database.
3. Notification is sent to authorized user of data to check.
4. User can either decline or accept the notification. If notification is accepted, the user is added to the authorized database otherwise user is marked as invalid.
5. Fake documents are sent to the malicious user. when user downloads the documents an .exe file is executed that extracts mac address of the attacker.
6. Mac address of the attacker is sent to fog node.
7. Fog node updates the malicious users' database and shares the information with other fog nodes to prevent an attack on other nodes.
8. Both the databases are updated on cloud by each fog node for backup and security.

CONCLUSION

Fog computing is latest technology that contributes an extension to cloud by providing services at the edge of the network. The users rely on fog nodes for computation and storage resources instead of cloud because of the enhanced features provided by fog computing. The features of fog computing were discussed in the chapter are the new benefits extended by fog. Fog computing eradicates many issues arising in cloud computing service. It retains computation and data local to end users by providing low latency, location-awareness and high bandwidth. Fog inherits some issues concerned with security and privacy of data and devices in fog architecture. Making data and other nodes secure is a vital task. Researches proposed a system that detects an intrusion into the fog application and planned measures to be taken after the intruder is detected. We need a more secure system that can avoid data loss due reasons like natural disasters and attacks. The real-time service of fog computing should not be interrupted due to privacy or security issues. Researches must focus on developing light weight secure system for fog nodes with minimal resources.

REFERENCES

Ahmed, E., & Rehmani, M. H. (2017). Mobile Edge Computing: Opportunities, Solutions and Challenges. *Future Generation Computer Systems*, *70*, 59–63. doi:10.1016/j.future.2016.09.015

Alliance, C. S. (2016). *The Treacherous 12 Cloud Computing Top Threats in 2016*. Retrieved from https://downloads.cloudsecurityalliance.org/assets/ research/top-threats/Treacherous-12_Cloud-Computing_Top-Threats. pdf

Bonomi, F., Milito, R., Natarajan, P., & Zhu, J. (2014). Fog computing: A platform for Internet of Things and analytics. In *Big Data and Internet of Things": A Roadmap for Smart Environments (Studies in Computational Intelligence)* (pp. 169–186). New York: Springer. doi:10.1007/978-3-319-05029-4_7

Bonomi, F., Milito, R., Zhu, J., & Addepalli, S. (2012). Fog computing and its role in the Internet of Things. *Proc. 1st Ed. MCC Workshop Mobile Cloud Comput. (MCC)*, 13–16. 10.1145/2342509.2342513

Bonomi, Milito, Zhu, & Addepalli. (n.d.). *Fog Computing and Its Role in the Internet of Things*. Cisco Systems Inc.

Chen, N., Chen, Y., You, Y., Ling, H., Liang, P., & Zimmermann, R. (2016). Dynamic urban surveillance video stream processing using fog computing. In *Multimedia Big Data (BigMM), 2016 IEEE Second International Conference on*. IEEE. 10.1109/BigMM.2016.53

Chen, R. Y. (2017). An intelligent value stream-based approach to collaboration of food traceability cyber physical system by fog computing. *Food Control, 71,* 124–136. doi:10.1016/j.foodcont.2016.06.042

Chiang, M., & Zhang, T. (2016). FogandIoT:Anoverviewofresearchopportunities. *IEEE Internet Things J., 3*(6), 1–11.

Cisco. (2017). *Fog Computing and Internet of Things: Extend the Cloud to Where the Things Are*. Available: http://www.cisco.com/c/dam/en_us/solutions/trends/iot/docs/computing-overview.pdf

Díaz, M., Martín, C., & Rubio, B. (2016, May). State-of-the-art,challenges,andopen issues in the integration of Internet of Things and cloud computing. *Journal of Network and Computer Applications, 67,* 99–117. doi:10.1016/j.jnca.2016.01.010

Do, C. T., Tran, N. H., Pham, C., Alam, M. G. R., Son, J. H., & Hong, C. S. (2015). A proximal algorithm for joint resource allocation and minimizing carbon footprint in geo-distributed fog computing. In *2015 International Conference on Information Networking (ICOIN)*. IEEE. 10.1109/ICOIN.2015.7057905

Heuser, S., Negro, M., Pendyala, P. K., & Sadeghi, A. R. (2016). Droidauditor: "Forensic analysis of application-layer privilege escalation attacks on android." Technical report. TU Darmstadt.

Li, M., Yu, S., Ren, K., & Lou, W. (2010). Securing personal health records in cloud computing: Patient-centric and fine-grained data access control in multi-owner settings. In *International Conference on Security and Privacy in Communication Systems*. Springer. 10.1007/978-3-642-16161-2_6

Monteiro, A., Dubey, H., Mahler, L., Yang, Q., & Mankodiya, K. (2016). *Fit a fog computing device for speech tele-treatments*. arXiv preprint arXiv:1605.06236

Ni, Zhang, Lin, & Shen. (n.d.). Securing Fog Computing for Internet of Things Applications: Challenges and Solutions. *IEEE Communications Surveys & Tutorials*. DOI 10.1109/COMST.2017.2762345

Prieto González, L., Jaedicke, C., Schubert, J., & Stantchev, V. (2016). "Fog computing architectures for healthcare": Wireless performance and semantic opportunities. *J Inf Commun Ethics Soc, 14*(4), 334–349. doi:10.1108/JICES-05-2016-0014

Ren, K., Lou, W., & Zhang, Y. (2008). Leds: Providing location-aware end-to-end data security in wireless sensor networks. *IEEE Transactions on Mobile Computing, 7*(5), 585–598. doi:10.1109/TMC.2007.70753

Roman, R., Lopez, J., & Manbo, M. (2018). *Mobile Edge Computing, Fog et al.: A Survey and Analysis of Security, Threats and Challenges* (Vol. 78). Futur. Gener. Comp. Syst.

Saqib, A., Anwar, R. W., Hussain, O. K., Ahmad, M., Ngadi, M. A., Mohamad, M. M., & .... (2015). Cyber security for cyber physcial systems: A trust-based approach. *J Theor Appl Inf Technol, 71*(2), 144–152.

Sarkar, S., Chatterjee, S., & Misra, S. (Forthcoming). Assessment of the suitability of fog computing in the context of Internet of things. *IEEE Trans. Cloud Comput.*

Shi, W., & Dustdar, S. (2016). The promise of edge computing. *Computer, 49*(5), 78–81. doi:10.1109/MC.2016.145

Shi, Y., Ding, G., Wang, H., Roman, H. E., & Lu, S. (2015). The fog computing service for healthcare. In *Future Information and Communication Technologies for Ubiquitous HealthCare (Ubi-HealthTech), 2015 2nd International Symposium on*. IEEE. 10.1109/Ubi-HealthTech.2015.7203325

Stantchev, V., Barnawi, A., Ghulam, S., Schubert, J., & Tamm, G. (2015). Smart items, fog and cloud computing as enablers of servitization in healthcare. *Sensors Transducers, 185*(2), 121.

Stojmenovic, I., & Wen, S. (2014). The fog computing paradigm: Scenarios and security issues. In *Computer Science and Information Systems (FedCSIS), 2014 Federated Conference On*. IEEE. 10.15439/2014F503

Stojmenovic, I., Wen, S., Huang, X., & Luan, H. (2015). An overview of fog computing and its security issues. *Concurrency and Computation.*

Vaquero, L. M., & Rodero-Merino, L. (2014). Finding Your Way in the Fog: Towards A Comprehensive Definition of Fog Computing. *ACM SIGCOMM Comp. Commun. Rev., 44*(5), 27–32. doi:10.1145/2677046.2677052

Varalakshmi, L., Sudha, G. F., & Jaikishan, G. (2014). A selective encryption and energy efficient clustering scheme for video streaming in wireless sensor networks. *Telecommunication Systems*, *56*(3), 357–365. doi:10.100711235-013-9849-0

Wei, X., Gomez, L., Neamtiu, I., & Faloutsos, M. (2012). Malicious android applications in the enterprise: What do they do and how do we fix it? In *Data Engineering Workshops (ICDEW), 2012 IEEE 28th International Conference on*. IEEE. 10.1109/ICDEW.2012.81

Yi, S., Hao, Z., Qin, Z., & Li, Q. (2015). Fog Computing-Platform and Applications. *IEEE Workshop on Hot Topics in Web Systems and Technologies*.

Yi, S., Qin, Z., & Li, Q. (2015). Security and privacy issues of fog computing: A survey. In *International Conference on Wireless Algorithms, Systems, and Applications*. Springer. 10.1007/978-3-319-21837-3_67

Chapter 6
EdgeCloud:
A Distributed Management System for Resource Continuity in Edge to Cloud Computing Environment

Jamuna S. Murthy
Ramaiah Institute of Technology, India

ABSTRACT

In the recent years, edge/fog computing is gaining greater importance and has led to the deployment of many smart devices and application frameworks which support real-time data processing. Edge computing is an extension to existing cloud computing environment and focuses on improving the reliability, scalability, and resource efficiency of cloud by abolishing the need for processing all the data at one time and thus increasing the bandwidth of a network. Edge computing can complement cloud computing in a way leading to a novel architecture which can benefit from both edge and cloud resources. This kind of resource architecture may require resource continuity provided that the selection of resources for executing a service in cloud is independent of physical location. Hence, this research work proposes a novel architecture called "EdgeCloud," which is a distributed management system for resource continuity in edge to cloud computing environment. The performance of the system is evaluated by considering a traffic management service example mapped into the proposed layered framework.

DOI: 10.4018/978-1-5225-6070-8.ch006

Copyright © 2019, IGI Global. Copying or distributing in print or electronic forms without written permission of IGI Global is prohibited.

INTRODUCTION

In the past few years we notice that there is a tremendous increase in the number of devices getting connected to the network. The raise in number of devices are concerned with two main resources i.e. the user devices and the sensors/actuators. The researchers from Cisco Company extensively report that there will be approximately 50 billion devices that will be connected to the network by the year 2020 (Evans, 2011). Today in the developing countries there is a major growth in the number of devices used by the people in terms of mobile phones, tablets etc. But very soon the usage of these devices will be over passed by the myriad of sensing/acting devices placed virtually everywhere (the so called Internet of Things, IoT, and pervasive sensor networks).

The new innovations such as the concept of Smart Cities(Nam & Pardo, 2011), Wearable Computing Devices such as smart watches and glasses, the Smart Metering Devices for monitoring energy consumption at homes, Visual Sensor Networks, Self Driving Vehicles with smart meters are such applications which are driving the ubiquitous computing to the next level of usage witnessing the presence of smart devices everywhere around us. This kind of technical achievements (i.e. invention of Smart devices) by the researchers is made possible by the usage of widely used technology called the Edge Computing or Fog Computing.

In the recent times Cloud Computing is slowly migrating towards the edge of network facilitating the routers to form an efficient virtualization infrastructure to support real-time data processing. This evolution of cloud to edge is labelled as Edge Computing or Fog Computing. Edge Computing is a scenario where in large number of heterogeneous devices (may be wireless or autonomous), ubiquitous devices and decentralized devices combine together in a cooperative manner to perform tasks such as storage and processing without any intervention of third party devices. The tasks performed are in nature of support for some network functioning or application interference or to provide new services in the sandboxed environment. They are generally fast since the operations take place at the edge of the network.

The main focus of Fog Computing is on improving the reliability, scalability and resource efficiency of cloud by abolishing the need for processing all the data at one time and thus increasing the bandwidth of a network (Vaquero & Rodero-Merino, 2014). Edge or Fog Computing provides wide range of benefits which is listed below:

- **Network Traffic Reduction:** There are billions of devices connected to the network world wide today. Amongst which the smart phones and tablets are in greater numbers being used by the people. These devices generally send, receive and generate data in such a way that the computing capabilities are related to the physical location nearest to the devices rather than being communicating with the data centres directly. Based on the frequency range configured for the devices, the sensor embedded in them collect the necessary data every few seconds. Therefore, it is neither necessary nor advisable to send all of the raw data to the cloud. Hence Edge Computing is very beneficial here by providing a platform for data collection, data filtering and data analysis at the edge of the cloud without being sent all the data at one time but perhaps sends only the absolutely necessary data for providing services (i.e. local data view). This in turn reduces the network traffic to greater extent.

- **Best Suitable for IoT Queries and Tasking**: As we know that the usage of smart devices and applications are increasing day by day. These smart devices are usually designed to collect the surrounding information and retrieve the information to the end user based on their service request. Most of the applications today use Edge Computing where in they serve the request without communicating with the global data present in the cloud. For Example, the applications such as Google Map is used for keeping track of surrounding information.

- **Low Latency Requirement:** Today most of the applications require real-time processing in order to quicken the tasks. One of the best examples is Cloud Robotics, which is a mission critical application where in we need to control the motion of the robot. Here the motion control depends on the data collected from the sensors and the processing is done based on the feedback control system designed. If in case the data necessary for the processing is present in the cloud then most of the times the sense-process-actuate loop processes become slow due to the continuous requests. This leads to communication failures and breakdown of application. This is where the Edge computing becomes beneficial where the controlling of the robot is done at the edge of cloud for every motion control request and helps in real-time processing of requests.

- **Scalability:** Most of the times we observe that the cloud with infinite virtual resources can also become the bottleneck when huge data generated by the end devices are sent to the cloud continuously. At this point Edge Computing becomes very essential where the processing of the incoming data is done close to the data source itself rather than communicating with the cloud data centre. This in turn increases the scalability of the endpoint devices to greater extent.

Edge Computing can complement Cloud Computing in a way leading to a novel architecture which can benefit from both edge and cloud resources. This kind of resource architecture may require resource continuity provided that the selection of resources for executing a service in cloud is independent of physical location.

Table 1. Resource continuity possibilities in the layered architecture

		Resource Continuity from Edge to Cloud			
		Edge			Cloud
		Edge Devices	Basic/ Aggregation Nodes	Intermediate Nodes	Cloud
	Device	Sensors, actuators wearables	Car, phones, computer	Smart building, cluster of devices	Datacenter
Features	Response Time	Milliseconds	Sub seconds, seconds	Seconds, minutes	Minutes, days, weeks
	Application Examples	M2M communication haptics	Dependable services (eHealth)	Visualization Simple analytics	Bigdata analytics Statics
	How long IoT data is stored	Transient	Minutes, Hours	Days, weeks	Months, years
	Geographic Coverage	Device	Connected devices	Area, cluster	Global

Let us consider few possibilities of resource continuity in layered architecture listed in Table 1. Table briefly lists out the characteristics of different computational layers from edge to cloud with different layers performing tasks associated with different devices. The different resources which are selected and categorized in the table address the optimization of service execution criteria wherein paving a way for providing solution to the problems such as privacy and security, resource efficiency, network overloading etc (Cisco. Inc, 2015). Even though there are many contributions (i.e. Business Models, Applications, Resource Models etc.) in the field of both Edge computing and Cloud Computing most of them lack Scalability, Resource efficiency and networking issues even today which are listed in detail in Literature Review Section.

By considering all the drawbacks from the existing edge computing architectures this research work proposed a new architecture called "EdgeCloud" which is a distributed management system for resource continuity in edge to cloud computing environment. The proposed architecture forms a foundational block to both edge and cloud computing resources being packed as different layers with various functionalities in order to support resource continuity while executing a particular service. A new service execution strategy is designed as a part of research work where different resources are assigned to different computational layers of the architecture based on their actual resource capabilities (i.e. storage, processing, computing and networking). The proposed "EdgeCloud" architecture is an open architecture and can be applied to any context or scenario at present. It is basically agnostic and support application extendibility to any real-time applications such as eHealth, visual sensors, military and hostile environments, language and speech processing etc to greater extent. However in case of extreme computing capabilities needed for any applications the requirements on demand may be added to provide better service. New algorithm, strategies and policies may be added based on the user requirements necessarily. A performance study is carried out at the end where in the scenario of Traffic Management is mapped on to the different layers of the proposed architecture to discuss the results in terms of scalability and resource efficiency. The database characteristics in relation to the proposed layer architecture is also discussed in detail which pave a way to further research studies in the field. The Chapter in organized as follows, Section 2 discuss the Literature review where existing architecture its drawbacks and proposed solutions are discussed in detail. Section 3 discusses the proposed "EdgeCloud" architecture with different layers and functionalities. Section 4 discussed the performance valuation of the proposed architecture with traffic management service deployed on a smart city and Finally Section 5 concludes the chapter.

LITERATURE REVIEW

In the past few years we witness that the concept of Edge Computing has turned out as a major research topic where the researchers are continuously involved in analyzing the benefits of edge or fog computing by applying it on the traditional applications (Baktir, Ozgovde, & Ersoy, 2017). The recent contributions are in the form of Cognitive Body Area Networks (BANs) (Quwaider & Jararweh, 2013), Smart Grid (Stojmenovic, 2014.), Augmented Reality (Zao, Gan, You, Méndez, Chung, Wang, ... & Jung, 2014), Assistance, Language and Speech Processing (Dubey, Yang, Constant, Amiri, Yang, & Makodiya, 2015), Military and Hostile Environments (Yaseen, AlBalas, Jararweh, & Al-Ayyoub, 2016), IoT and Wireless Sensor Networks (Aazam & Huh, 2016), Video Streaming and Analysis (European Telecommunications Standards Institute Industry Specifications Group, Mobile-Edge Computing – Service Scenarios, 2017), etc. Also "OpenFog Consortiums" are organized by the industrial sectors to discuss the new ideas and opportunities in the Fog Computing field.

Kirak Hong et al. (2013) designed a framework called "Mobile Fog" which is a programming model for large scale applications on the Internet of Things which are basically geospatially distributed and are latency sensitive and large scale. The Mobile Fog model is analysed to find out the performance issues by considering the use case of vehicular network and the simulation results were tabulated. But the results showed large differences in execution time and the resource were allocated only using the distributed layered approach. But the proposed EdgeCloud model supports resource continuity from edge to cloud environment by combining both cloud and edge resources efficiently and hence increases the performance of the system in terms of bandwidth and network traffic reduction to greater extent.

Clinton Dsouza et al. (2014) designed a framework for management of resources in fog computing environment using some policy. The architecture extended the existing fog computing architecture to support privacy and security management plane which is collaborative and interoperable to the user requests in Fog environment. The framework was applied on Smart Transportation scenario to evaluate the performance. The performance was evaluated based on the network traffic load with high and lower load points. But the results were satisfactory. Proposed system showed best results by reducing network traffic load to 2-3Kbps.

Bo Tang et al. (2015) designed a distributed, hierarchical fog computing framework for Bigdata analysis in smart-cities. The framework consists of different components and services that pave a way for a multi-ownership infrastructure deployment in smart cities scenario with Bigdata analytics. The main motive of the framework was to optimize the response time and identify the anomalies and hazardous events. Fibre optic sensor technology was use to monitor distinct events in smart cities. A performance analysis was carried out to check the response time and bandwidth of three fog layer. The result showed bandwidth reduction of 0.02% only but the proposed framework reduced the bandwidth to 2-3% hence proposed system can be more applicable to smart city scenario.

Xueshi Hou et al. (2016) designed a Vehicular Fog Computing (VFC) infrastructure which uses the collaborative approach of edge devices and end user clients for communication and computing of resources of each vehicle. The aim of VFC is to provide better QoS and application service by aggregating resources of each vehicle. Four types of scenarios are discussed for moving and parked vehicle to carry out the quantitative analysis in terms of resource capability, connectivity, and mobility of vehicles. But if we compare the VFC architecture to proposed EdgeCloud model the main features such as Resource management, security and privacy and the reduction of bandwidth and network traffic are missing which are very important for any Fog/Edge computing scenario. Thus VFC is less efficient and not secure compared to proposed system.

Arslan Munir et al. (2017) designed an Integrated Fog Cloud architecture called IFCIoT that aims at reduction of network traffic, quick response time, reduce latency and to increase scalability so as to facilitate better performance for future IoT applications. IFCIoT consist of different fog nodes that are used as edge servers, smart routers, base stations that receive computational requests from the user. Finally, a layered approach of five different layers is used here to increase the efficiency and enhance communication between each Fog layers and edge servers are deployed for collecting the information regarding user request. The framework is applied on transportation management service in smart city to analyse the results. Even though the framework is very similar to proposed layered approach the performance of IFCIoT shows large difference since in proposed system uses resource continuity which showed best results in network traffic reduction and also proposed layered architecture is simple compared to IFCIoT which is very complex to understand.

PROPOSED SYSTEM

From the Section 1 study on benefits of Resource Continuity model we infer that the combination of fog and cloud resources deliver very useful services when managed efficiently. Hence this section describes the main architectural features of the proposed system in two major subsections. The first architecture is lined out as a *Layered, hierarchical and distributed management architecture* and the second one as "Functional block design". The two architectural approaches describe the proposed system in such a way that they lead to one main objective of designing a distributed management system for resource continuity in edge to cloud environment called the "EdgeCloud" model. The proposed architecture is illustrated by considering the concepts of smart city scenario for better understanding purposes.

Architecture of Proposed "EdgeCloud" Model

Figure 1 shows the envisioned layered, hierarchical and distributed architecture of the proposed system. The system describes the allocation of fog and cloud resources to different layers based on their functional capabilities such as response time, storage, processing, geographical coverage etc. listed in Table 1 of Section 1. The coordinated Edge and Cloud architecture in Figure 1, illustrates four different layers with Cloud being the top most layer and the other three being the Edge Devices layer, Basic or Aggregation Layer and Smart nodes layer. The design follows the bottom up approach where the functional capabilities of the layers increase from lower to higher layer (i.e. Cloud layer). Cloud layer is the most efficient and the layer with highest capability. We imply on the "Edge Devices" layer that if the number of devices is considered to be less then it leads to much higher security and privacy. The main aim behind the proposed resource continuity model is to abstract the resources allocated to each layer in such a way that the performance of the system turns out to be efficient in delivering services at request time. The categorization of the physical resources remain to be similar as mentioned in Table 1, provided the categorization of the resources from edge to cloud coordinate in such a way that the abstraction between the layers facilitate resource continuity with abstracted entity being distributed within one unique layer. Clearly the above scenario of abstraction is described in Figure 1 as two different views such as Physical view and Logical view. The Physical view is more of detailed layered view where the four different layers are clearly visible as Edge Layer 1(EL1), Edge Layer 2(EL2), Edge Layer 3(EL1) and Cloud Layer (CL). EL1 consist of set of Edge devices namely Sensors, actuators, wearables etc. EL2 consist of Basic/Aggregate nodes such as cars, mobile phones, tablets, PCs etc. EL3 consist of Intermediate nodes such as Smart buildings, Cluster of devices etc. and finally CL later consist of Data center. These layers are mapped on to a single abstract view in order to facilitate resource continuity known as the Logical View. Each of the abstracted resources is envisioned to be managed using resource management functioning uniquely designed in the proposed system.

The abstraction of resources from edge to cloud environment can be implemented using virtualization technology. But here the important factor is; how to provide the coherent view of all the abstracted resources. In case if we consider virtual machines to manage the data centers in the cloud layer, then it is also necessary to consider virtual machines for managing the abstracted resources from edge devices. Or else

Figure 1. Architecture of Proposed "EdgeCloud" Model

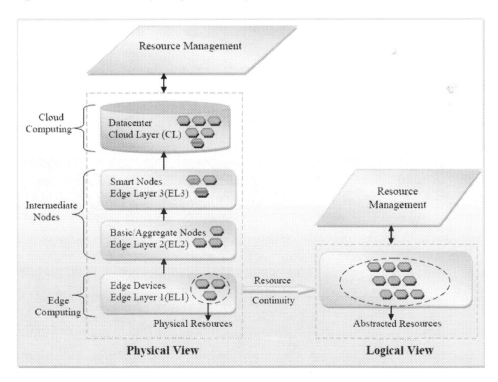

we must use different abstraction and management strategies for different layer such that they are adaptive to provide essential services at the request time such as the container and virtual machines. Any system that guarantees resource continuity must meet the following requirements:

- Firstly it must possess the coherent view of all the set of resources present in the system so that optimization of service request can be possible.
- Secondly there should be a "Control and Management" plane specially designed only for managing resources such that it independent of physical location and ownership.
- Thirdly there should be a proper and efficient strategy for Selection of resources, classifying them and allocating them in such a way that they deliver essential services on demand.
- Fourthly the resource selection, classification and allocation strategies should be decided mainly by considering the functional capabilities of resources listed in Table 1.
- Lastly the set of resources used in the system must be efficiently in a manner so that the performance of the system remains to be high.

Application of "EdgeCloud" Model on Smart-City

To study the proposed "EdgeCloud" Model in detail lets apply it on one of the well-know examples of today i.e. Smart-City. Figure 2, shows the "EdgeCloud" Model mapped Smart-City architecture which consist of three main layers i.e. two Edge layers (Layer A and Layer B) and one Cloud layer (Layer C) with all the edge devices, computing resources, storage resources, processing resources and networking resources to be combined. If we consider the two Edge layers Layer A and B, in the lowest layer simple edge devices such as sensors, actuators and wearables are implemented and the upper layer consists of cars, smart phones and PCs. Let us assume that from now on the devices are grouped into Edge domain referred to as "Edges" based on the some policy laid down based on factors such as capability, proximity, real-time connection and business benefits. Next the Cloud layer, i.e. Layer C is implemented as three different clouds i.e. public, private and hybrid clouds based on the requirements. In Layer A there are four different Edges (Edge domains) i.e. Edge A1, Edge A2, Edge A3 and Edge A4. Also in Layer B there are two different Edges such as Edge B1 and Edge B2. The Figure 2 consists of other two important coordinated management artefacts such as Zone and Base elements. A Zone is an area which consists of an Edge orgroup of Edges present in different layers to facilitate vertical coordination of resource among the different layers. Configuration of different zones and their control mechanisms is out of scope of to research work and the details such as definition is open to the research and can be found in related research articles. Base elements are the control elements required for facilitating the real-time functioning of the system. Two Base elements are proposed in the system here, they are Access Points (AP) and Zone Supervision Units (ZSU). Access Point is a control element which helps in delivering different services that are required for specific Edge. It also consist of a Control Block (CB) to facilities the network functioning over real-time efficiently. In Figure 2, each of the Edge layer consist of two different Zones, Zone 1 and Zone 2. In particular the Zone 1 of "Edge layer B" consists of a Access Point embedded with Metro Station of Edge A1 which in-turn is implemented with a vehicular network and edge premise in building (i.e. a building with smart camera, face recognition systems etc.) . A Zone Supervision Unit (ZSU) is a control element which helps in management and supervision of different zones designed in the system based on factors such as location identification, security and privacy etc. There are two ZSUs implemented in the system i.e. Zone Supervision Unit-A and Zone Supervision Unit-B. The functioning of ZSU in the proposed system is; firstly the ZSUs are connected with different Access Points of the nearest zones such that the vertical coordination among the resources allocated in different layers happen efficiently based on their capabilities. Secondly the ZSUs are connected as "Inter-Zone Control Communication" by enlarging the distinct resources available from different ZSUs such that to facilitate horizontal coordination efficiently in the system. Finally the ZSUs are connected even with the Cloud Layer consisting of cloud resources through "Control Communication" channel thus enabling a concept of deploying a distributed system for resource continuity in edge to cloud environment.

Management and Coordination Module System for Resource Continuity

In an earlier section, we studied a concept of application of proposed "EdgeCloud" model on Smart City. The architecture diagram was brief and clearly paved a way for deploying a distributed framework for resource continuity in edge to cloud environment. But the main idea behind the research work is how exactly we manage resource continuity in edge to cloud environment. Thus in this section new set of modules are designed for proper management functionalities. Figure 3 illustrates the coordination and management of resource continuity in edge to cloud environment based on three major functional blocks. The three modules are Instantiation, Processing and Brokering.

The major part of the module system includes the Processing Component. It consists of three major blocks namely User/Context Side Block (USB), Service Side Block (SSB) and Resource Side Block (RSB). Each block differs in their own way

117

Figure 2. Application of EdgeCloud model on Smart-City

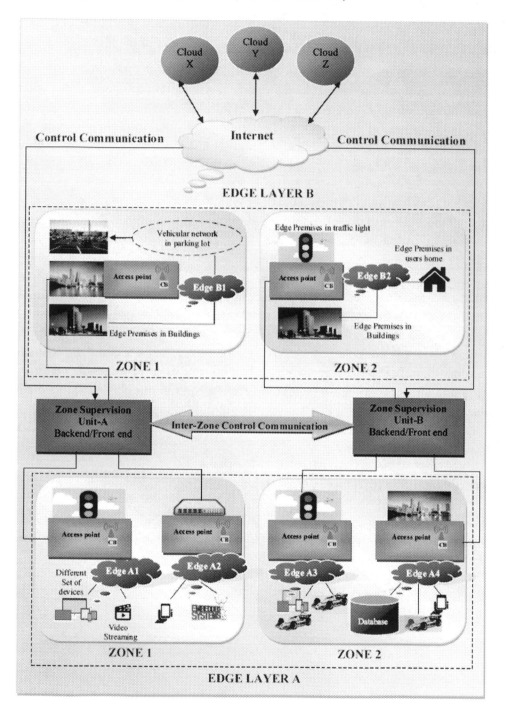

Figure 3. Distributed management architecture for Resource Continuity

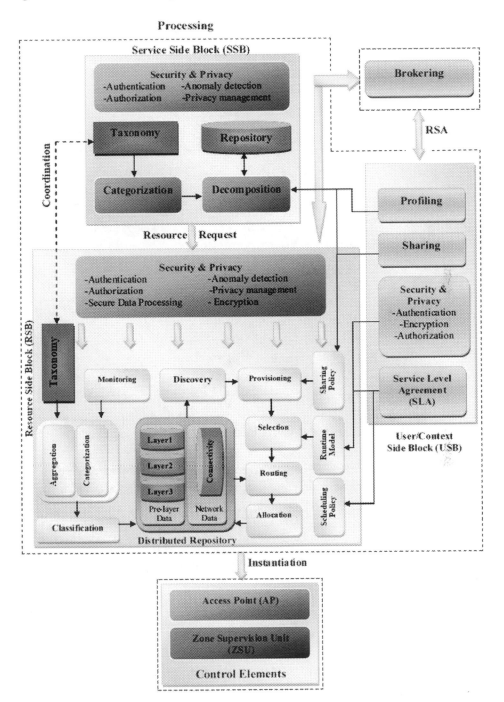

based on their functionalities. The third component is brokering which is used at the times of multi-ownership infrastructure. If the Edge or the Cloud layers in the system belong to different parties then brokering helps in joint deployment. The three major functional blocks in the proposed module system are explained in detail.

Functionalities of User Side Block(USB)

From Figure 3, we notice that the objective of USB is to facilitate user interaction in the system and to contextualize how the user service requests are made and how exactly those service requests are handled and executed in the system. In USB first and the most important step for resource continuity in edge to cloud environment follows "Profiling" which means, a user must first register or provide required contextual information so as to deliver the necessary services on-time based on the demands. Second step is any user who registers can benefit the "Sharing" of resource because of the presence of Edge/Fog service in the system. Third step is any user who stores and shares the information must follow Security and Privacy rules such Authentication, Authorization and Encryption. That is any user who wishes to share his resources for example, details of his car and vehicles at his house may strictly follow rules and regulations of privacy since other users may not be loyal and can't be trusted. Also, the fourth step says a while deploying the corresponding functionalities in the real world they all the functioning must be under business policies i.e. Service Level Agreements (SLA).

Functionalities of Service Side Block(SSB)

The main aim of designing SSB is to handle the user requests effectively in the system. As soon as the user makes any request it goes to SSB and the service made by the user is categorized based on dynamic service taxonomy, where-in a service can be neither pre-configured nor created instantly. User request on the other hand can be decomposed into atomic service i.e. subservices for handling them easily. The main goal behind this decomposition is atomic services may generally require less computing resources, and facilitates parallel execution. This can reduce the processing time so that in-turn can increase the performance of the system. The Repository is a database which generally stores the of set of atomic services which are pre-configured based on predictions from previous user requests and also adds the new services made by the user. One of the challenges that arise here is how to maintain the performance of the system (i.e. taking into consideration the computing resources and service execution time) while allocating a place for subservice in repository during decomposition. Also a very interesting issue arise here while defining the extent of service that can be associated with the Access Points in the system such as subservices and their relationships, defining graph rules and dependencies, decision making for giving preference to search the available resources from Layer-Zone or Zone-Layer, find out the missing subservices in the Zone or Edge Layers and planning strategies at time where the user may not to be satisfied from the services provided by the SSB etc. Also to handle security and privacy issues within the system such as anomaly detection and privacy management.

Functionalities of Resource Side Block(RSB)

The objective of RSB is to facilitate coordination and resource management functionalities in the system. The first and the fore most steps are Monitoring and Discovery. These steps help to acquire the domain specific knowledge of resources for each device and also the accurate representation of each device based on factors such as tablet or mobile or PC, virtual device or Physical device, shared resource or exclusive etc. After performing the above steps, the information or knowledge gathered is categorized and classified (i.e. same strategy as used in SSB for categorization) stored in an interactive database called the Distributed Repository. The distributed repository consists of two main components. First is pre-layer for storage and computing of resource. Second one is network connectivity feature which enables topology information gathering. Each service is executed based on Provisioning which include whether to decide the service is free and given by the system or it is on-demand service by the users. After the decision is made the resources are selected based on some runtime policies Routing techniques Resources are assigned to the service to be executed, depending on the service demands, runtime model or policies and are finally allocated by initiating any routing. Usually representation of resources to each layer is a hideous task due to the hidden complexities and relationships within the layer, the heterogeneity of the edge devices and also at extreme cases the business policies when we have multi-ownership infrastructure. Hence in the proposed framework resource continuity is envisioned as open source where the services and the users benefit from the open source resources for performance optimization.

PERFORMANCE STUDY

In this section we study about the potential benefits obtained when the proposed resource continuity management architecture is deployed on Smart City application. Here we highlight the performance issues concerning to the traffic management service example discussed. The performance study or analysis made here is purely envision and doesn't guarantee any profits or benchmarking. They state the potential performance benefits that can be obtained when proposed resource continuity concept (i.e. EdgeCloud model) is deployed using layered approach and in fact to encourage the further research in this area. With the above objective performance study starts with description of the Traffic Management Service which is deployed on smart city application using proposed EdgeCloud model. Different Edge layers and its functionalities are clearly mentioned including the topologies which are configured for three different cities in real-world i.e. Bangalore, Mumbai and Pune. The preliminary results are shown on proposed traffic management database.

The illustration of the Traffic Management Service is shown in Figure 4. The figure consists of three different Edge Layers i.e. Edge Layer A, Edge Layer B and Edge Layer C. Each layer collectively function for providing traffic monitoring service and differ based on the resource capacity i.e. from Layer A to C the resource capabilities keep on increasing. Edge Layer A consist of three different sub layers i.e. Edge Layer A1, A2 and A3 where A1 and A2 function for traffic monitoring and A3 functions for Car monitoring in Zone. Edge Layer B possesses more computing capabilities such as storage, processing and networking than Layer A and hence it is deployed to serve as Bus stop monitoring system. The Zone Control Unit is assumed to be deployed in Edge Layer B. The Edge Layer C has highest resource computing capability and hence it is deployed for resource sharing in parking lot. All the layers are assumed to be present in one single zone and the resources are published to the Brokering module present in the system which takes care of global policies of multi-ownership.

J.J. Fernndez Lozano et al. (2015) discussed a unique approach for collecting the data regarding the vehicles travelling in certain routes based on its source and destination city using a data matrix. This is based on the sensor technology where sensors are present at distinguished locations and the locality information is collectively processed and reported eventually to the centralized data centre. Thus to manage and coordinate traffic management service here a well-defined approach discussed above is incorporated. But the difference is in proposed approach single specific city zone is used instead of multiple cities. Thus here the approach is much simpler and need on make decision regarding geographical shifts of distinct data centers. Different Edge layers are used to collect the required vehicular information and are forwarding to single data centre located in the same city zone. A traffic management sub-matrix is defined for each city i.e. Bangalore, Mumbai and Pune which consist of required information for local decision making in order to facilitate the traffic management service smoothly. The potential benefits such as latency, bandwidth reduction and execution time are however present in the system since edge computing for traffic management service here. In addiction the impact of analysis of database size, traffic load and lookup time for updating proposed traffic management database is also shown here. Since the information gathered here is using the real-time sensor technology the database size and lookup time will be comparatively higher. The database results are discussed for two different scenarios such as cloud management and distributed layered approach for three real-world cities based on the following assumptions.

- Edge A1, Edge A2 and Edge A3 are defined as Traffic Sensor Nodes (TSN) which detect the Car IDs or numbers with MAC address.
- TSN in Edge Layer A are separated by 100m linear distance in the city streets. The baseline city will have 10,000m street area in the city.
- A car is assumed to occupy 4m alone and distance between two cars can be 1m and distance between a car and lane is an average of 1 meter.
- The data collected by the sensors of same city zone will be used for providing the traffic management service of that particular zone.

Bangalore city has 1,319,125 street meters and here let us assume that the TNS are 100m away from each other. Thus there are approximately 13k TNS that register eventually to the data centre about the number of cars and its MAC address. Again let us assume that there are two lanes in each street separated by 100m under each Edge layer of zone which may have 20 cars separated by 4 meters each and 1m distance between a car and a lane. This turns out as single TNS that stores 40 car ids (MAC address of 48 bits). Thus in cloud approach the centralized database stores $40*48*13k = 3$Mbps of car data and updates it for every few seconds. Whereas in the distributed layered approach only the city specific information or data is stored. Here the size of each area within the city is considered for defining the trend of the city. Here it is assumed that each city area is considered as a layout.

In Bangalore city there are hundreds of areas but for an instance around 10 areas are considered with each of 1.3k TNS (i.e. all present in Edge Layer A). Thus information stored in database is $40*48*1.3k= 300$Kbps. But on the other hand if we consider large set of 130 areas with each of 100 TNS then the information stored in database is around $40*48*100=23$Kbps (i.e. updated every few seconds) as shown in Table 2. The time complexity here is assumed to be O (log(S)), where S is the size of the database. Table 2 clearly differentiates the cloud and distributed approach for traffic management service considering other cities such as Mumbai and Pune as well.

Figure 4. Traffic Management with resource continuity concept

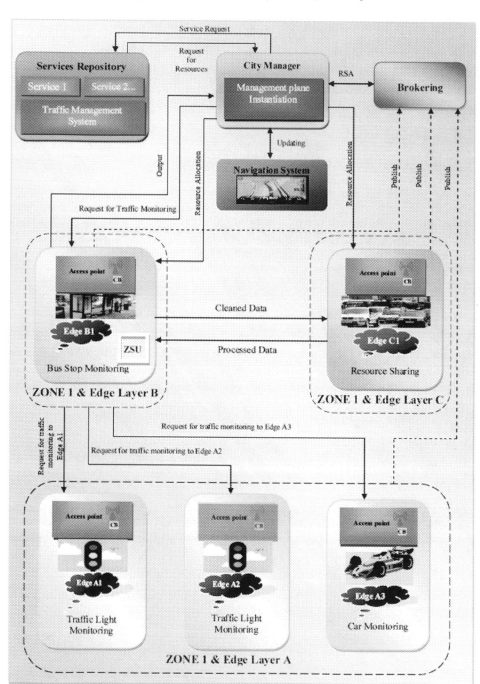

Table 2. Proposed database approach for updating network traffic

City Database Information				
Bangalore City	**Edge Computing and Management**			
Mean length between Traffic sensor Nodes(m)	*Total no. of Traffic sensor Nodes in Zone*	*No. of City Zones*	*Size of the table in each zone(KB)*	*Average Lookup Time*
100	1300	10 (layouts)	300	1,21
100	100	130	23	1
Bangalore City	**Cloud Computing and Management**			
Mean length between Traffic sensor Nodes(m)	*Total no. of Traffic sensor Nodes in Zone*	*Size of the table in all city zones(MB)*		*Average Lookup Time*
100	13,000	3		1,40
Mumbai City	**Edge Computing and Management**			
Mean length between Traffic sensor Nodes(m)	*Total no. of Traffic sensor Nodes in Zone*	*No. of City Zones*	*Size of the table in each Zone(KB)*	*Lookup Time*
100	708	6 (layouts)	165	1,17
100	100	43	23	1
Mumbai City	**Cloud Computing and Management**			
Mean length between Traffic sensor Nodes(m	*Total no. of Traffic sensor Nodes in Zone*	*Size of the table in all city zones(MB)*		*Average Lookup Time*
100	4,250	1		1,31
Pune City	**Edge Computing and Management**			
Mean length between Traffic sensor Nodes(m	*Total no. of Traffic sensor Nodes in Zone*	*No. of City Zones*	*Size of the table in each zone(KB)*	*Average Lookup Time*
100	3,680	15 (districts)	860	1,29
100	100	550	23	1
Pune City	**Cloud Computing and Management**			
Mean length between Traffic sensor Nodes(m	*Total no. of Traffic sensor Nodes in Zone*	*Size of the table in all city zones(MB)*		*Average Lookup Time*
100	55,000	12		1,52
Database Updating Traffic				
Management Approach	**City**	**1 sec (Mbps)**	**5 sec (Mbps)**	**10 sec (Mbps)**
Cloud	Bangalore	3	0,6	0,3
	Mumbai	1	0,2	0,1
	Pune	12	2,4	1,2
Layered	Any city	23	4,6	2,3

The results from Table 2 clearly show the potential benefits of proposed distributed layered approach concerned to the size and lookup time of the database. We can observe the trade-off between the number of city areas and the services that can be provided in each city. This gives us a clear picture that the lookup time and size of the database increases with the increase in the area of the city. This in turn increases the services that have to be provided as well. The database also defined the amount of traffic load that was handled by the proposed database system and its impact creates a motivational factor for future research on extension of database. Database characteristics of Pune city gives us a motive that for every 5 seconds around GBs of data is sent over the network thus provisioning the impact of other factors such as network dimensioning, energy consumed and optimization of infrastructure only on the updation of proposed database.

CONCLUSION

Edge Computing can complement Cloud Computing in a way leading to a novel architecture which can benefit from both edge and cloud resources. This kind of resource architecture may require resource continuity provided that the selection of resources for executing a service in cloud is independent of physical location. Hence this research work proposed a new resource continuity model called "EdgeCloud" which consist of three different Edge layers operating in a unique way paving a way for reducing network traffic at greater extent. Initially the proposed EdgeCloud model is applied on a smart city scenario by implementing two important control elements called AP and ZSU. Later detailed distributed management architecture with three functional blocks was deployed to facilitate resource continuity in edge to cloud environment. The architecture clearly described the security and privacy issues, selection of strategy for resource computations and also how each edge layers communicate to allow resource continuity to provide better services to user. Finally the proposed approach was evaluated for performance using traffic management service example by considering three real-world cities Bangalore, Mumbai and Pune. The network traffic was calculated for each city using cloud and layered architecture approaches and was tabulated using proposed database structure. Clearly it indicated that proposed EdgeCloud model reduces the network traffic to greater extent than the cloud computing approach alone. Hence it draws to a conclusion that proposed model is well suitable for implementation on any smart city scenario which include resource pooling. Future research objectives many include simulation of proposed approach or to implement the proposed resource continuity architecture using visualization technology.

REFERENCES

Aazam, M., & Huh, E. N. (2016). Fog computing: The cloud-iot\/ioe middleware paradigm. *IEEE Potentials*, *35*(3), 40–44. doi:10.1109/MPOT.2015.2456213

Baktir, A. C., Ozgovde, A., & Ersoy, C. (2017). How Can Edge Computing Benefit from Software-Defined Networking: A Survey, Use Cases & Future Directions. *IEEE Communications Surveys and Tutorials*, *19*(4), 2359–2391. doi:10.1109/COMST.2017.2717482

Dsouza, C., Ahn, G. J., & Taguinod, M. (2014, August). Policy-driven security management for fog computing: Preliminary framework and a case study. In *Information Reuse and Integration (IRI), 2014 IEEE 15th International Conference on* (pp. 16-23). IEEE.

Dubey, H., Yang, J., Constant, N., Amiri, A. M., Yang, Q., & Makodiya, K. (2015, October). Fog data: Enhancing telehealth big data through fog computing. In *Proceedings of the ASE BigData & SocialInformatics 2015* (p. 14). ACM.

European Telecommunications Standards Institute Industry Specifications Group, Mobile-Edge Computing – Service Scenarios. (2017). Retrieved from http://www.etsi.org/deliver/etsi_gs/MEC-IEG/001_099/004/01.01.01_60/gs_MEC-IEG004v010101p.pdf

Evans, D. (2011). The internet of things: How the next evolution of the internet is changing everything. CISCO. *Int. J. Internet*, *3*(2), 123–132.

Fernández-Lozano, J. J., Martín-Guzmán, M., Martín-Ávila, J., & García-Cerezo, A. (2015). A wireless sensor network for urban traffic characterization and trend monitoring. *Sensors (Basel)*, *15*(10), 26143–26169. doi:10.3390151026143 PMID:26501278

Hong, K., Lillethun, D., Ramachandran, U., Ottenwälder, B., & Koldehofe, B. (2013, August). Mobile fog: A programming model for large-scale applications on the internet of things. In *Proceedings of the second ACM SIGCOMM workshop on Mobile cloud computing* (pp. 15-20). ACM. 10.1145/2491266.2491270

Hou, X., Li, Y., Chen, M., Wu, D., Jin, D., & Chen, S. (2016). Vehicular fog computing: A viewpoint of vehicles as the infrastructures. *IEEE Transactions on Vehicular Technology*, *65*(6), 3860–3873. doi:10.1109/TVT.2016.2532863

Munir, A., Kansakar, P., & Khan, S. U. (2017). IFCIoT: Integrated Fog Cloud IoT: A novel architectural paradigm for the future Internet of Things. *IEEE Consumer Electronics Magazine*, *6*(3), 74–82. doi:10.1109/MCE.2017.2684981

Nam, T., & Pardo, T. A. (2011, September). Smart city as urban innovation: Focusing on management, policy, and context. In *Proceedings of the 5th international conference on theory and practice of electronic governance* (pp. 185-194). ACM. 10.1145/2072069.2072100

Quwaider, M., & Jararweh, Y. (2013, December). Cloudlet-based for big data collection in body area networks. In *Internet Technology and Secured Transactions (ICITST), 2013 8th International Conference for* (pp. 137-141). IEEE.

Satyanarayanan, M., Schuster, R., Ebling, M., Fettweis, G., Flinck, H., Joshi, K., & Sabnani, K. (2015). An open ecosystem for mobile-cloud convergence. *IEEE Communications Magazine*, *53*(3), 63–70. doi:10.1109/MCOM.2015.7060484

Stojmenovic, I. (2014, November). Fog computing: A cloud to the ground support for smart things and machine-to-machine networks. In *Telecommunication Networks and Applications Conference (ATNAC), 2014 Australasian* (pp. 117-122). IEEE. 10.1109/ATNAC.2014.7020884

Tang, B., Chen, Z., Hefferman, G., Wei, T., He, H., & Yang, Q. (2015, October). A hierarchical distributed fog computing architecture for big data analysis in smart cities. In *Proceedings of the ASE BigData & SocialInformatics 2015* (p. 28). ACM.

Vaquero, L. M., & Rodero-Merino, L. (2014). Finding your way in the fog: Towards a comprehensive definition of fog computing. *Computer Communication Review*, *44*(5), 27–32. doi:10.1145/2677046.2677052

Yaseen, Q., AlBalas, F., Jararweh, Y., & Al-Ayyoub, M. (2016, September). A fog computing based system for selective forwarding detection in mobile wireless sensor networks. In Foundations and Applications of Self* Systems, IEEE International Workshops on (pp. 256-262). IEEE. doi:10.1109/FAS-W.2016.60

Zao, J. K., Gan, T. T., You, C. K., Méndez, S. J. R., Chung, C. E., Te Wang, Y., . . . Jung, T. P. (2014, June). Augmented brain computer interaction based on fog computing and linked data. In *Intelligent Environments (IE), 2014 International Conference on* (pp. 374-377). IEEE. 10.1109/IE.2014.54

Chapter 7
Security and Privacy Issues in IoT:
A Platform for Fog Computing

S. R. Mani Sekhar
Ramaiah Institute of Technology, India

Sharmitha S. Bysani
Ramaiah Institute of Technology, India

Vasireddy Prabha Kiranmai
Ramaiah Institute of Technology, India

ABSTRACT

Security and privacy issues are the challenging areas in the field of internet of things (IoT) and fog computing. IoT and fog has become an involving technology allowing major changes in the field of information systems and communication systems. This chapter provides the introduction of IoT and fog technology with a brief explanation of how fog is overcoming the challenges of cloud computing. Thereafter, the authors discuss the different security and privacy issues and its related solutions. Furthermore, they present six different case studies which will help the reader to understand the platform of IoT in fog.

INTRODUCTION

Internet of Things (IoT) is on the cutting edge of Technology, connecting humans, devices and systems intelligently. It is a network of connected physical objects that are reachable through the Internet. The 'Thing' in the IoT could range from a "Smart Home" to a "Connected Inhaler", that is assigned a unique address and has

DOI: 10.4018/978-1-5225-6070-8.ch007

Copyright © 2019, IGI Global. Copying or distributing in print or electronic forms without written permission of IGI Global is prohibited.

the potential to fetch and handover the data collected, over a network without any assistance, making our lives more easier. IoT enables a device to represent itself digitally over the internet and gets connected to its surrounding devices triggering interaction among various such connected devices.

The word "Internet of Things (IoT)" was coined by Kevin Ashton in 1999 and is defined as the network of physical nodes with other items embedded with it like software, sensors, actuators, and network connectivity which enable these objects to collect and exchange data. IoT integrates the real world with the computer-based systems precisely and efficiently, reducing the human intervention.

Though the term "Internet of Things" is two decades old, it is in limelight since 2010 as there has been an exponential growth in the number of devices connected to the internet. Starting from a 'Connected Home' having remotes, smart refrigerator, security keypads to the present-day mobile-controlled devices, smart-temperature learning device (thermostats), connected fitness tracker we have seen our lives evolving around the internet. Medical field is tremendously improving by the application of IoT as it aims to empower people to lead a healthier life by wearing connected devices. The impact of IoT is challengingly growing in the Agriculture, Poultry and Animal Husbandry fields.

There is an exciting future in the field of IoT. Growth of Artificial Intelligence and Machine Learning will result in a new range of connecting devices in the coming decade with improvised technologies. Concepts like "Monitoring and Reporting" will ensure clean and safe surroundings with smart traffic systems resulting in lessening the accident numbers, ensuring security. Applications of IoT to Plants and Animals sector will lead to a smarter way of growing, processing and storing food. Smart Home would automatically manage our most standard house activities and its energy consumption.

The evolution of IoT has started with remote computing infrastructures like data centers and moved on to the recent Cloud Computing environment to meet the demands of enormous data that the devices generate by making use of virtual storage applications in turn it will take off to "fog computing" in the coming days. Fog Computing features a cloud on the edge of the device where data is generated resulting in reducing the access time to the cloud.

Boon of IoT would be Machine to Machine (M2M) Communication leading to an automation of daily tasks which in turn provide a controlled, efficient, timely, and a better quality of life. Setback of IoT would be technology taking over our lives, lesser employment of menial staff, risk of losing privacy, any failure or bug in the software will result in serious consequences.

HOW IS IoT LINKED WITH FOG?

The Internet of things is developing gradually and is leaving a mark in almost all domains. High-speed data processing, analytics and with less response times has become mandatory in all applications and software's and it is turning out to be a tough task to meet these requirements in the current centralized cloud computing technique used by the present IoT systems. Organizations storing large amounts of data on the cloud find it difficult to cope with the swift changes in the cloud technologies, making them dependent on the service providers. Security, Privacy and Complexity in building their private cloud still seems challenging for the Cloud Computing Sector (Lebied, 2017).

To overcome the challenges faced by the Cloud Computing Technology, researchers have come up with an idea of bringing Cloud service features closer to physical IoT devices. This computing infrastructure where the cloud is placed in vicinity of data being generated featuring as "mini-cloud" is referred to as Fogging or Edge Computing or Fog Computing, often associated with Cisco. The metaphor "fog" is coined since it refers to the cloud near the ground. Substantially, the fog layer acts as a junction between the produced data and cloud capabilities. It aims to increase the efficiency by reducing the movement of data to and fro the Cloud. Here, the processing and storage of computing resources and its applicant services are closer to the edge of the network. Any device with computing, storage and network connectivity is referred to as a fog node which can be installed anywhere in a network connection. Fog nodes are the building blocks of the Fog Computing Infrastructure allowing short-term analytics at the network edge.

IoT Applications which require mobility support such as geo-distribution and location-awareness can be implemented by Fog Computing. Besides these, real time gaming augmented reality and real time streaming which require high speed processing and low latency can use Fog over Cloud. Ultimately, Fog computing can be used in Big Data sector as it supports edge analytics and stream mining, helps in reducing data volume at a very early stage, cutting down delay and saving bandwidth.

Fog computing brings forward some evidential benefits (Bonomi, Milito, Zhu & Addepalli, 2012) such as:

- **Low Latency:** The proximity to end users makes possible the support of real-time services (e.g. gaming, video streaming).
- **Geographical Distribution of Network:** The Fog provides distributed computing and storage resources to, for example, large and widely distributed sensor networks.

- **Mobility:** It delivers rich services analogous to location for moving users and location constrained devices.
- **Flexibility and Heterogeneity:** This technology allows the interaction of different physical environments and infrastructures among multiple services.
- **Scalability:** The closeness to the edge of the network enables scaling the amount of connected devices and services.
- **Delay Jitter:** High in Cloud Computing, very low in Fog Computing.

Below section explains the different applications related to IoT and Fog Computing:

- (Yi, Hao, Qin & Li,2015) has proposed a Smart Home concept by connecting different devices and sensors which are capable of computing and storing data. Fog computing can be used to integrate all the individual components into a single system with elastic resources.
- Health-Care Information (Yi, Hao, Qin & Li, 2015) has to be handled with great security and privacy thereby paving way for the Fog Computing technology to be used in the Medical Sector. It can be used to store a patient's information in separate fogs and can be updated on regular intervals directly into the patient-owned fog
- A smart traffic light (Bonomi, Milito, Zhu & Addepalli,2012) system illustrates the role of fog computing in IoT in which a smart traffic light node interacts locally with a number of sensors, which detects the presence of pedestrians and bikers and also measures the distance and speed of the approaching vehicles. Based on this information the smart light notifies the approaching vehicles or may modify its own cycle to prevent accidents.

SECURITY IN IoT

By the end of 2020, around 38.5 billion devices are expected to be connected to the Internet which has already crossed 13.4 billion in 2015 (Raval, 2016). The count of the connected devices makes it obvious that the amount of data which will be flown across the network will be massive and this would completely challenge the capture, storage, and analysis of data, something that will transform the types of database technologies we have.

DATA SECURITY ISSUE

Due to the predominance of Cyber Security malfunctions, people are finding it difficult to secure their personal gadgets like Mobiles and laptops from security threats, whereas in IoT where there are billions of devices, securing the devices will definitely be a tedious task. Ensuring cyber security of all these devices does not seem to be an easy task. The volume of data is also so huge that tracking and identifying malicious traffic over the network is quite challenging. With the rise of IoT, phishing attacks are definitely going to increase. The systems, appliances and the embedded systems which are a part of the IoT network have the power to control the utility grids and communication systems of the world. An interruption in the functionality of these devices by a cyber-attack may have dreadful consequences. The Internet of Things may range from a thousand to millions of identical devices, so if a hacker is able to sneak an attack into one of these devices, then a similar attack can be reproduced across all devices.

THREATS TO IoT AND FOG COMPUTING

In these sections we discuss the different threats related to smart meter, smart watch and device kidnapping.

THREAT TO ELECTRICITY SMART METER

The users of the connected devices which are part of the Internet of Things network must try to understand what kind of data their connected devices collect and how much of that data is being shared with other devices and what sort of modes are used for the transmission and retrieval of the data, where the data is being stored and how strongly this data has been secured. These connected devices must run the latest version of any software so that the devices remain bug-free else it may fall prey to unauthorized access. For example, if there is a smart meter which sends energy-usage data to the utility services companies for billing, it must be ensured that this data is safely secured. Else if on hacking this information reaches the hands of thieves, they can burgle houses based on their power usage information, that is, if the power usage of a house is less, it would mean that there is no one in the house. Hacking of a smart-meter of a house would peril on various personal information like our email-id, phone number, bank account details or Government-Id details as they are linked with smart meters. Thus if we have good security mechanisms to protect all our smart devices which are connected, then we will be free from such threats.

THREAT DUE TO DEVICE KIDNAPPING

Another threat to the security of data in the field of IoT would be Device Kidnapping (Suthar, 2016). Some device owners claim that their device was hacked and the hackers were demanding certain amount as ransom, to get it unlocked. Suppose a home security system or a webcam or any other optical device gets hacked, a hacker can gets access to the surveillance system. It would become easier for someone to keep an eye on that person, in their house, without them even having the slightest of idea about it.

Due to the possibility of information getting stolen from the smart devices, consumers are very concerned about the security of their data and thus they would hesitate to purchase IoT enabled smart connected devices. Researchers (Meola, 2016) have been able to hack into real, on-the-market devices with enough time and energy, which means hackers would likely be able to replicate their efforts.

THREAT TO SMARTWATCH AND FITNESS TRACKER

Wearable devices like smart watch and fitness tracker carry a lot of information on the health data of a person. Data sent between smart watch and an android phone can be intercepted by hackers as data exchange between these devices through Bluetooth communication which relies on a six digit pin which can be easily cracked using a brute force technique in turn providing easy access to the health data of the user and manipulate it thereby leading to fatal consequences on patients' health. It is very crucial to ensure that motion sensors embedded in such devices do not disclose any such information to the neighboring fog nodes.

SOLUTIONS TO SECURITY ISSUES IN IOT AND FOG

Below section provide the overview of present solution for Malware protection, authentication, data encryption and access control etc. in the field of IoT and Fog computing

MALWARE PROTECTION

The fog nodes in the Fog Computing Platform which are affected by malware like virus Trojans, ransom are worms, spyware rootkits etc. can reduce the performance of the fog network and also damage the data permanently. The above stated can be resolved by installing anti-malware software programs in the fog nodes with a deployment of certain intrusion detection systems at vulnerable points in the fog network and stringent regular data backups can be performed.

Instead of carrying out computing and device control in the remote data centers as in Cloud Computing, with fog it can be carried out at the end-user devices thereby making it difficult for threats and attacks to pass through all the fog nodes as these nodes can quickly identify strange activity and tranquilize them before the malware enters the core system. When it comes to data storage, the data collected from the IoT devices are managed by the distributed fog nodes, then these data will be more easily available and can well protected in comparison to the data stored in the user remote data centers.

AUTHENTICATION

Authentication is considered as an important issue in fog computing as these services are made available to a huge mass of end-users by the front fog nodes. When a device is connected to a network, authentication of the device is required prior to transmitting and receiving data. Balfanz has put forward a cheap and user-friendly solution using biometric authentication through fingerprint or face which can be used to simplify the authentication procedure in a fog network thus providing security of user data. Outsourcing of data to a fog node leads to difficulty in ensuring data integrity as this data may be lost or modified and in turn can be manipulated by some unauthorized alliances. In order to provide integrity, confidentiality and verifiability for a cloud storage system, the client can verify its data stored on untrusted services, auditable data storage services, by providing the different approaches such as combination of homomorphic encryption and searchable encryption.

DATA ENCRYPTION

Data encryption is an extensively used approach to secure data confidentiality. Encryption may lead to increased resource allocation issues, so only subtle and crucial information like user's identity in vehicular networks, patient data in healthcare systems, cached data should be encrypted. Efficient data integrity scrutinization must be performed to ratify the received and sent information both before and after communication.

Due to the lack of available dedicated and contiguous memory in the fog platform, there is an absence of malware protection in the fog devices. One solution for this issue would be using a physical malware device such that it does not use any fog resources. Tools like Bare Cloud (Kirat, Vigna, & Kruegel, 2014) can be used to automatically recognize dangerous malware and zero day threats can be identified using some machine learning algorithms.

ACCESS CONTROL

In order to restrict the privileges of the device components and applications, access control measures must be built into the operating system of the fog network devices so that only the required resources can be accessed. As access to all resources is not essential for the devices to perform a function, the principle to minimum privilege would minimize the intervention of security. A good practice would be to keep the devices in the fog network relatively secluded thereby allowing only few delegated persons to have access, making these devices tamper-proof or tamper-evident might be favorable. This type of endpoint hardening can help restrict intruders from reaching the data. The endpoints can be secured by using (Corser, Fink & Aledhari, 2017) small simple plastic devices, port locks and camera covers, which would shut out the USB and Ethernet ports and camera webcam apertures. Port locks also help in avoiding undesirable malware from entering. When a device gets tampered, some of the tamper-resistant techniques paralyses the device. This security countermeasure of endpoint toughening creates a sort of a layered path that would require the attackers to bypass a variety of difficulties planned to protect the device and its information from illegal access.

NEED FOR PRIVACY

Digitalization of the physical world through sensors and connectivity using Internet of Things (IoT) is widely extended to various fields making Environment Monitoring, HealthCare, Industry Automation, and Precision Agriculture and so on possible. These applications of IoT tend to produce enormous amount of data and is estimated by the International Data Corporation (IDC) that the data stored in the "cloud" would go up by two folds by 2020. Increase in the data produced by the connected devices makes the data more vulnerable to Hackers and Cyber Criminals, urging for the need of Security and Privacy for Data.

Most of the IoT applications measure variables related to consumption, velocity, temperature, pressure, heartbeat or control some physical systems, power circuits, automated lights, valves and brakes. Also, financial, criminal, political, medical records maybe collected by the IoT devices. Sometimes, this may result in the gathering of very private and sensitive data related to an individual giving rise to some Data Privacy issues.

DATA PRIVACY ISSUES

Some of the issues related to Data Privacy in the IoT domain (Meola, 2016) are:

- **Tremendous Data:** The data generated by devices is massive as per Federal Trade Commission there are more than ten thousand household devices which can produce more than 150 million data points every day. This makes more access points for Hackers and Cyber Criminals.
- **Unwanted Public Profile:** Some personal information of an individual which might be very crucial to a company may be handed over to the company by that individual consciously, but later the company might misuse the data for acquiring benefits. For instance, an insurance company may collect data related to one's driving habits through a connected car.
- **Eavesdropping:** Manufacturers and Hackers can use a connected device to invade a person's activities by collecting private data about the individual.
- **Customer Confidence:** All these factors create void in the day-to-day usage of IoT by Customers as the customers are concerned regarding the privacy of their data.

PRIVACY IN IOT AND FOG

Privacy of Data in IoT devices is accomplished using Authentication, Encryption and Data Masking (Madakam & Date, 2016) ensuring that the access to data is authorized. Various devices that are connected to each other to communicate should ensure that they are reliable and credible. Some security standards are to be set up and followed by the devices which gather sensitive data. The mobile nodes in IoT which often move from one cluster to another should be embedded with cryptography-based protocols that provide quick identification authentication and privacy protection.

THREATS TO IOT AND FOG

Looking on to Fog Computing, fog devices face similar Security and Privacy threats as the conventional Data Centers used in Cloud Computing. Security and Privacy is to be tended into every layer in constructing the Fog Computing System resulting in a better Privacy mechanism.Though the Privacy of data and information in Fog Computing is better when compared to the conventional Cloud Computing and other technologies as the data is collected, inspected and stored locally in the fog located over the device, there are still some problems related to the Privacy of Data in Fog Computing.

MALICIOUS FOG NODE PROBLEM

Malicious Fog Node Problem is a threat to the Data Privacy in Fog Computing in which when a fog node receives heavy workload from one of the connected devices, if there exists a malicious user amongst those nodes, then there might be a difficulty in maintaining the integrity of data resulting in some privacy threats to the data, as the fog nodes should trust each other before splitting the computational work amongst themselves. In order to handle this issue, only the fog nodes which are authenticated by the cloud should be located in that particular fog domain.

DATA ENCRYPTION AND DECRYPTION

When there is a large volume of data to be processed by the IoT device which cannot be computed by itself then the IoT device sends messages to its nearby fog nodes. In such cases, the data is split and sent to the nearby fog nodes to process it where the data is expected to be processed without exposing it to the other nodes. Later, on completing the process, integration of the processed data from each associated node should take place ensuring the integrity of data. This brings in the need for the encryption and decryption algorithms for the data on IoT device. This gives rise to some concerns as the fog nodes have limited resources and a lightweight encryption algorithms and masking techniques have to be used to hide the original data.

MAN-IN-THE-MIDDLE ATTACK

Man-in-the-Middle attack is another Privacy and Security threat faced by Fog Computing. Here, some of the fog nodes in the Fog Computing Environment are replaced by some fake fog nodes which cannot be identified by the traditional Detection Mechanism. This brings the need for the Encryption algorithms to protect the communication between the IoT devices and the Fog node, but these methods take away a large amount of space on the IoT enabled devices.

VARIOUS TYPES OF PRIVACY ISSUES RELATED TO FOG COMPUTING

Here we discuss the different privacy issues which are related to a Fog computing such as Usage, and location privacy.

USAGE PRIVACY

Another privacy issue which comes into picture regarding the utilization of the Fog Computing Services by the IoT devices is referred to as Usage Privacy (Yi, Qin & Li, 2015). The IoT devices store all the sensitive information regarding the activities and statistics of its user in the fog nodes violating the Data Privacy. One proposed solution to this problem would be that the IoT device stores the actual task along with some created dummy tasks into various fog nodes, resulting in the masking of the actual task. However, this will increase the usage of resources and storage which may result in some wastage but it helps in securing the Data.

LOCATION PRIVACY

The IoT devices (fog client) generally store the data in their nearby available fog nodes leading to some location privacy issues (Yi,Qin & Li, 2015) of the Data. Sometimes the fog client uses multiple fog nodes at multiple locations to store its data, it might reveal its path trajectory to the other fog nodes assuming that the fog node would be intrigue, causing some Location Privacy Issues to the IoT device. One solution to this issue would be through identity obfuscation of the IoT device(fog client) such that even if the fog node knows its fog client it wouldn't be able to detect and identify it, but it might know the approximate location of the fog client but not its precise location. Identity Obfuscation can be done by trusted third party applications generating some fake IDs for the fog client(IoT device).

SOLUTIONS TO PRIVACY ISSUES IN IOT AND FOG

Various solutions that have been proposed to secure the Privacy of Data are Verifiable Computing and Data Searching and Access Control.

VERIFIABLE COMPUTING

According to Verifiable Computing (Yi, Qin & Li, 2015), an IoT device can shift its process of computation to some insecure server or to another fog node, where the incoming results are verified. The server computes the given task and returns the result to the node along with a proof. To infuse confidence into the computation offloaded onto the fog node, the fog user can verify the correction of the results. (Gennaro, Gentry & Parno, 2010) have proposed a Verifiable Computing Protocol that allows the server to return a computationally impressive and a unreciprocated proof to the client(fog node) that can be verified by it. The protocol makes sure that the server does not keep any information regarding input and output.

DATA SEARCHING

Data Searching (Yi, Qin & Li, 2015) using keywords is another technique to secure Data Privacy. Generally, sensitive data from the IoT devices is encrypted and then stored in the fog node. This makes Data Usage Services quite challenging. One of the important usage services is the Keyword search which is used to search a particular keyword over the encrypted data. Researchers have come up with various searchable Encryption schemes that can be used by the user to search over encrypted data without decrypting it. Using the Data Searching technique, the data can be secured as there is ample secrecy for encryption, controlled searching and also there is a support for the hidden query. As the data is not decrypted at any point of the search this ensures privacy for the data.

ACCESS CONTROL

The most reliable technique for seclusion of Data is through keeping a control on who should be accessing the data, resulting in safeguarding and ensuring the privacy of user. The Access control mechanism in the traditional Cloud Computing is done through the cryptographic methods for its expandable data (Yu, Wang, Ren & Lou, 2010) have come up with the technique of attribute based encryption (ABE) which is finer than the other techniques like symmetric key management and couple open key course of action. In case of Fog computing, authors of (D'souza, 2014) have come up with the policy-based resource access control in order to support interoperability between resources and assure joint exertion (Fakeeh,2016). However, arranging the access control on the fog cloud as well as meeting the goals with the limited resource would be a tedious job.

CASE STUDIES

Below section illustrates the different case studies such as smart grid system, Surveillance Video Stream, Agriculture and Food Traceability System, Disaster Management and Web Optimization system.

ELECTRICITY CONSUMPTION MONITORING SYSTEM- SMART GRID

Introduction

Production of Electricity by utilization of fossil fuels has adverse effects on the environment causing climate changes, global warming and increase in the carbon and greenhouse gases in the atmosphere bring in the need of alternative sources of Energy like Solar and Wind Energy. The Conventional Electricity Distribution System (Okay & Ozdemir, 2016) which transmits electricity from power stations to the customers does not integrate these eco-friendly alternative sources of energy to the its transmission grid and further it does not provide any chance to the customer to monitor and control their energy consumption. These drawbacks have been overcome by the Smart Grid which has incorporated a two-way flow of both electricity and data creating a more advanced and dynamic Energy Distribution System.

Smart Grid employ Smart meters to collect information regarding the electricity consumption of a user and also to gather sensitive data like energy exhausted by various devices. This data is often stored in Cloud based Data Centers, making this private data prone to hackers, service providers and other intruders. Smart Grid must ensure Security, Scalability and Flexibility while handling and storing the data. As data managed by smart grid increases, it becomes difficult to handle these issues.

ISSUES FACED BY CLOUD COMPUTING IN SMART GRID IMPLEMENTATION

Fog Computing provides a resolution to these problems as the data storage and computation could be done locally near the edge of the network securing privacy of data and processing it with low-latency. In smart grids, Fog Computing is not the replacement of Cloud Computing and it provides some additional features as follows:

- **Scalable Real-Time Services:** This allows the users to keep a check on their energy consumption.
- **Private Data:** Since Cloud Data Center is a shared environment it is affected by the privacy issues. Fog Computing secures the private data of the users.
- **Proximity:** The fog nodes are close to the users allowing direct access to the source can also simplifies the extraction of key information from the big data.
- **Latency:** Latency is highly interrelated with Proximity as the more the closer the fog node to the user the faster is the reaction time and further reduces congestion issues.
- **Geo-Distribution:** Power generators, distribution network and transformers that form Smart Grid are naturally distributed where fog services can be located at the edges of network making fog computing is advantageous.

PROPOSED SOLUTION

A proposed method for implementing Smart Grid (Okay & Ozdemir, 2016) by the application of fog computing is a three-tier architecture where the first tier consists of Smart Meters, second tier consists of the Fog Servers and the third tier composes the Cloud Data Center, overall facilitating four types of communications - device to device, device to fog server, fog server to fog server, fog server to cloud server.

First-Tier

The first tier is accountable for communication between the smart grid devices like electrical vehicles, mobile phones, smart meters and various other electrical appliances. This communication in first tier between the appliances could be related to business purposes, billing reasons or location-based services. Data from the electric appliance is fetched and computed by smart meter and then transferred to the fog server. Smart Meters measure the consumption of energy by various electric devices so that the consumers can keep a check on their usage. This fetching of sensitive information lead to certain privacy issues which is taken care by the smart meter as it classifies the data into public and private data. Private data generally consists of electricity consumed by each appliance, and this data is encrypted using an encryption function authenticating them with a key and then transmitted to the corresponding fog server in an interval of fixed time. Further, a certain amount of renewable energy (solar, wind) that is being produced in the house is sent to the smart grid. The sum of the energy consumption by various devices and also the sum of the energy produced by the house is termed as Public data.

Second-Tier

In second-tier, there is communication between the fog servers and the smart meters and the fog server connects the smart meters with cloud. The fog servers process the gathered public and private data coming from the smart meters separately. To secure the private data, the fog servers collect the public data as unencrypted data and private data as encrypted data. Fog servers aren't capable of decrypting the private data as the key of the encryption function is only shared with the consumer and cloud. The fog servers aggregate public and private data without violating consumers privacy and then it sends this data to the cloud, in order to reduce the amount of data storage in the cloud. Fog servers store the detailed information regarding the consumption of energy of each appliance temporarily so as to respond to the customer requests quickly.

Third-Tier

The third tier consists of the cloud data center storing all the information (public data) coming from various fog nodes and processing it. The data from the cloud can be easily accessed by the customer by using a mobile application or a web interface. A smart home can be taken as a use case for the above proposed solution where the smart meter produces a report on the energy consumed by various appliances and classifies them as public and private and stores it on the fog servers, further connecting itself with the cloud via fog server.

In the proposed model the fog server stores private data of the customer which can be periodically erased from it. Further, only the aggregated consumption and production values are stored on the cloud thereby increasing the privacy of data. The model is geometrically distributed providing reliability and extending the capabilities of cloud in terms of privacy and latency for smart grid. Thereby, Fog Computing increases the efficiency of the Cloud Computing in Smart Grids.

HEALTHCARE MONITORING SYSTEM-ECG FEATURE EXTRACTION

Introduction

Internet of Things provides an adequate and organized approach to enhance the health and prosperity of mankind. Fog computing which is an extension to cloud computing is implemented in the healthcare and elderly care systems (Khan, Parkinson & Qin,2017) where self-automated wireless sensors send data to the fog nodes instead of sending them directly to the cloud.

CLOUD AND FOG COMPUTING IN HEALTHCARE SYSTEM

A smart healthcare infrastructure can be created using many sensors. In the fog layer, semantic tagging and classification of data is performed and this polished data can be later sent to the cloud systems for further processing and analysis. Human health can be monitored in real-time by retrieving bio-signals from sensor nodes and transmitting them to the gateways using wireless communication protocols. This data is then sent to a cloud server for real time processing, visualization and diagnosis. Fog computing is used in such health monitoring systems by facilitating services like embedded data mining, distributed storage and notification storage at the edge of the network.

ECG FEATURE EXTRACTION USING FOG COMPUTING

Electrocardiogram(ECG) feature extraction plays an important role in the diagnosis of many cardiac diseases. In smart gateways (i.e, the edge of the network), the ECG signals are examined and features (Gia, Jiang, Rahmani, Westerlund, Liljeberg & Tenhunen, 2015) like the heart rate, P wave and T wave are extracted. One of the elementary technologies in healthcare IoT is the Wireless Body Area Network (WBAN), which is used for retrieving real-time signals such as the Electrocardiogram(ECG), Electromyography(EMG), body temperature and blood pressure a systematic manner. In most of the healthcare examination systems, the data collected from the sensors implanted in the wearable devices is sent to the cloud server for analysis, but during this process of transmission, the data might get corrupted or lost, thereby leading to errors in the analyzed data of the patient. Even a minute error in the health report of a patient may lead to faulty treatment decisions for a health problem. Thus there is a need for reducing the length of path travelled by the data and also guarantee good quality of service. This can be fulfilled by the fog layer where the fog nodes can process the data at the edge of the healthcare monitoring systems and also diminishes the network bandwidth used. For the convenient utilization of the network bandwidth between the health monitoring system's gateway and a cloud server, a flexible arrangement has been put forth where in light-weight algorithms are used to extract the heart rate, P and T waves which can be cited at the end-user's browser.

- **WBAN Systems:** When data needs to be aggregated from a patient's body, many devices and sensors need to be attached to their body using many wires and cables. For diabetes and cardiovascular patients, their health needs to be monitored for a long duration like for an entire day, in such cases the patient may require to spend an entire day with many cables and sensors attached to the body. Due to the body movement of the patient, the data which may be recorded in the sensors may be incorrect. These incorrect results may lead to inaccurate report of the patient's health. A health monitoring system which works on WBAN can overcome this drawback because of its characteristics of mobility and wireless transmission. The WBAN systems have three main components- a sensor node, a gateway and a backend, fulfilling the following functions.
- **Sensor Node:** A medical sensor node consists of devices and wearables which accumulate the health data and then transmit the data to the gateway by means of communication protocols like Bluetooth, WiFi or ZigBee. The gateway or the fog node is a medium for the health data to flow from the sensors to the cloud server. It is considered as the most important part of the WBAN architecture as if any problem occurs in the gateway the entire system will fail.
- **Gateway:** The smart gateway engineering incorporates physical and organizational structures. The physical structure consists of an embedded router which endorses communication protocols like Bluetooth, Wifi and Ethernet but this router does not support communication with sensor nodes which require low power communication protocols like 6LoWPAN. This requirement is fulfilled by another component of the physical structure called sink nodes which incorporates 6LoWPAN protocol into the gateway. On the other hand, the operational structure consists of the embedded operating system, a hardware layer and a fog computing service layer.

A flexible template at the smart gateway is used to extract the ECG feature which consists of three main parts.

1. First part is the ECG preprocessing which contains notch filters which is used for removal of artifact movement.
2. Fast computation techniques and some wavelet algorithms are included in the second part of the template called the Wavelet Transformation.
3. The third part is the ECG extraction which deals with implementing algorithms for extracting data such as P-R interval, Q-T interval, S-T segment, QRS area and QRS energy.

At the smart gateway, Graphic User Interfaces can be used by users such as caregivers, medical doctors and system administrators for apprehending the ECG and bio-data. These interfaces can be accessed by logging in.

The smart gateway provides some real time notification services to update about anomalous situations. Real-time signals are sent to the cloud which then sends notification signals to the users when one of the three situations occurs, either:

1. When data is not received by the gateway from the sensor nodes.
2. An embedded gateway or a sink node temperature is higher than a predefined threshold.
3. When the heart rate is not in the normal heart rate range as per the American Heart Association.

- **Back - End Part:** Backend consists of the cloud server and the other backend services. The cloud server is responsible for the storing and processing of data whereas backend services are liable for the dynamic data analysis and visualization. High portability and 90% increase in bandwidth efficiency is witnessed in the propounded system.

SURVEILLANCE VIDEO STREAM PROCESSING USING FOG COMPUTING

Introduction

When coherent processing and immediate decision-making is necessary, fog computing comes into picture as it has a vital role. Urban surveillance which is an important component of circumstantial cognizance deals with heterogeneous data from a stratified sensors environment which is useful for the improvement of urban planning and management.

CLOUD AND FOG COMPUTING IN VIDEO STREAM PROCESSING USING DRONES

When tracing of targets objects is being carried out using a drone video stream, instead of sending the dynamic real-time video content to the cloud platform, it can be sent to the fog node so that transmission and processing time can be cut down and the possible network congestions can be shunned. By fog nodes, we mean any smartphones or laptops or tablets which support the tracking algorithms and can process the live streaming feeds. On an average, around thirteen percent (Khan, Parkinson & Qin, 2017) of the processing time has been reduced due to the introduction of an intermediate fog platform between the surveillance area and the Cloud. Sending video feeds from every camera sensor to the cloud is a very tedious task to perform, but due to the high processing services provided by the distributed Edge computing, each video can be processed separately at the fog nodes and then sent to the Cloud where all the data can be accumulated and a proper final result can be obtained. Thus, Fog Computing proves to be an optimistic solution for this operation.

With the aid of huge trajectory data gathered from various sensors that are installed, Urban Traffic can be monitored. The city administration and law enforcement department can use this data collected from sensors and provide services efficiently. For example, pedestrians can be victims to over-speeding vehicles. Such fatal accidents can be minimized by a dynamic traffic surveillance system. The sensor on a drone records the videos of vehicles commuting on the road and sends these videos to the controller on the ground.

The urban surveillance system has three layers (Chen, Chen, You, Ling, Liang & Zimmermann, 2016)- a surveillance application layer, a Fog Computing layer and a Cloud Computing layer.

- **Surveillance Application Layer:** The surveillance application layer contains the drone devices which are used to monitor the regions of interest and capture the video. The controller station at the ground level also is a part of this layer where the video data generated from the drone is displayed on a monitor screen. Upon finding any sceptical vehicle speeding beyond a limit, only that particular region of the video can be locked and transmitted to the next layer for further processing.
- **Fog Computing Layer:** The fog layer contains fog nodes which are usually computer systems on which tracking algorithms can be run. One key issue in the fog nodes is the video processing time. If the output frame rate is made equal to or greater than the input frame rate, then the requirement of real-time video streaming can be satisfied. This issue can be solved in two

ways. Decreasing the video frame rate or discarding a few frames without altering performance could be one method. As in this method some frames are dropped, it might result in a big gap between any two frames thereby leading to loss of suspicious targets as the target might have moved a large distance in this interval. Another method would be decreasing the resolution of the surveillance video which would reduce the data size but some crucial information in the video might be lost. If in safety or security related applications, information is lost, then the consequences might be disastrous. For better situational awareness and decision making, a high resolution video is required.

The controller or operators on the ground are the police officers who on receiving the video data sent from the drone sensors, identify over-speeding vehicles and capture or lock that vehicle in the real-time frames for further inspection. Using the divide-and-conquer technique, only the sub-area containing the suspicious vehicle is obtained from the original video and is transmitted to the fog computing units. As only a sub-area is extracted from the original frame, the data size is toned down and thus transmission time also is reduced.

- **Cloud Computing Layer:** The fog computing units stores this data for a short duration and then sends this data to the Cloud server for further analysis. Precise speed information of the vehicle of interest can be deliberated from the frames using powerful and efficient algorithms such as L1 tracker using accelerated proximal gradient approach. The mostly likely time during which over-speeding can happen can be a concern so that during those times extra care can be taken by the police officers to avoid accidents. This scheme on implementing using two DJI drones and a laptop server as a fog computing device gave results which were encouraging as this urban surveillance system had the ability to track only one target object, but even multiple targets using the two simple algorithms mentioned above.

AGRICULTURE AND FOOD TRACEABILITY SYSTEM

Introduction

Population inflation (Goel, Bhagwan, Chaturvedi, Rai & Pandey, 2015) over the years has led to the ever-increasing demand for food, cloth, etc. which has led to researchers and scientists trying to innovate new technologies to fulfill this requirement. Farmers grow crops in the fields, harvest them and vend them to the markets by seeking knowledge from other co-farmers on various ways to maximize profits. This insight of the farmers influences the outcome of their yield as they repeatedly growing the same crops again and again without paying attention to the weather conditions, soil fertility or pests and diseases. Due to this, a need for information on better farming techniques has risen. Fog Computing can be extensively used in the improvement of the agricultural sector.

PROPOSED SOLUTION

A Fog Computing model initiated by the ICT has two major parts-Cloud Agro System and Food Traceability Management.

- **Cloud Agro System:** This System is used to observe and meet the obligations with a user-friendly and quicker approach by providing services like e-knowledge sharing, demand-supply, communication devices and conducting research. The other part is the e-Data Bank which stores all necessary analyzed data like the crop-related or weather and soil related propaganda, crop growth progress data provided by the farmers, etc. in a consolidated location. Information Technology enabled agricultural farming techniques (Chavali, 2014) like precision farming which is information profound affects the economy of the farmers extensively. Therefore, technologies like cloud computing and fog computing are adopted to comply with the requirements of the farmers in terms of affordability and convenience.
- **Food Traceability Management:** Another domain where Fog Computing is applied is that of the Food Traceability Management (Khan, Parkinson & Qin,2017) where impoverished kind of items are removed from the supply chain using value-based processing. Using the traits such as processing and transportation gadgets and location, the food products can be easily traced. The Cyber Physical System(CPS) which gives judgments based on Fuzzy rules is responsible for determining the quality of the food component. The complete food supply chain is made track-able in the Fog Network when it receives the food traceability and quality information. The undocked data on all the food items which were pursued are stored in the Fog Network which finally conveys this information to the Cloud System which can be accessed by the allies of the Internet.

This Food Traceability System prevents harmful substances from entering the food Chain and also removes ambiguous products from the food supply conglomerate.

DISASTER MANAGEMENT

Introduction

These days every country is witnessing sudden natural calamities like earthquakes, floods, hurricane, typhoon and artificial disasters like bombing, fire accidents, traffic jam and so on. Government and Safety Organizations have to take up instant actions when these occur as it involves millions of lives. IoT technology can be very useful during those situations.

DRAWBACKS OF CLOUD COMPUTING

Implementation using Cloud Computing has some drawbacks like low-latency resulting in delay and jitter, as it involves real-time events. These downsides of Cloud Computing can be overcome by using Fog Computing in such situations. Any devices facilitating processing, storage and connectivity features can act as a fog node.

PROPOSED SOLUTION

Crowdsourcing-based Disaster Management model (CDMFC)(Rauniyar, Engelstad, Feng & Thanh, 2016) is proposed to manage disasters using Fog Computing. This model makes sure that the real-time disaster related IoT data reaches the fog nodes. The structure of CDMFC consists of four layers - sensing, crowdsourcing, CDMFC and cloud computing layer.

- **Sensing Layer:** The sensing node facilitates the sensing of any disaster event like earthquake or typhoon. Massive amount of Data is generated by humans or any IoT device during a calamity, this data may or maybe not be related to the calamity. This layer is dedicated to sensing all types of data transmitted during the disaster.
- **Crowdsourcing Layer:** The data from the sensing layer comes to crowdsourcing layer where all the data is further transferred to Cloud Layer where various algorithms and techniques of Data Mining is applied for further analysis of data. Since a large number of devices generate data during a calamity a huge amount of data gets piled up at the cloud which may reduce the processing speed of the data by increasing the latency. To avoid such situation first the crowdsourcing layer sends only data related to emergency

events to the CDMFC layer where a filtration technique based on emergency keyword search is applied to only allow such data to enter it. In addition to this there might be situations where a link between a fog node and CDMFC layer is broken due to poor network infrastructure at the disaster site, in such cases that fog node send information to another fog node using CDMFC layer.

- **CDMFC Layer:** Data generated at the disaster site consists of Time and Location details which can be used by CDMFC layer to precisely identify the disaster location. This layer also consists of some emergency phone numbers of safely organizations who can rescue people from disaster site. Data related to the disaster like photographs, videos are stored in the fog and are accessible to the people near the affected regions so that they are aware of the present situation at the site. CDMFC layer facilitates machine to machine, device to device and also human to machine interactions.

- **Cloud Layer:** The data which has to be stored for long duration can be sent to the Cloud. Finally the cloud layer can be used to store certain data coming from various other layers in the model can here data mining algorithms and visualization techniques are applied to derive various conclusions from the disaster related data.

CDMFC model implemented using Fog Computing results in easier planning and reacting to disasters. CDMFC model conserves bandwidth as only data related to disaster is computed at the fog nodes and the other data which has to be used to draw conclusion and for long-term storage is transmitted to the Cloud. Further CDMFC model can operate on IoT data inside the fog nodes using certain security and privacy algorithms.

WEB OPTIMIZATION

Introduction

The speed in which web pages are displayed on the user's browsers is referred to as Web Performance and the techniques adopted to increase the web performance are Web Optimization. Researchers have been focusing on various methods on optimizing the speed with which the web page load. Web Optimization (Zhu, Chan, Prabhu, Natarajan, Hu & Bonomi, 2013) improves the user's experience as the web pages load faster. It is estimated that about 80-90 percent of the load-time happens at the end-user's browser(client side) and this can be optimized by reducing the number of HTTP requests, intelligently using style sheets on the web page and maximizing the cache.

PRESENT SOLUTION AND ITS DRAWBACK

Various optimization tools like Google Page Speed and Yahoo! YSlow measure the performance of the website when the developer physically submits their website that is to be optimized. There is no idea of automatic optimization of a webpage based on the data of the client which is known or which can be measured by devices at the client's network like the clients' feedback getting worn out when it passes more than the predefined number of hops or the data traffic could be measured by the gateways at the client side network. Here, Fog computing can be used to optimize the Web Performance.

CLOUD COMPUTING AND FOG COMPUTING IN WEB OPTIMIZATION

In Cloud Computing the web applications are computed on the Centralized Data Cloud resulting in low latency and also raise issues for applications requiring mobility support, location awareness and geo-distribution which could be overcome by integrating fog computing to the system. Computation and storage, Data management and analysis become easier on using fog computing as an extension of Cloud Computing.

There are certain informal rules laid down by researchers that can be used to speed up the web performance by using Fog Computing. Optimization tools use these rules to check the performance of a particular website and optimize them accordingly. One factor that could help in the optimization of website is the reduction in the number of HTTP requests. More the number of HTTP requests, slower are the execution of the webpage as there are more round trips between the server and the client.

METHODS TO INCREASE OPTIMALITY OF WEBSITE USING CLOUD AND FOG COMPUTING

- **Styled Websites:** A website consists of several styling elements (CSS), images and scripting data (JavaScript) that would increase the number of HTTP requests. Resolution to this problem would be to combine all the style sheets into a single file and scripting sheets into another file and then broadcast it to the user. If the website has multiple background images then all can be combined into one and then be transmitted to the user. Further, the HTML file has to be examined and if there are links for redirection, then that HTTP link should be replaced by the complete URL. All the embedded objects on the web page should have an expiration head with time that is in accordance with Fog server caches' expiration time so that the browser would reduce its requests to objects.

- **Minimization of Web Objects:** Another factor that could improve optimization is by minimizing the size of web objects. HTML, Style Sheets, Scripting Files can be zipped before sending it to the user and mentioning 'giz' in the HTTP response. Minification should be applied to remove inessential characters from the CSS and JS code. Munge Procedure should be applied to JS file to reduce the length of the symbol names. Graphics and GIF animations should be optimized before transmitting to the user.

- **Website Requested for First Time:** While if the webpage is been requested for the first time by a client on that network or requests for a webpage that was present in the fog server cache but later has been expired then, the incoming parts of the web page that comes from the data center can be inspected by fog server and then sent to the user. Although, optimization of the complete web page is not possible however, the small incoming portions of the webpage can be optimized by applying relevant optimization techniques. The optimization of web pages should be acceptable by both the end user and also by the website.

  In Wide Area Networks(WAN) fog nodes are advantageous as they are closer to the user and the fog servers were aware of the network condition near the user, like congestion, data rate in the wireless channel. This information can be utilized by the fog nodes for optimizing the web pages.

- **Browsing Behavior of User:** Web Pages can be optimized better if the fog node knows about the browsing behavior of the user. If a user views a particular website many times then the performance can be improved by using external approach where the web pages are cached and stored in the fog server and can be utilized by other clients. Identification of user can be done by cookies or by track by using the IP address of the user but this is not possible if the user belongs to a network behind a firewall. Fog Server can identify the user in such cases as the fog server belongs to the same network and it can track the users via their MAC address.

Rendering speed of the webpage on the client's browser can be measured by adding code fragments to the HTML file. This measurement is accurate only if the client and web server are present in the same network, as the fog nodes can assist the flow of data to the client browser based of this speed thus making it efficient and reducing computation and cost. Thus, Fog Computing features dynamic and automatic optimization of websites only based on the Client Network Conditions.

CONCLUSION

Security and privacy are the challenging areas in the field of IoT and Fog computing. It provides lots of observation from academic, researcher and manufacturing peoples. This chapter has illustrated the overview of different security and privacy issues in IoT and Fog Technologies. Each of these issues has been discussed with present available solutions. By the end of these chapter we have discuss the different case studies which covers the different domain of computing technologies.

REFERENCES

Bonomi, F., Milito, R., Zhu, J., & Addepalli, S. (2012).Fog Computing and Its Role in the Internet of Things. *Proceedings of the first edition of the MCC workshop on Mobile cloud computing*, 13-16. 10.1145/2342509.2342513

Chavali, L. N. (2014). Cloud Computing in Agriculture. In Agricultural Bioinformatics. Springer. doi:10.1007/978-81-322-1880-7_12

Chen, N., Chen, Y., You, Y., Ling, H., Liang, P., & Zimmermann, R. (2016). Dynamic Urban Surveillance Video Stream Processing Using Fog Computing. *Second International Conference on Multimedia Big Data*, 105-112. 10.1109/BigMM.2016.53

Corser & Aledhari. (2017). *Internet Of Things(IOT)Security Best Practices.* IEEE Internet Technology Policy Community White Paper.

Dsouza, A., & Taguinod, M. (2014). Policy-driven security management for fog computing: Preliminary framework and a case study. *Information Reuse and Integration (IRI), 2014 IEEE 15th International Conference,* 16-23.

Fakeeh. (2016). Privacy and Security Problems in Fog Computing. Communications on Applied Electronics. *Foundation of Computer Science FCS.*

Gennaro, R., Gentry, C., & Parno, B. (2010). Non-interactive verifiable computing: Outsourcing computation to untrusted workers. In Advances in Cryptology--CRYPTO 2010. Springer.

Gia, T. N., Jiang, M., Rahmani, A.-M., Westerlund, T., Liljeberg, P., & Tenhunen, H. (2015). Fog Computing in Healthcare Internet-of-Things: A Case Study on ECG Feature Extraction. *15th IEEE International Conference on Computer and Information Technology*, 356-363. 10.1109/CIT/IUCC/DASC/PICOM.2015.51

Goel, Bhagwan, Chaturvedi, Rai, & Pandey. (2015). Application of cloud computing in agricultural sector. *4th International Conference on Agriculture & Horticulture. Agrotechnol*

Khan, Yongrui, & Qin. (2017). Fog computing security: a review of current applications and security solutions. *Journal of Cloud Computing.*

Kirat, D., Vigna, G., & Kruegel, C. (2014), Barecloud: Bare-metal analysis-based evasive malware detection. *USENIX Security Symposium*, 287–301.

Lebied, M. (2017). *6 Cloud Computing Challenges Businesses are facing in these days.* Retrieved from: https://www.datapine.com/blog/top-6-cloud-computing-challenges

Madakam, S., & Date, H. (2016). Security Mechanisms for Connectivity of Smart Devices in the Internet of Things. Springer. doi:10.1007/978-3-319-33124-9_2

Meola, A. (2016). *How the Internet of Things will affect the security & privacy?* Retrieved from http://www.businessinsider.com/internet-of-things-security-privacy-2016-8?IR=T

Okay, F. Y., & Ozdemir, S. (2016), A Fog Computing based Smart Grid Model, Networks, Computers and Communications (ISNCC). *2016 International Symposium IEEE*, 1-6.

Rauniyar, A., Engelstad, P., Feng, B., & Thanh, D. V. (2016). Crowdsourcing based Disaster Management using Fog Computing in Internet of Things Paradigm. *Collaboration and Internet Computing (CIC), 2016 IEEE 2nd International Conference,* 490-494. 10.1109/CIC.2016.074

Raval, K. (2016). *The Big Data of IoT – Understanding Privacy and Security Threats.* Retrieved from: https://www.letsnurture.com/blog/the-big-data-of-iot-understanding-privacy-and-security-threats.html

Suthar, S. (2016). *How is Security important to IoT devices?* Retrieved from: http://www.cxotoday.com/story/how-is-security-important-to-iot-devices/

Yi, S., Qin, Z., & Li, Q. (2015). Security and privacy issues of Fog Computing: A Survey. In *International Conference on Wireless Algorithms, Systems, and Applications.* Springer. 10.1007/978-3-319-21837-3_67

Yi, S., Zi, J. H., Qin, Z., & Li, Q. (2015). Fog Computing: *Platform and Applications. Workshop on Hot Topics in Web Systems and Technologies.* IEEE.

Yu, Ren, & Wenjing. (2010). Achieving secure, scalable, and fine grained data access control in Cloud Computing, Infocom. *2010 Proceedings IEEE,* 1-9.

Zhu, J., Chan, D. S., Prabhu, M. S., Natarajan, P., Hu, H., & Bonomi, F. (2013). Improving Web Sites Performance Using Edge Servers in Fog Computing Architecture. *Service Oriented System Engineering (SOSE), IEEE 7th International Symposium,* 320-323.

KEY TERMS AND DEFINITIONS

Cloud Computing: Network of servers hosted over the internet to store and process data.

ECG Extraction: Technique to monitor the performance of human heart.

Fog Computing: Infrastructure in which storage and computing is distributed between cloud and data source.

IoT: Network of physical devices that can connect and exchange data.

Privacy: Various techniques used to protect private data.

Security: Protection of data from threats and damage.

Smart Meter: Electrical device which records electricity usage over various intervals.

Web Optimization: Knowledge about increasing web performance.

Chapter 8
Software Engineering in Internet of Things

Naresh E.
Ramaiah Institute of Technology, India

Vijaya Kumar B. P.
Ramaiah Institute of Technology, India

Aishwarya Hampiholi
Ramaiah Institute of Technology, India

Jeevan B.
Ramaiah Institute of Technology, India

ABSTRACT

This chapter gives an overall role of software engineering in internet of things domain. In this chapter, the following topics are included: glimpse of complete software engineering, main motivation of IoT, how IoT evolved, usage of software engineering concepts in IoT, role of CBSE in IoT, role of aspect-oriented software engineering, heterogeneous boards in designing IoT systems, importance of integration phase in IoT systems, comparison of different IDEs of IoT, testing of IoT systems, and a case study illustrating all the concepts for online blood banking system and forest fire detection.

DOI: 10.4018/978-1-5225-6070-8.ch008

Copyright © 2019, IGI Global. Copying or distributing in print or electronic forms without written permission of IGI Global is prohibited.

SOFTWARE ENGINEERING: THE SCIENCE OF CREATING EFFICIENT SOFTWARE

Suppose we want to build a new house or any infrastructure in common, what do we do? Well, we approach an engineer who has great experience and good name in the industry. For a great result, it is important for the engineer to plan out the construction process. It is also important for the customer to brief the engineer about what exactly is he looking for in the building. If the customer is not sure about what he wants, it becomes difficult for the engineer to carry out the further process. Once the requirements are clearly defined, the engineer plans out the rest of the process based on his level of expertise.

The same theory applies for the software and computer systems of today. We are surrounded by enormous number of computer systems. To create each of these systems, there is a certain process that needs to be followed. This process needs to be planned very well and needs to be executed in the same order. The study of Software Engineering teaches the aspect of planning and executing the process of building a software system.

Software Engineering involves identifying the best practice to plan and execute the creation of new software. Be it, the traditional method like waterfall model or adaptive models like agile or spiral models. Every software needs to be developed in a different and unique way. The software needs to be developed using the waterfall model when it has all the requirements fixed in the initial stage of development. Whereas, in a few cases the requirements keep changing every now and then. In such cases, we go for adaptive models like agile or spiral. If the software development plan is not made in a proper way, it does not turn out to be the way we expect it to behave.

Software Engineering also provides the methods to test the final software product such as verification and validation. Not just that, it also includes the techniques to manage the whole process be it in estimating of cost and effort or in managing the staffing issue. It also throws light on the various types of software services/ development techniques (Sommerville, 2011).

- **Component Based Software Engineering:** This technique mainly involves the idea of reusing already existing components instead of creating new modules everytime from scratch while creating a new software. Components are the pre-existing modules that have a definite functionality and can be adapted while building a new software. More about CBSE is explained in the part 1.5 of this chapter (Niekamp, n.d.).
- **Service-Oriented Software Engineering:** This technique mainly promotes reusability of code. It is similar to component based software engineering but, here, instead of smaller modules for individual functions, we use smaller

modules that provide services. For example, webservices. This includes third party service providers as well (Cervantes, Humberto & Hall, 2004).

- **Aspect-Oriented Software Engineering:** This is one of the software engineering techniques that is a little more advanced than the component-based software engineering. In this technique, we can not only reuse the modules for a particular functionality, we have the liberty to add many more functionalities without changing the existing code(Kiczales, Lamping, Mendhekar, Maeda, Lopes, Loingtier, & Irwin, 1997).

- **Model-Based Software Engineering:** While component-based software engineering, gives the ability to reuse functional modules, model-based software engineering gives the abstract models that can be reused for building any new system (Schmidt, 2006).

Even though Software Engineering has been the backbone of software development process, the new trend in software and technology called the Internet of Things (IoT) has proven to be a challenge to this subject. IoT is essentially the emerging trend in technology that involves connecting various physical systems to easily accessible network like the internet so that they could be operated from anywhere in the world. Its development process is totally different from that of the traditional and well-established rules and regulations that are a part of the present Software Engineering philosophy.

Before we get into the comparison between IoT and Software Engineering, lets have a small look at what exactly IoT is, and why is it necessary to implement it in the present day.

MOTIVATION BEHIND IOT SYSTEMS

As we know in the past few years, the usage of internet has become very popular. Information about anything and everything in the world is available on our finger tips with the help of internet. In the world driven by technology like artificial intelligence, internet, cyber space, our lives have become super easy to lead. To make our lives easier and more comfortable, the concept of integrating physical things to internet came into picture. This integration is now popularly called as the Internet of Things (IoT).

Initially, machines were made to reduce the human effort. But now, we are finding out ways to make the machines intelligent and interactive with the human beings. Using any machinery becomes a lot easier when you can communicate well with the machine itself just by the press of a button or just by talking to it just like talking to a friend. In an attempt to make the machine more efficient and user friendly, we have now come up with ways to directly talk to the machines in order to get our work done.

Due to the growth in technologies like Artificial Intelligence, Big data, Embedded Systems and Wireless connectivity, etc., the concept of Internet of Things came into picture. Not just these, but there are many other aspects that motivated the growth and usage of IoT systems. They are:

- Real-time production and usage of data for various other purposes
- Optimization of process
- Adding Analysis-as-a-service(AaaS) as an important service in a cloud setup
- Self-aware and self-acknowledging intelligent systems
- All devices connected through a single network

HISTORY AND EVOLUTION OF IOT

The concept of Internet of Things came into picture in the year 1999. The term was coined by Kevin Ashton. It was in this year that the concept of IoT came into existence. Although this term was modified a little from its actual name: "Internet for Things", it seemed appropriate for the actual process that took place (Mattern, Friedemann, Floerkemeier, & Christian, n.d.).

It all started with a coke vending machine that was connected to the internet. People used to check the availability of coke cans and if the cans were cold or not, using the information given by the vending machine. This gained popularity very quickly and the idea of connecting many other such machines to the internet came up. Then in the early 2000's the research on this concept started. But, this concept mainly gained most prominence from the year 2010 and onwards.

Initially, IoT was known to help only those "things" that had the option of on/off. And also, it was physically connected through wires and cables to the local network. As the research began, the local network was replaced by the internet that was accessible worldwide. This was the major turning point in the evolution of IoT. Slowly, the connectivity with the internet got rid of the physical wires. Instead of the wired setup, the researchers proposed the option of wireless connectivity to the "things" in Internet of Things (Cervantes, Humberto & Hall, 2004).

Now, as the advancement in sensors and embedded systems has increased, the "thing" in IoT need not be a machine that could be in on/off state. Infact, the technology has gone a step ahead in identifying and controlling even the smallest of the small things that do not have any electric connection like pens, gates, doors, chairs, plants, etc.

The evolution of IoT led to the development of new technologies like Big Data, Data Analytics, Smart "things" concept, etc. As we know, in IoT, any "thing" could be connected to the internet and its information could be collected instantaneously. As the data flow is instantaneous, the growth of data flow raised drastically. This gave rise to the concept of Big Data. And, as Big Data came into picture, we needed better way to use this huge amount of data that was collected. Hence, the Data Analytics part also grew drastically.

After the introduction of Big Data and Data Analytics, IoT spread across various domains like (Borne, 2014):

- Agriculture
- Health
- Smart cities
- Weather monitoring system
- Energy (Smart Grids)
- Retail
- Logistics
- Industry
- Home Automation

SOFTWARE ENGINEERING AND INTERNET OF THINGS

As we have seen earlier, Process of software engineering is developing a product on software. It has been our practice to follow the Software Engineering concepts while developing any software. And it has been in the market since the time of start of software development. But, IoT is a relatively new concept and has been in the market for just a few years.

IoT takes a totally different approach to produce software systems. It does not implement the age old methods of SE like the waterfall model. But, it could use the approach of agile methodology for the development of systems. Ultimately, there is a huge difference in the development of an IoT system and Software Engineering. A few differences are listed below:

- **Standardization of the System:** In usual product development using Software Engineering methodology, the developer need to keep in mind that the product must obey certain standards so that it could be released to the customer. But, in case of IoT systems, there are no predefined standards that the system needs to meet in order to get released to the customer. As there's still a huge number of researchers working towards finding a suitable standard for the IoT systems, it seems impossible to do so, because, IoT systems are very easily prone to frequent changes.

- **Component-Based Software Engineering:** IoT makes use of the newer version of Software Engineering called the component-based software Engineering in which the system is built using the existing modules called components. It saves a lot of time and also has a large number of pre-defined functionality. In case of traditional SE, each system needs to be started from the scratch. This is more time consuming. But, this approach helps in having flexible functionalities which is unavailable in CBSE.

- **Code Re-Usability:** As IoT uses CBSE, the system is completely made of reusable code. It has a set of predefined functionalities. Whereas in the traditional SE, the concept of code re-usability does not exist. The code is unique for each system.

ROLE OF SOFTWARE ENGINEERING BASED ON COMPONENT IN IOT

Component Based Software Engineering is the part of Software Engineering in which a few functionalities that are most widely used are combined to form small modules called "packages". These packages are mainly used in adding generic functionalities while developing a software. This process helps in saving a lot of time to the developer. CBSE also helps in saving a lot of amount spent on development of a new software. CBSE mainly comprises of two entities:

1. Component Interface
2. Component Models

Component Interface

Component interface mainly has two activities:

1. Providing interface i.e., the services that are provided by the component to other components.
2. Requires interface: i.e., the services that specifies what services must be made available for the component to execute as specified.

Figure 1. Component Diagram

Required Interface .... Compnent .... Provided Interface

Component Models

A component model is a model that gives a brief introduction about the standards for component implementation, documentation and deployment as shown in Figure 1. The main objective of a component model (Figure 2.) is to specify how interfaces should be defined and the elements that should be included in an interface definition. It is mainly used to integrate loosely coupled lesser functionality components to form one huge product.

A few examples of component models are:

- EJB model (Enterprise Java Beans)
- COM+ model (.NET model)
- Corba Component Model

The Process of Component Based Software Engineering

We need to be very careful while making use of the components while developing any new software product. We must know what the ideal requirements are and

Figure 2. Component Model

how to achieve it using the pre-existing modules or packages and also know which functionalities are given by the packages if they are adapted in the software. This mainly involves as follows and as shown in Figure 3.

- Developing abstract but clear requirements.
- Searching for the existing but most suiting components and then modifying the software requirements according to available functionality.
- Searching again to find if there are better components that meet the revised requirements.

During the CBSE process, the processes of requirements engineering and system design are interleaved. Combining of components together or "Wiring" of components in order to create a whole new system is called as Component composition. When composing reusable components, you normally have to write adaptors to reconcile different component interfaces.

When choosing compositions, one needs to be aware of what functional and nonfunctional requirements are covered if that package is used and also about how the system requirements may undergo change as the time passes. Hence the components must also be ready to undergo slight changes in the meantime.

ASPECT ORIENTED SOFTWARE DEVELOPMENT

AOSD is technology which keeps the aspects in mind and implements the new developmental modularization which helps in improving the business logic let's consider a scenario of smart environment where by considering the various aspects related to the protocols of for the given feature IoT derives some various challenges collected from the Internet in which we explain the context of scalability, heterogeneity, undefined topology and point information regarding data, user preferences has incomplete metadata and conflicts. The non-availability of data point information is a major consequences in an unknown topology details in which no more suitable device can be available at the geographical site in order to provide required information or a device may not have collected the data points from the various site. So there is a strong need in collecting the various points of data without any human intervention. Similarly, the information related to the services has been manually entered by the human operator at the installation time. As device strength grows, the manual information given can be incomplete or inaccurate. SO this reason makes the system to get all the data properly. So there is a need of a method which can use the IoT devices such as sensors and actuators to gather data and provide the proper information required by the system.

The savvy condition is given gadgets that can shift as for memory, preparing capacities and network. This requires the middleware part itself ought to be reconfigured powerfully in the part of runtime sending and reconfiguration of administrations subsequently making it conceivable to include, evacuate, and supplant the administrations amid running. In addition the administrations are disseminated in nature, which empowers the non-utilitarian prerequisites like security and adaptability to be considered for execution. The proposed middleware is intended to join the dynamic reconfiguration ability keeping in mind the end goal to appropriately adjust to the ceaseless changes in the earth and circumstance mindful administrations to give client bolster.

Recommending a five layered design for the IoT. Those layers incorporate Edge Technology layer which comprises of RFID labels, sensors, actuators and equipment gadgets constituting things in the IoT worldview, Access Gateway Layer managing distributing, subscribing administrations gave by the things, message steering and correspondence, Internet layer for associating source and goal, Middleware layer including functionalities like administrations revelation, benefit choice and security, and application layer to convey the administrations. Our imagined angle arranged IoT middleware is delineated in Figure 3. The commitments of our proposed work are triple as takes after:

- Design and execution of angle arranged middleware.
- Multi-specialists to present the usefulness of checking the running condition and adjusts in light of changing client and ecological changes by running new design.
- Deploying practical substitution and on-request estimation benefits as angles in middleware and empowering impairing at whatever point vital.

The basic parts of the proposed middleware system incorporate shrewd condition observing administration (SeMS), reconfiguration benefit for adaptability(RSA) and angle administration benefit (AMS). RSA contains the required rationale for reconfiguration in light of the setting information provided by the SeMS. SeMS comprises of portable operators and insightful specialists for keen condition checking and extricating the data. Specialists are fit for moving and dispersing themselves to play out their observing undertaking lead. They are utilized to take care of issues by utilizing a decentralized approach where a few operators add to the arrangement by participating each other. The essential favorable position of programming operators is the insight that can be epitomized into them as per some aggregate counterfeit consciousness approach that necessities participation among a few specialists that can keep running on a parallel or dispersed PC to accomplish the required superior for taking care of substantial complex issues keeping execution

Figure 3. Aspect Oriented Software Development

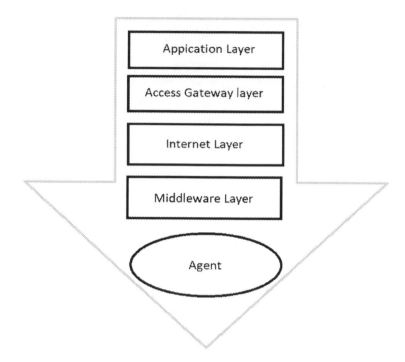

time low. AMS helps in woven and unwoven of usefulness demonstrated as angles. When we have built up the fundamental administrations of the middleware, test application situations reasonable for IoT condition will be planned and assessed. The application administrations are reconfigured in light of the setting data gave by the checking specialists and suitable useful segments are substituted in view of the setting information. In light of the setting information and administration depiction International Journal of Intelligent Engineering and Systems, Vol.8, No.4, 2015 24 the design storehouse is populated. The RSA module will choose proper setup in view of the setting information.

TESTING

Testing Internet of Things (IoT)

Testing is something the we check weather the system that we build is working properly and also is it fulfilling the necessary features that are asked for so in testing IoT devices we check for the various factors of the IoT which is discussed below.

Now we have to decide on how to approach the testing mechanism we have to put ourself few questions as:

- How do we do it now? How is it so different?
- We need to understand these first after which we can learn how to test them.

Approaches Used to Test the IOT Devices

Usability

- Each device usability has to be verified so that it's used properly.
- Medical tracking devices has to be portable enough so that its transferable to various segments.
- Every equipment has to be smart enough to display notifications along with the error messages and warnings.
- In order to provide clarity to the end users the system has to be having the option to view log events and those system who don't have the option to store the log should store in the database.
- Notification display has to be handled properly in the system.
- Testing of data in terms of display, processing and job scheduling should be done thoroughly.

IoT Security

- Security challenge of IoT could be the data availability where data is stored in data center and only available if the data is present and connected.
- There is chance to steel or sneak the data when the data is being transferred from source to destination.
- Before testing we have to make sure the nature of the data weather it is protected or encrypted when they are transferred.
- We have make sure to protect the UI based application with a password to avoid unauthorized access.

Connectivity

- Connectivity plays a very importation roles as without connection we cannot achieve anything.
- There should be a seamless connection to the server so that it could provide the services to the stakeholder 24x7.

- Two things are very important in connectivity;
  - Data transfer should be up and running when every there is connectivity.
  - When the connectivity is offline there should be method to inform the users that the system is off-line and should try to fix the problem or establish the signal soon.

Performance

- We have make sure the system is scalable.
- As a tester we have to make sure that the system performance is even for all the users at every time.
- We have make sure the system consumes less power and provide high data efficiency.

Compatibility Testing

- Testing is a must as the architecture of the IoT system are very complex.
- Testing has to done for all the various kind of system environment such as OS, machine etc.

Pilot Testing

- Pilot testing is a must as far as the IoT is concerned.
- Pilot testing should be done on a real-time basis taking a handful of the users and getting the feedbacks from them.
- The feedbacks got from the testing can be a backup and makes the system robust to solve the issues.

Upgrade Testing

- Combination of various OS, devices and firmware etc. makes a IoT machine/device.
- When we upgrade the system we have to make sure the legacy features of the system has to be verified along with the changes made to the system.

Challenges Faced During Testing in IOT

The following are the challenges faced during the testing in IOT by the tester:

Mesh of Hardware and Software

Architecture of an IOT, where hardware and software components are closely coupled. Software applications are not only the ones who makes the system it also depends on the hardware and play a vital role.

In certifying the system not only functionality testing helps but also there are dependency on each other in terms of the environment or even a data transfer. It becomes a tedious task as compared to generic system of testing.

Interaction Module for Device

The architecture of both hardware and software are very different so it becomes mandatory to talk between them before the real time or even close to that time. Then both are integrated and then testing on security, upgrade issues are the main obstacle from now on.

Testing on Real Time Data

We know that pilot testing/regulatory testing is must for this kind of system and it also becomes very tough obtain such data.

As a part of test team getting the data from checkpoints and other from the deployed system is very difficult.

UI

Based on platform IOT is spread on every one of them and now testing on every platform is pretty impossible whereas testing can be done on a specific machine alone for various case.

It is not possible to omit from a device to access UI which do not have the possibility of simulation. Which is a very tough challenge to overcome.

Availability of Network

Connection of network plays a very important role in IOT as it's all about the data being communicated in a very fast manner at all time so it has to be tested for all kinds of speed.

In order to test the above we need a virtual network simulators which could help to vary the network load and the connectivity etc. but in a real world data is a real time depended so it's very hard to test and solve.

Tools Used for IOT Testing Mechanism

There are many tools that are used to test the IOT device lets discuss few of them. Based on the Target Lets Classify the Tools as Follows:

1. Software:
    a. **Wireshark:** It's an open source tool used for stimulating the network related stuff by creating a model and introducing the various variations.
    b. **Tcpdump:** This application does a similar work of a above application but doesn't have a GUI and its completely based on command line interface.
2. Hardware:
    a. **JTAG Dongle:** It's similar to a PC application performing debug operation on a given target platform code and the various variable step by step.
    b. **Digital Storage Oscilloscope:** This could be used to check various events based on the time stamp and the variation in power supply and signals.
    c. **Software Defined Radio:** Used to transmit and receive the large amount of signal of wireless gateways.

In the world that is drastically developing, IoT is a growing market and provides a lot of opportunities. The time is not far when Internet of Things becomes an essential requirement for the testers to mark their presence in the development world (Aspect Oriented Software Engineering).

The IoT-enabled smart gadgets, devise application, and communication module play an important role in studying and evaluating the performance and behavior of various IoT services.

Poor design of IoT-enabled devices and services can deteriorate the quality of functioning of the application and in turn negatively affect the end-user experience.

CASE STUDY

Case Study 1

Title: Blood Bank Application

Introduction and Description

Online Blood Banking is especially purpose for hospital that needs blood to the patient regularly or for blood bank so to collect blood to be given for different hospital. Here we maintain the information about the donor in the database. It helps the doctors to find the donor at right time and help the patient in need.

They have tried to maintain few of that information of donor which can be easily understandable to the doctors which makes them easy to find the donor whenever essential or for the patient directly. Using this schema donor to be attracted to donate the blood. Our system encourages the blood communication between the donor and doctor product is delivered within time and delays are minimized. Proper tools are used which require low cost for the development of our system.

We have used PHP, HTML to build the system which is generally feasible for the development of the system as well as suitable for coding which makes our project more attractive.

Some of the objectives of the project are:

1. Making Time Consumption less for searching for blood in many blood bank centres' as user can login and see the various blood bank centre's on these application.
2. Customer won't have to wait for long queue to get blood as they have many other options for collecting blood at various Blood Bank Centres.
3. To make everything fast, that is from searching for blood bank centres to polio vaccine reminder and Emergency Notifications.
4. To properly manage detail of each and every customers.
5. Maintain a high level of surveillance.
6. Promote, support and raise the effective establishment of national blood donor programs and the also eliminating the dependency on the paid blood donation.
7. To encourage every people to donate their blood voluntary on unpaid basis.
8. To ensure that the citizen can access the availability of blood units by using our applications. And to make every child diseases free and make the future of our nation bright and wonderful.

Architecture

-   **Donor:** Donor first register himself into the application where he shares his information with the application and later the data is stored and only required data is shown on the website where the information like phone number blood type and his name is shown and can be called when its required by the patient.
-   **Patient/Receiver:** Patient should also register and then search for the required blood type based on their location where we have used pin code as their location then search for the donor and contact them so that it saves time and as well as life in case of emergency and should make sure that the donor is given the address of the nearby police station.
-   **Application Manager:** It manages donor and patient data by providing and maintaining the database in the backend where we maintain the centralized

database to store the data which provides integrity to the data and can provide security for the data that is obtained by the users so it provide authorization, authentication, privacy and other aspects providing the data quality improvement.

- **Some Non-Functional Factors:** It provides some of the nonfunctional requirements which are provide as the additional service to the given system such as about page which helps the user to understand about the system and the agreement page to provide safety for the users such that if anything goes wrong the user himself is responsible for any invalidated data entry or so.

Obstacles in Development of the Project

- Proper GPS location is hard to find as GPS keeps on fluctuating.
- Motivate people to donate blood.
- Authenticity of the application.
- Connectivity of the network in all the area.

Advantages and Disadvantages

So it is a simple and easy to use application that people groups in need at whatever point basic likewise it gives wellbeing, security, protection and we keep up approval and confirmation to the application.

In the up and coming form we are running consolidate with Google maps so that the correct area of the giver can be discovered and can pick him if essential or give

Figure 4. Architecture of simple Blood bank application

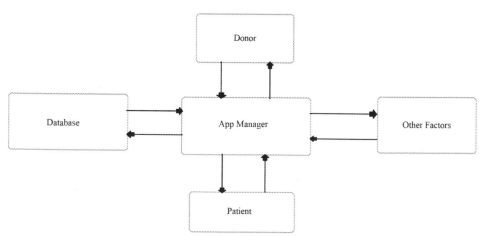

a taxi to him driven the clinic so this gives an unmistakable preferred standpoint in sparing existence of the general population.

Cons of this are individuals may abuse the application and can cut down the fundamental use of the venture so with a specific end goal to overcome in this application we have an assertion so we can enhance it by the following adaptation.

Case Study 2

Title: Forest Fire Detection

Introduction

Forests are the biggest providers of natural resources on earth and they help maintain a balance in the ecosystem. But, now a day, they are getting destroyed because of various reasons. One among the most important reason for depletion of forests is forest fires. Forest fires are usually detected only after it has spread over a wide area and has almost consumed most of the place. Sometimes, it is impossible to control these fires. The result of this action is devastating and it causes irreversible damage to the environment. Not just that, forest fires contribute to the production of 30% of carbon dioxide (CO_2) in the atmosphere (Bahrudin, & Kassim, 2013), in addition to irreparable damage to the ecology. Impacts on weather patterns, global warming, and extinction of rare species of the flora and fauna are just a few of the many terrible long-term consequences of forest fire. These results are no less than a disaster.

As forests are filled with trees, dry wood, leaves, etc., they act as a fuel source. Also, the forests are usually found on the outskirts of the city where human vigilance is very less. Hence, it is very difficult to manage these forests. These elements form into highly inflammable material and become the perfect context for initial-fire ignition. The fire ignition may be caused due to various reasons. To name some, we can consider: human actions like smoking or barbeque parties; natural reasons such as very high temperatures on hot summer days; a piece of broken glass working as a lens focusing the sun light on a small spot for a very long time, leading to ignition of forest fire. Once the ignition takes place, combustible material act as fuel that feed the fire's central spot helping it become massive. The starting stage of ignition is referred to as "surface fire" stage. This may then lead the fire to spread to adjoining trees and the flame becomes higher and higher, thus becoming "crown fire." Mostly, at this stage, the fire becomes uncontrollable and damage to the locality/ lands in that area may become excessive and could last for a very long time depending on existing weather conditions and the terrain.

Millions of hectares of forest are destroyed by fire every year. The lands and locality affected and destroyed by these fires are massive and produce more carbon monoxide (CO) than the overall automobile traffic. Analyzing and monitoring of the possible risk areas and early detection of fire can significantly lessen the reaction time, potential damage and the cost of firefighting. A few known rules can be applied here: 1 minute ->1 cup of water, 2 minutes -> 100 liters of water, 10 minutes ->1,000 liters of water. The main objective is to detect the forest fire as fast as possible and its exact localization and early notification to the fire units is vital. This is the kind of situation, the present invention attempts to remedy, by detecting of a forest fire at a very early stage, and to enhance the probability of putting it out before it has grown beyond control or causes any significant damage. There are a number of detection and monitoring systems used by authorities. These include observers in the form of patrols or monitoring towers, aerial and satellite monitoring and increasingly promoted detection and monitoring systems based on optical camera sensors, and different types of detection sensors or their combination.

Technical Requirement

- ARDUINO UNO
- LCD 16*2 Display
- MQ-7 Semiconductor Sensor for Carbon Monoxide
- Fire Sensor

Figure 5. Architecture of Forest Fire Detection system

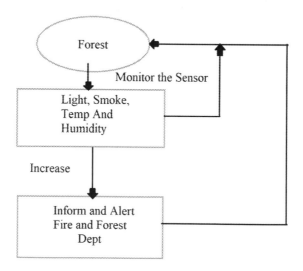

- Light Sensor and
- Temperature Sensor

Issues and Recommendation

The points in the previous part, interest a few of the central review sources that have motivated the advancement of the exploration work in this proposition. It demonstrates that the best accessible answer for forest fire location is utilizing wireless sensors, just because it can give all required data that impacts nature at any minute precisely. Remote sensor arrange innovation regularly that conveys vast number of little, minimal effort sensors that can watch and impact the physical world around them by collecting the physical data, changing it into electrical signs, sending it to a remote area to do some examination, and sending the outcomes in various applications. By along these lines there is no compelling reason to develop towers or set entangled correspondence connections, for example, microwave and satellite. It can be sent anyplace even in difficult to reach places.

This innovation can give constant checking, where it can give data at the start case or at little postponements, contingent upon the hub utilized as a part of wake-up/rest plan. This innovation takes a shot at short correspondence joins form. Thus, more precise data with less deferral can be accommodated the fire warriors.

Utilizing this innovation for timberland fire application requires countless conveyed hubs to give a dependable system.

REFERENCES

Cervantes, H., & Hall, R. S. (2004). Technical Concepts of Service Orientation. In Service-oriented software system engineering: Challenges and practices. Idea Group Inc. (IGI).

Kiczales, G., Lamping, J., Mendhekar, A., Maeda, C., Lopes, C., Loingtier, J. M., & Irwin, J. (1997). *Aspect-oriented programming. ECOOP'97. Proceedings of the 11th European Conference on Object-Oriented Programming*, 220–242. 10.1007/BFb0053381

Mattern, F., & Floerkemeier, C. (2014). *From the Internet of Computers to the Internet of Things*. ETH Zurich.

Md, S. B. B., & Abu Kassim, R. (2013). Development of Fire Alarm System using Raspberry Pi and Arduino Uno. In *Electrical, Electronics and System Engineering (ICEESE), 2013 International Conference on*. IEEE.

Niekamp. (2011). *Software Component Architecture*. Gestión de Congresos - CIMNE/ Institute for Scientific Computing, TU Braunschweig.

Schmidt, D.C. (2006). Model-Driven Engineering. *IEEE Computer, 39*(2).

Sommerville, I. (2011). *Software Engineering* (9th ed.). Academic Press.

Chapter 9

IOT and Data Analytics Solution for Reducing Pollution, Accidents, and Its Impact on Environment

Chetan Shetty
Ramaiah Institute of Technology, India

Sowmya B. J.
Ramaiah Institute of Technology, India

Anemish S.
Ramaiah Institute of Technology, India

Seema S.
Ramaiah Institute of Technology, India

ABSTRACT

The goal of this chapter is to inspect and consider the answer for accidents and reactions to the accidents in the urban zones. Modules have been made to manage the colossal datasets and to bring interesting bits of knowledge into the outcomes. This is done by utilizing decision tree analysis.

DOI: 10.4018/978-1-5225-6070-8.ch009

Copyright © 2019, IGI Global. Copying or distributing in print or electronic forms without written permission of IGI Global is prohibited.

INTRODUCTION

The overview by NSW demonstrates that from 2005 to 2013, around 30 individuals are hospitalized by crashes on streets every day. Analysts utilize normal information mining and prediction models on the measure of accident related data. The goal of this paper is to inspect and consider the answer for accidents and reactions to the accidents in the urban zones. Modules have been made to manage the colossal datasets and to bring out interesting bits of knowledge into the outcomes. The module including the assurance of the severity of the accidents, based on specific factors, for example, the city, driving under influence, speed zone, the state of the light and so forth. The above prediction is done by utilizing Decision Tree analysis which produces a decision tree due to prediction.

Consistently, many lives are lost because of accidents, chiefly on the grounds that emergency care fails to reach the accident spot on time. Currently, we totally depend on bystanders to call for help. At times, accidents may happen in remote areas where relying upon human's assistance isn't conceivable. Likewise, the victim may not be in a position to call for emergency vehicle. Considering such circumstances, it would be useful if the way toward distinguishing accidents is computerized.

To robotize the path toward recognizing and reporting accidents, we composed a model, containing System-On-Chip and distinctive sensors in each vehicle. Exactly when an accident happens, the data is sent to the Cloud. This data is used to immediately, advising the concerned specialists, for instance, nearest Ambulance and on the spot medical care.

Air contamination is the presence of particulates, organic atoms, or other unsafe materials in the atmosphere, causing to sicknesses to people or harm to other living life forms i.e. animals and crops, or the natural and manmade structures. Air contamination can be caused because of different human exercises i.e. industries, vehicles and due to the consumption of non-renewable energy sources like wood, coal and so forth or normally. In spite of the fact that there is increment in the advancement of technology and human race, we have neglected the surroundings in which we live in. Along these lines we pollute the nature and thereby lessening the quality of the air in the place we live into. One such significant giver is Motor Vehicles. Roughly 25% of the unsafe gases that are discharged into air are because of internal combustion engine. With the expansion in the quantity of vehicles because of urbanization, air contamination has expanded quickly in the previous couple of years. The essential toxins transmitted from these vehicles are carbon monoxide, oxides of nitrogen and unburned hydrocarbons. CO is thought to be the most harmful among all these. Due to these harmful gases causes different sicknesses i.e. cancer, asthma, Cardiovascular Disease, diabetes, bronchitis and furthermore putting the elderly and the children at a higher hazard. Thus different measures are taken to lessen the vehicular contamination. The variables that add to vehicular contamination are poor fuel quality, old vehicles, insufficient upkeep, old car technology and traffic. Subsequently vehicles that are more fuel efficient and those that create less discharges are a portion of the methods by which we can diminish transport related air contamination. Discharge from vehicles can't be totally reduces, it unquestionably can be controlled.

Rapid industrialization and urbanization have achieved an exponential development of IC engine vehicles everywhere throughout the world and India is no special case. Such developing urbanization, joined with rising number of vehicles, which has led to a new field for exploration regarding traffic analysis, prediction and traffic control. The expansive measure of information accessible today makes information mining strategies to a great degree helpful in rush hour gridlock related research. The work aims for proposing the plan of a model which would address the above issue. Bangalore is the sixth most excruciating city on the planet for traffic jams. The normal speed of private vehicles is 25 km/hr and the speed of public vehicles is 15 km/hr. A 20 km drive in the city can take as long as 3 hours in the peak hours. This Exponential development in the huge number of vehicles and absence of city wide development plan has led to traffic analysis, prediction and traffic control. This undertaking tries to see the traffic video information so as to give an outline of clog level at various intersections over the city. This is done adequately by utilizing data mining strategies

A car, as observed from a layman's view is only a means for transportation, to go from point A to point B. In any case, from the vehicle's point of view, it is a source that encounters a ton of ongoing variables. The vehicle stalls out in rush hour gridlock, traverse long distance through fluctuating climate conditions and air quality, accidents. In the cutting edge age of the car, it is outfitted with choice sensors-a rain sensor, a light sensor, a temperature sensor, a humidity sensor, an collision sensor, sensors for different functions, alongside is an embedded system that logs this information. An issue of real concern is the breakdown of public transport or other huge vehicles amidst the street. Quite a while is taken to take care of these vehicles, in this way prompting serious congested roads and burden to a ton of workers. This issue can be successfully tended to by: 1) caution the vehicle proprietors well ahead of time of the vehicles with deteriorating health, and; 2) alarming the closest service center so they can dispatch help if there should arise an occurrence of a breakdown.

The meteorological offices anticipate climate, particularly rains, utilizing the information from cloud cover (acquired by means of satellite pictures) and furthermore in view of their past predictions. Be that as it may, these prediction relies on real time data and the precision is missing the goal by a lot. Thinking about the ubiquity of vehicles in a locale, and the way that the greater part of them are as of now outfitted with humidity sensors, we can give all the more constant rain information to these organizations. This information can supplement the satellite information to make more exact forecasts.

Data mining is a computational procedure that aides in finding patterns in substantial informational collections. Data sets can be mined at various levels with analysis, representation, gauge and streamlining systems so as to uncover its inborn properties and enhance better decision making. Data mining includes strategies at the crossing point of simulated learning, machine learning, insights and database frameworks.

A definitive objective of data mining process is to separate information and patterns from a substantial informational index and change it into an understandable form for future use. A specific field in which data mining can be connected is street activity information. This field creates gigantic measures of data consistently and with the developing number of automobiles the information produced should be mined so as to extricate just the applicable data which is effortlessly justifiable and valuable. This mined information can be additionally grouped and can be utilized for different research zones, for example, traffic control, Accidents analysis, seriousness of mischances and so on. One such region can be in traffic control and prediction of traffic alongside mischance investigation for clear course for emergency vehicles. This will be useful in controlling the expanding issue of traffic and will likewise be useful in anticipating pointless loss of time for emergency vehicles as in that circumstance every moment is valuable.

LITERATURE SURVEY

(Sangeetha, Archana, Ramya & Ramya, 2014) Emphasizes on the prerequisites on the emergency vehicle side i.e., for arriving at the accident site in time. This is done by controlling the signal lights at whatever point a rescue vehicle is recognized adjacent movement intersections in order to give an unmistakable way to the emergency vehicle by giving green light to the path in which the emergency vehicle is right now moving. The creators have developed 2 units to be specific: emergency vehicle unit, to impart the position of the rescue vehicle and movement intersection unit, to control the activity lights as and when the rescue vehicle draws close to its region. In the rescue vehicle unit, a GPRS 3G modem is introduced in order to give position of the emergency vehicle and in addition to get the directions of the accidents site.

The position is displayed as latitude and longitude, which is shown on the LCD. In the rush hour gridlock intersection unit, the signal received from the emergency vehicle will make the hardware change the signals to green. Subsequently the essential belief system in this work is the programmed control of traffic signals. In this work, other imperative transportation vehicles which need to reach on time to the conveyance site will endure because of the disturbance in the traffic lights and furthermore it will require investment to disentangle the genuine position in view of latitude and longitude to pin point the real area and to give the location to the emergency vehicle driver.

In (Gotadki, Mohan, Attarwala & Gajare, 2014), the creators have executed smart rescue vehicle framework by giving instruments to quantify imperative patient data, for example, heart rate and body temperature. The rescue vehicle is likewise furnished with the ability of changing traffic signals to give a smoother ride of emergency vehicle. A visual framework is outlined and actualized in the doctor's facilities concerned with the goal that the fundamental arrangements can be made as appropriate for the casualty and as fast as could be possible.

The plan of the work is as per the following. There are 3 principle parts to be specific namely Ambulance unit, Hospital unit and Traffic signal unit. In the emergency vehicle unit sensors to check patient's condition for example, heart beat/ pulse rate and body temperature is installed on to the micro controller. It likewise has a simple to computerized converter and a Zigbee module. Zigbee module keeps up energy effectiveness, subsequently it functions admirably on low power batteries. The simple to computerized converter changes over the simple signal recognized from the inserted sensors so necessary operation can be performed. The microcontroller peruses the parameters and shows on the LCD. It is then sent to the Zigbee module to send the data to the hospital.

The traffic signal unit comprises of RFID reader, microcontroller, relay driver and light flag. RFID reader identifies the signals emitted by the emergency vehicle and every rescue vehicle will have unique RFID. After receiving the signals, the signals are passed on to the microcontroller which is then passed on to the hand-off to change the traffic signals. The healing center unit comprises of Zigbee which is associated with a visual framework to show the patient parameters so the doctor's facility staff can influence the necessary arrangements to even before the arrival of the patient.

The work proposed by the creators in (Jadhav, Satam & Salvi, 2016) comprises of an android application which acts like a caution framework amid medical need. At whatever point a man encounters a medical need, the application sends an alert message to his family and his medical care professional so the prescribed medicines and the measures to be taken reduce the casualties can be sent. An interior database is kept up with the goal that the gathered can be sent to trusted health care analyst so the required examination can be done. It utilizes 3G network as a hotspot for speedy data transmission and GPS and remote highlights to give the location of the patient.

The design of the application is as follows. Personal Information Gathering, this module gathers the required personal information from the user. Account details, to manage the details and also to edit any information necessary. Emergency system, this module sends the emergency message to the patient's family and his doctor along with the nature of the emergency and also the location of the patient. Prescriptions, the information in this module is sent by the doctor to the patient prescribing the required medicines for those particular emergencies.

In (Moje, Kumbhar, Shinde & Korke, 2016) the creators have proposed keeping sensors on vehicles in order to recognize impact. At whatever point a crash is identified the data in regards to the position of the casualty is sent to the main server, where the primary server chooses the closest emergency vehicle, closest health care center and the shortest course to the site. Subsequent to ascertaining the required parameters, the location is sent to the emergency vehicle unit which is embedded in the rescue vehicle to get the patient. An activity control unit is additionally actualized to influence the movement to make the signals green at whatever point a rescue vehicle is recognized close to the unit with the goal that the emergency vehicle can reach the clinic as fast as possible.

The fundamental outline of the work is as per the following. The vehicle unit, at whatever point an impact is recognized the location of the casualty through GPS module is sent to the main server. The main server, at whatever point the data is gotten from the vehicle unit, the server checks the database to discover the list of ambulances, finds the closest emergency vehicle, closest medical facility and the briefest course from the rescue vehicle to the casualty. The rescue vehicle unit likewise comprises of GPS module to pass on its location to the main server and furthermore a map with the shortest route to the casualty. The traffic signal unit after accepting the signals emitted from the emergency vehicle unit judges the distance and turns the signal green quickly so the rescue vehicle can pass the activity with no hiccups. The work proposed by the creators in (Manjunath, Nikschal, Mohta & Sindhuja, 2016) tries to give an answer for the to the traffic congestion which are the principle factor for the smooth going of crisis vehicles like ambulances. This work utilizes RFID module to limit the impediments caused by the changing traffic light for the crisis vehicle yet in addition in the smooth entry of the crisis vehicles. The proposed framework comprises of RFID, GSM, UART and RS-232 microcontrollers for the communication and data transmission.

The plan of the proposed work is as per the following. The RFID is for the most part used to find the closest crisis vehicle and furthermore to identify the priority of the crisis vehicle. For whatever length of time that the said RFID of the specific vehicle is close to the region of the getting unit implanted close to the movement intersections, the traffic signal on that path will be green and every single other path will be red in order to give a smooth movement stream to the rescue vehicle or some other crisis vehicle. When the crisis vehicle leaves the region of the intersection the traffic unit resume normal activity. The proposed work sparkles in the way containing multi-paths. At whatever point the said crisis vehicle go through way containing different paths, just the activity signals for that path is controlled in order to not turn out to be excessively nuisance general society.

(Samani & Zhi, 2016) Emphasizes the requirement for getting an outer robot instance of extreme fatalities, for example, serious heart attacks. This paper focuses on just the fatalities caused by heart attack. They have actualized anautomated external defibrillator, with the goal that at whatever point the casualty experiences a severe heart attack, quick medical aid can be given. The robot works utilizing GSM network, a mobile application, a sensor connected to the casualty's body and a WAN to control and monitor the robot.

(Ali & Eid, 2015) Emphasizes the need to maintain a strategic distance from traffic at whatever point a accident happens and such mischance must be advised to the closest medical facility with the goal that the ambulances can be sent in a brisk and convenient way. At whatever point a mischance is recognized the specialists will be advised of the accident to take activities against the developing traffic congestion because of the mishap, with the goal that the casualty can be transported to the healing facility as quickly as time permits. The work uses fluffy logic to identify accidents and in addition to reroute the traffic without making any problem the overall population.

(Megalingam, Nair, & Prakhya, n.d.) Emphasizes on mishap identification and answering to the closest crisis specialist organization so the specialist organization can advise the same to the doctor's facility and furthermore to the police. The sensor used is accelerometer. The yield from the server is inputted to the PIC16F877A microcontroller. The microcontroller transmits the information through RF transmitter module to the Emergency Service supplier control room. The control room is introduced with the RF recipient and at whatever point it gets data important advances are taken to tell the police and the hospital.

(Amin, Jalil, & Reaz, n.d.) Emphasizes on identifying accidents and revealing them utilizing GPS, GPRS and GSM tech. This work screens the speed of the vehicle through the GPS framework. The GPS unit will continue contrasting the speed of the vehicle and the speed of the vehicle one moment some time recently. At whatever point the speed comes to beneath certain edge it will assume an accident has happened and sends the warnings to the concerned specialists through GSM and GPRS modules.

(Prabha, Sunitha, & Anitha, 2014) Emphasizes on automatic accident location detection utilizing GSM and GPS module. This work has used piezoelectric sensor to distinguish accidents. At whatever point a accident is identified, the data will be passed on to the ARM7 microcontroller and the required messages will be sent to the concerned experts which are stored in the microcontroller.

(Almadani, Bin-Yahya, & Shakshuki, 2015) Emphasizes on giving different treatment to the patient inside the rescue vehicle. This is done if the patient condition is critical and some kind of emergency treatment must be given to stabilize the state of the patient. This work uses different biosensors to screen the state of the casualty. These sensors form a network so the data can be gathered in a brief and systematic way. This data is then sent to the control room introduce in the healing center so medical care professionals can judge the state of the patient and instruct the emergency vehicle faculty so that treatment can be given to the casualty.

As the fixation is on aversion and expectation of air contamination from vehicles, we utilize two gas sensors i.e. MQ-7 and MQ-135. MQ-7 is an essentially as CO gas sensor as CO is one of the primary substance in the vehicular fumes. It is a continuous work where a demo application has been made in which Arduino processor is utilized and a controller board is made where every one of these gadgets get incorporated and work in like manner. The vehicle is controlled by this circuit. At the point when a vehicle achieves certain edge contamination level then a SMS is created and sent to the pre-characterized number put away in the memory through the GSM module about the day and age which he has been apportioned for the adjusting of the vehicle. The GPS module is utilized to find the vehicle position where it is stopped. This paper shows a successful use of innovation by which we spare our condition by controlling the contamination of vehicles.

The point of (Kulkarni & Teja, 2014) is that the system depends on a smart sensor microcontroller with a network capable application processor that downloads the toxins level to a PC for additionally processing. The system screens and transmits the parameters of climatic condition to a command center (administrator's server). From this paper, we got the idea to transmit the information gathered from the sensors to the administrator's server, for further analysis and this would likewise keep track about the proprietor's vehicular discharges. This information gathered from the sensors will be useful in information portrayals and rankings for the specific districts/territories.

(Al-Ali, Zualkernan, & Aloul, 2010) gives us bits of knowledge about the power administration for the system. Any sensor framework must be exceedingly efficient as far as power utilization and management. The lesser the framework utilizes power; the more extended time it can be used. Likewise, from this paper, we thought of the possibility of having an android application which will give you routing between regions not founded on traffic but rather in light of contamination levels. This thought of having an android application gives an edge to this system as well as will help the proprietor to have his very own records to vehicle's emanation. This android application will likewise be the methods for spreading the mindfulness about the control of air contamination by our "Tip of the day" highlight of the system.

Derhorng et al. (2004) have proposed a Computer based reenactment and representation instrument that discovered new algorithm for incident location and systems for incident management. They examined circumstances, for example traffic incident investigation utilizing different information mining techniques. From the investigation, it created the impression that information mining gave the chance of better understanding the effects of an occurrence, and was as an imperative instrument for expanding effectiveness of their analysis.

Ying et al. (2006) have proposed a system on the Gary-Chicago-Milwaukee (GCM) Corridor Transportation System, it was done to collect the interstate activity. They had put intelligent sensors on roadways to gather real traffic streams data to accomplish the idea of savvy streets and utilized the idea of distributed traffic stream mining system. The objective was to outline the distributed activity stream mining system to screen the present roadway.

Nicholas et al. (2011). In their exploration article they researched the chain of events that prompt a crash in light of investigating tiny information. The advancement of techniques independent of the event of the impact for street wellbeing had likewise been explored by them. The examination was done for the most part utilizing decision trees and k-means algorithm and in light of the outcomes designs were identified. The clustering analysis yield prove that not all conflicts ought to be utilized as surrogates for all crashes and indicated how gatherings of comparable clashes and crashes could be recognized.

Wei et al. (2012) have proposed an Artificial Neural Network(ANN) that was utilized to recognize the activity conditions in the rush hour gridlock data is determined using the information mining technology. The approach they utilized was Self-Organized Feature Map (SOFM) to bunch the traffic information through an unsupervised learning and gave the names to these data. The order result demonstrated that the concealed examples could be distinguished effectively by the SOFM and consequently a dependable ANN model could be built with those marked groups.

Jayasudha et al. (2012) have proposed to decrease the death rate and increment the rate of loss of lives by utilizing a few instruments, techniques or various algorithm of information mining utilizing the activity information. They did the investigation of different papers that have been done in accident databases by analysing them with data mining techniques. They made use of sensors to assemble the points of interest from the GPS and put away it in the database after which it was grouped, identified and sent to the driver as an alert.

As per look into by Krishnaveni et al. (2008), in the year 2011, they utilized characterization models to foresee the level of damage because of road accidents. They looked at Naive Bayes Bayesian classifier, AdaBoostM1 Meta classifier, PART Rule, classifier, J48 Decision Tree classifier and Random Forest Tree classifier for arranging the level of damage of different car crashes. The primary goal of their exploration was to discover the pertinence of information mining procedures to help street car crash examination in avoiding and controlling accidents .Random Forest calculation was observed to be the most productive.

Tibebe et al. (2007) they concentrated on developing adaptive regression trees to build a decision tree to deal with street activity analysis and the level of seriousness of the damage because of accidents. They did the investigation with the assistance of the traffic information of Addis Ababa, Ethopia. They utilized coordinated data mining for prediction and undirected data mining to distinguish the patterns.

Miao et al. (Miao Chong, 2004). The significant concentration was to decide the seriousness of damage because of an accident by utilizing a practical model. This research was for broadening earlier research about and effectively predicting the seriousness and the most essential variables influencing the same amid an accident. Of all these the decision tree approach was the best regarding precision and it elevated the decision tree approach in vehicle information mining.

This paper concentrated on the significance of classification algorithm in prediction of the vehicular impact patterns in the idiosyncrasy of grouping of crashes. Different classification algorithm, for example, C4.5, C-RT, CS-MC4, Decision List, ID3, Naïve Bayes and RndTree were connected in anticipating vehicle impact patterns. Of all the arrangement systems utilized the arbitrary tree approach was the best and another outcome acquired was that the classifier precision was enhanced when the component choice strategy was connected with it. The Internet of Things, viewed as "the following huge mechanical transformation", is assessed to create about US $746 billion income opportunity worldwide in the assembling business (counting car) (Worldwide Internet of Things Spending by Vertical Market 2014-2018 Forecast," IDC, June 2014). The IoT is a intelligent system which encourages trade of data and correspondence through the data detecting gadgets by interfacing everything to the Internet. It accomplishes the objective of clever distinguishing, finding, following, observing, and overseeing things (Stankovic, 2014) It is an augmentation and development of Internet-based system and grows the correspondence from human and human to human and things or things and things. In the IoT worldview, many items encompassing us (for our situation, vehicles) will be associated into systems in some frame. Customary practices and procedures in the vehicle business are being changed always with the appearance of IoT. It has empowered car industry to have coordinate contact with the clients by grasping the most recent innovation and making vehicle overhauling a smooth assignment. In Predictive Maintenance, the imperative vehicle data and cautioning alarms furnished through telematics abilities are joined with other information focuses to empower propelled continuous examination to distinguish patterns, foresee machine wellbeing, and more (Intel Galileo2 versus Raspberry Pi2).

Vong et al. (2011) have connected IoT in vehicles to tell auto proprietors and legislative experts of the emission data of the automobiles so they can get their cars fixed before the compulsory vehicle emission test is done. Alam et al. (International Conference on System Science and Engineering, 2011) have depicted the Internet of Vehicles (IoV) as one of the key individuals from IoT. Utilizing this tech, to improve safety, proficiency, infotainment and comfort related data with other vehicle and infrastructures utilizing vehicular ad-hoc network (VANETs).

DESIGN AND IMPLEMENTATION OF DIFFERENT CASE STUDIES

Case 1: E-Medical Emergency Monitoring System

A. Graphical User Interface

The following pictures depict the graphical user interface of the E-Medical Emergency Monitoring App. Figure 2 shows the GUI of Ambulance Service Provider (ASP) side, which mainly consists of the potential victims that might have met with accident. Figure 3 shows the GUI of Hospital side of the app which shows the victim to be admitted and Figure 4 shows the GUI of Ambulance side of the app

The android app consists of 3 modules namely: ASP part, Ambulance part and the hospital part of the app. The algorithm for the work is depicted below.

Algorithm for the Collision Detection Module

- **Step 1:** Setup the sensors and the GPS/GPRS module on the Arduino Uno board.
- **Step 2:** Monitor the sensor data continuously.
- **Step 3:** When the data collected by the sensors is beyond the collision threshold activate the GPS/GPRS module.
- **Step 4:** Determine the location of the accident through the GPS module and store it.
- **Step 5:** Through GPRS send the location of the victim as well as the details of the victim to the real time database.

Algorithm for the Ambulance Service Provider (ASP) Part of the App

- **Step 1:** Log in to the app with the required credentials.
- **Step 2:** Give a unique username to any new ambulances if at all present.

Figure 1. Represents the workflow the system

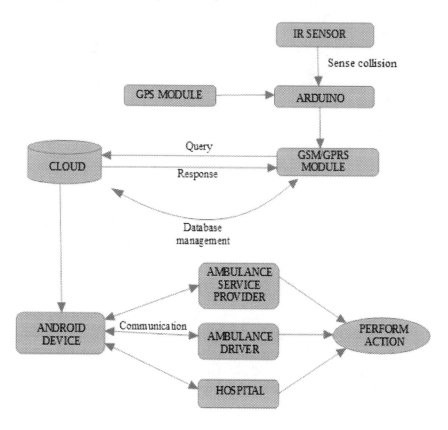

Figure 2. GUI of ASP side of the app

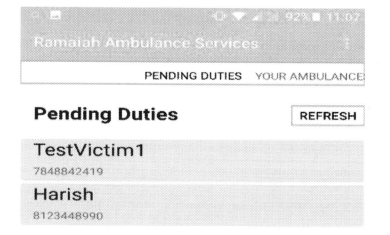

Figure 3. GUI of Hospital side of the app

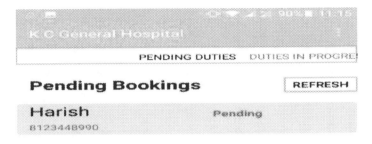

Figure 4. Navigation displayed on the Ambulance side of the app

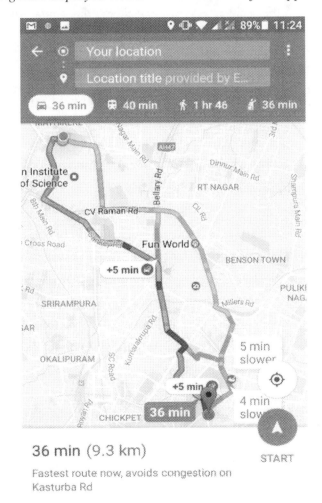

- **Step 3:** Connect to the real-time database to detect if any accidents have occurred.
- **Step 4:** When an accident is detected provide an option to call the victim for conformation.
- **Step 5:** If the supposed victim confirms that he does not require emergency service, abort the job.
- **Step 6:** If the victim confirms the emergency service requirement, or if there is no reply from the supposed victim, assign an off duty ambulance to the victim and notify the nearest hospital of the required number of beds.

Algorithm for the Ambulance Part of the App

- **Step 1:** Login to the app using the unique username provided by the ASP.
- **Step 2:** Locate the accident occurred place and navigate to the victim using Maps.
- **Step 3:** After reaching the location determine the actual number of victims and notify the hospitals of the same.
- **Step 4:** Drop the patient at the nearest hospital and drop the subsequent victims to the next nearest hospitals, if any.
- **Step 5:** After dropping all the victims, abort the duty thus alerting the ASP as well as the concerned hospitals about the completed job.

Algorithm for the Hospital Part of the App

- **Step 1:** Login to the app using the required credentials.
- **Step 2:** Whenever an alert is received from the ASP or other hospital, book the required number of beds.
- **Step 3:** If less than required number of beds are available, then perform partial booking.
- **Step 4:** If partial booking is selected, notify the next nearest hospital of remaining required number of beds.
- **Step 5:** Steps from 2-4 carried out in the subsequent hospitals if at all partial booking is selected by the subsequent hospitals.

Case 2: Prediction and Controlling of Air Pollution Caused Due to Automobiles Using IoT and Data Analytics Techniques

The objective lies in reducing the air pollution and finding a technical solution for the same. The project aims at enabling facilities such as:

1. Message intimation by the system to the owner of the vehicle for the service that is required by the vehicle on excess of the carbon monoxide and/or nitrogen oxides.
2. Warning message to be sent to the owner as a reminder to the inactivity towards servicing of the vehicle.
3. A device to be developed that blocks the supply of fuel to the engine thereby deactivating the vehicle if the owner fails to get the vehicle serviced after series of intimations.
4. Ranking the various areas of the city based on the air pollution levels. Graphical representations for various parts of the city based on various parameters should be provided.
5. Predictions should be provided based on the current levels of the pollution and certain precautionary measures to be suggested.
6. Routing of vehicles based on Air pollution at different locations.

The project overall has been done in three different modules. The three modules are:

1. IOT module,
2. Data Analytics module, and;
3. Android app module.

The flow of the project in shown in Figure 5. The overall functioning of the project is as follows:

The sensors i.e. MQ-7 and MQ-135 sense the outflow levels from the vehicular fumes. These data are then sent to the Arduino for handling. In the event that the emanation levels are underneath the predefined safe esteem or hasn't crossed limit, the system will again gather the following arrangement of values. In the event that the emission levels gathered from sensors have crossed the limit, at that point notification is sent to the proprietor of the vehicle about the surpassing discharge level and is designated a time for getting his vehicle adjusted. Sensors are as yet gathering the information from vehicle. In the event that the vehicle emission still keeps on surpassing the limit, suggestion is sent to the proprietor as an update for overhauling. Indeed, even after the second notification if emission level surpasses the limit then his fuel supply is cutoff by the utilization of solenoid valve activating it through a relay circuit. The information gathered by the sensors are sent to a server for effective analysis.

Presently, data analytics module manages by giving the ranking of the territories in light of the contamination levels in regions. This information is gathered from the Karnataka State Pollution Control Board and Sunitha Narain, head of center for

Figure 5. Workflow of the system

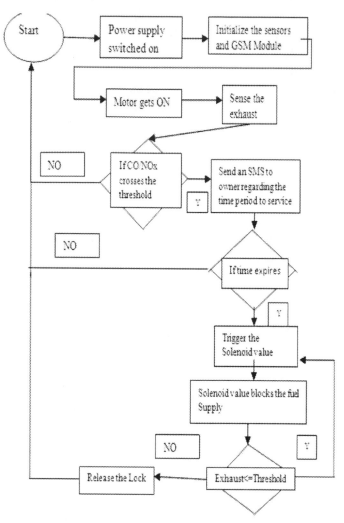

science and Environment. Indian focal information gathered from Center for Science and Environment. The information is analyzed and afterwards a ranking is created for the zones. This ranking is utilized by the App module for navigation in view of the contamination levels in regions. The administrator keeps up the most recent year's information and also the dynamic information gathered from the sensors and has a dashboard which is available just to the head which has the diverse graphs and tables. This dashboard has a great UI and is utilized for effective data analysis.

At long last, the Android App module is an application which is produced to proposes a route for navigation between two locations. The route depends on the level of contamination in the course and propose the most ideal briefest, slightest polluted course. Application additionally has client validation and gives basic and simple UI.

The Figure 6 shows the Arduino IDE where the CO and NO extraction code are run and the output is seen through serial monitor which can be accessed in the backend.

After the connection with the server, the information gathered from sensors are sent to the web server for observing and storage of gathered information. The Figure 7 demonstrates the website page which will enable the admin to monitor and control the system. The web server gives the data about the CO and NO on various days in various areas. Data gathered from the sensors can be seen in visualizations. All the required information is put away on the Cloud. We got Dataset from Karnataka state contamination control board for the year 2015 of 6 unique regions in Bengaluru. The stored information can be analysed at anytime and place. The Figure 5 demonstrates the information gathered from these sensors and are region wise. And furthermore it presents the date, NO, CO and PM emission values. This data is stored in the AWS and is accessed by utilizing the administrator webpage. This is made open just to the administrator.

Figure 6. Snapshot of Arduino IDE

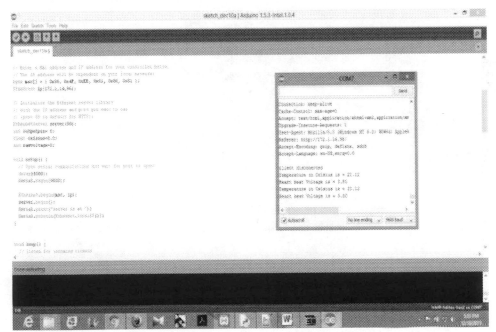

Figure 7. Snapshot of web page

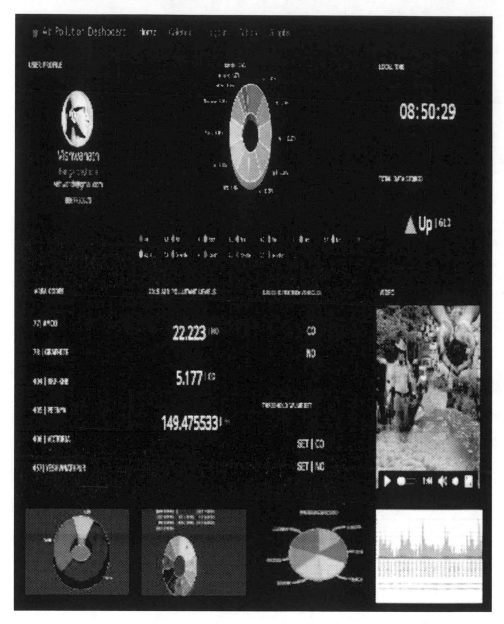

The graph in the Figure 8 gives the analysis of CO discharge level for the year 2015 month to month premise. This graph dipicts to the change in CO levels for consistently. What's more, in which month the CO discharges are low/high. The diagram appeared in the Figure 8 gives the analysis of CO emission level for the year 2015 month to month basis.

194

Figure 8. Visualizations on dashboard

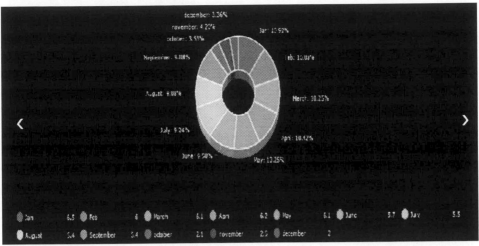

An android application is additionally created for client's. In which they login as a client and can get the route between two locations in view of minimum pollution levels. This depends on the information gathered. It additionally furnishes the time span alongside the direction. Figure 9 demonstrates the guide which gives the route in view of least pollution levels Notifications on approaches to diminish pollution are sent every day to make awareness among individuals. And furthermore different news, online journals are shared utilizing this application to lessen air pollution.

Case 3: Traffic Analysis, Prediction and Congestion Control Using Data Mining

To analyse the traffic data we created a model and trained it using various machine learning algorithms. The dataset is divided into two groups, the first group is utilized to train the model and the second group is used to test numerous scenarios. Since, the input form for WEKA is arff (attribute relation file format) or csv(comma separated values), so the matrices are converted into csv format and then using the arff loader option in WEKA the appropriate arff format is generated. The training set has a string type column which indicate the congestion level by the string- hc (high congestion), nc(no congestion) and mc(moderate congestion). To begin with ZeroR, a machine learning algorithm which is the simplest classification method relying on the target value was used. The below logic is used for the ZeroR algorithm:

Construct a frequency table for the target.

ZeroR:

Figure 9. Android App

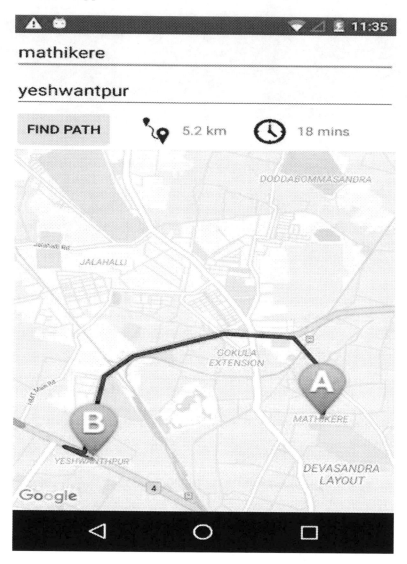

1. *Construct a frequency table for the target.*
2. *Select most frequent value from the table.*

Post completing the baseline value using the ZeroR algorithm, we used the J48 algorithm, which is an open source Java Implementation. The logic behind this approach has been detailed below:

J48:

1. *Check for base cases.*
2. *For each attribute a. Find the normalized information gain from splitting on a.*
3. *Let a best be the attribute with the highest normalized information gain.*
4. *Create a decision node that splits on a best.*
5. *Recourse on the sub lists obtained by splitting on a best, and add those nodes as children of node.*

The last algorithm used to train the model was Naïve Bayes, which for each class, the mean and variance of every attribute of all instances belonging to that class is computed.

Naïve Bayes:

1. *for i 0 to no of classes do*
2. *Calculate prior probabilities.*
3. *end for*
4. *for i 0 to no of attributes do*
5. *Calculate mean and variance for all the tuples.*
6. *end for*
7. *Input test set.*
8. *for each tuple in the test set do*
9. *Compute the posterior probabilities for all the classes.*
10. *Classify the tuple into the class with the maximum posterior probability.*
11. *end for*

The test set matrices have a string type column with a question mark ("?") in all rows. This is then fed as an input file to the prediction model generated earlier. The model then predicts the value of the column with the "?" and fills in the appropriate string- hc (high congestion), nc (no congestion) or mc(medium congestion) which is in line with the logic fed into the training model. The predicted output of Weka is converted back to normal .csv format. Dijkstra's algorithm is used to find the shortest path to the destination from the source in terms of distance among the available routes.

Step 1: Assign to every node a tentative distance value: set it to zero for our initial node and to infinity for all other nodes.

Step 2: Set the initial node as current. Mark all other nodes unvisited. Create a set of all the unvisited nodes called the unvisited set. For the current node, consider all of its unvisited neighbours and calculate their tentative distances.

Step 3: Compare the newly calculated tentative distance to the current assigned value and assign the smaller one.

Step 4: When we are done considering all of the neighbours of the current node, mark the current node as visited and remove it from the unvisited set. A visited node will never be checked again. If the destination node has been marked visited or if the smallest tentative distance among the nodes in the unvisited set is infinity then stop. The algorithm has finished.

Step 5: Otherwise, select the unvisited node that is marked with the smallest tentative distance, set it as the new "current node", and go back to step 3.

After the evaluation results obtained from the initial analysis on Paramics the next step involves capturing the map of New Bel road from open street map and importing it on SUMO (Simulation of Urban Mobility), and analysing the traffic conditions for this situation. The prediction should be accurate as that output will be given as input to our self-written Route Selection algorithm.

SUMO allows us to simulate traffic on a real map and we can capture the traffic simulations and analyse them. So the input for this will be screen grabs ofSUMO. Stationary vehicles can also be generated in SUMO and those have also been taken into consideration as they provide a distinct advantage for our project over google maps where stationary vehicles are not considered while finding out the congestion as infrared rays generated by cars are used to find the congestion. Also, priority vehicles such as the emergency vehicles, authority vehicles are also shown with the help of SUMO as to how they will reach the destination in case of congestion.

The two outputs of Weka and Dijkstra's is used in our ROUTE SELECTION algorithm which is used to find the shortest path to the destination based on the distance and the congestion level so as to provide a less congested shorter route for the vehicles. The logic behind the algorithm is detailed below:

1. *Copy the output of WEKA in an array.*
2. *Divide the predicted value into no of routes.*
3. *for each route do*
4. *for $i \leftarrow 1$ to no of predicted values in each route do*

5. *Find which is maximum class label.*
6. *end for*
7. *Assign to the route, the congestion equal to label corresponding to maximum obtained.*
8. *end for*
9. *if shortest route has high congestion compared to others*
10. *if distance difference with the consecutive shortest distances is less than double*
11. *take second shortest.*
12. *else take shortest*
13. *else if shortest routes has medium congestion and other routes no congestion and distance difference less than double than*
14. *take other route.*
15. *else take shortest route*
16. *else take shortest route*

The above logic is implemented in the output feed from the Dijkstra algorithm and it displays the route to be selected by the simulated vehicle in case of congestion. In this section, we have presented the experimental results of the proposed system for traffic flow prediction. The implementation setup of the proposed system comprises of, spatial data extraction from simulated images using MATLAB and prediction done with ZeroR, Naïve Bayes and J48 classifiers using WEKA. The input to the system is the simulated traffic generated in the PARAMICS and SUMO simulator which is converted to matrix form and used for mining and predicting the congestion level. The expected output is a matrix with the string type column filled by predicted congestion level as indicated by- hc, nc or mc. If the prediction accuracy is more than 90% the model passes the test stage.

Initially zeroR was used for training the classifier; it gives an accuracy of 90% but it takesthe maximum value during prediction so cannot be used for prediction. The maximum accuracy was achieved using J48 which gives above 93% during prediction. Based on the results obtained for the simulation dataset the next real data testing was approved.

The confusion matrix for prediction:

a b c ← classified as
413 1 11 | a = nc
5 65 5 |b = hc
14 2 56 |c = mc

In the confusion matrix, column a represents the count of 'nc', b represents count of 'hc' and c represents count of 'mc'.T he first row shows that 413 instances out of 425 were correctly classified as nc, 1 as hc and 11 as mc. The second row shows that 65 instances out of 75 were correctly classified as hc, 5 as mc and 5 as nc. The third row shows that 56 instances out of 72 were correctly classified asmc, 2 as hc and 14 as nc.

The ROC curve for the three classes hc, nc and mc is shown in Figures 10-12.

Once the simulated data was correctly classified, the output obtained is used in our ROUTE SELECTION algorithm which is used to find the shortest path to the destination based on the distance and the congestion level so as to provide a less congested shorter route for the vehicles. The below layout of an actual street 'New BEL Road, Bangalore, India' was imported into SUMO using OpenStreetMap.

Using SUMO, vehicles and pedestrian traffic was simulated into the imported structure and multiple scenarios were designed. To test our Route Selection algorithm, we implemented our algorithm for a priority vehicle to reach from Point A to Point B and take the fastest route with less congestion.

Figure 10. Threshold curve for the class value nc

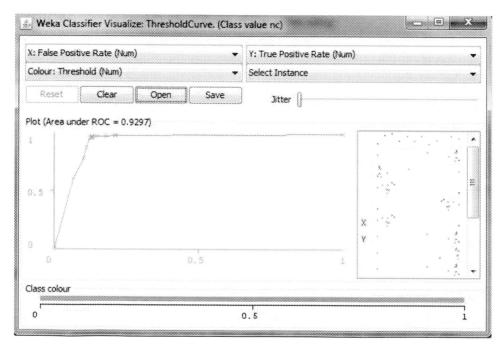

Figure 11. Threshold curve for the class value mc

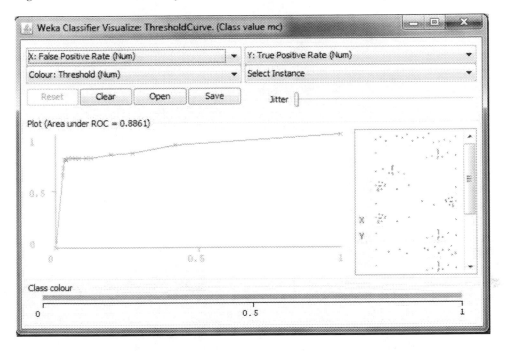

Figure 12. Threshold curve for the class value hc

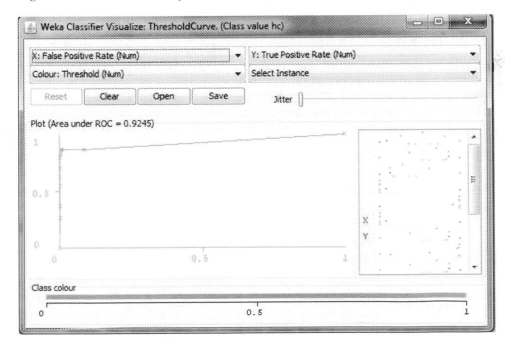

Figure 13. Vehicles and pedestrian traffic

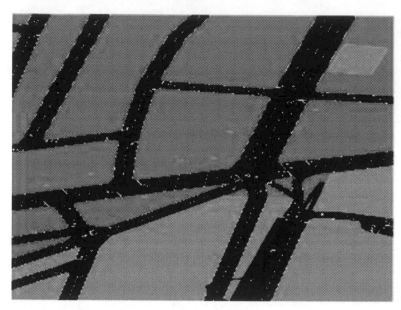

Case 4: Data Analytics on Accident Data for Smarter Cities and Safer Lives

A. Analysis of Severity of Accidents Based on Consumption of Alcohol

In this module, we analyzed the seriousness of the accident because of DUI. The value on the X-pivot relate to the severity of accidents being highly, moderate and less severe. The Y-pivot demonstrates the number of accidents which have happened because of the DUI and non-consumption of liquor. The conclusion which is derived from this is that greater part of the situations when the driver of the vehicle has consumed alcohol, the severity was more, which would have caused accidents. The number of severe accidents which have happened because of DUI is almost double the number of serious accidents happened due to the non-utilization of alcohol. Figure 15 demonstrates the graph for this analysis.

B. Analysis of Severity of Accidents Based on the Condition of Light

In this way, accidents were higher in number and were more extreme, when it was pitch-dark and road lights were missing (more noteworthy than 40,000 in number). The X-axis demonstrates the different light conditions, for example, total darkness

Figure 14. Workflow of the system

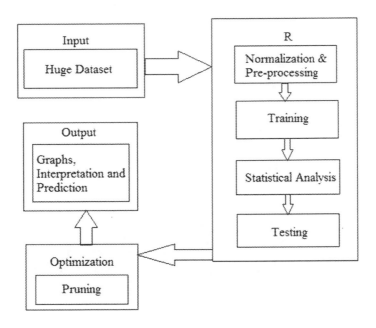

Figure 15. Analysis of Severity of Accidents based on consumption of alcohol

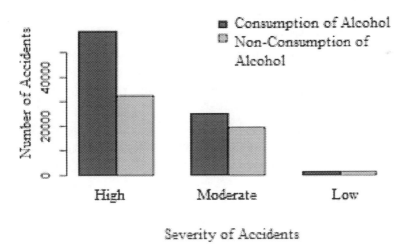

with no road lights, day break, sunset and evening. The number of accidents caused amid the nightfall time is more than the mishaps amid the sunrise and evening. The number of direct accidents happened amid the first light and nightfall are especially considerable as well as they are substantial in number.

Figure 16. Analysis of Accidents based on the light conditions

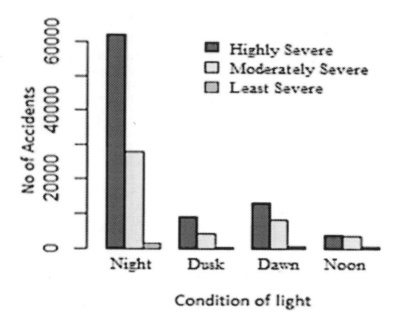

C. Analysis of Severity of the Accidents Based on the Speed Zones

The value 1, 2 and 3 on the X-axis relate to the severity of the accidents being high, modestly and less severe. The number of serious accidents happens in the speed zones where admissible driving speed is 60 km/hr. The reason could be due to excessive number of vehicles moving in those zones. The number of accidents occurred in the zones where admissible speed is about 50 and 80 km/hr. is likewise considerable. The greater part of moderately severe accidents happens in the zones where as far as possible is 70 km/hr, trailed by 40 km/hr. One imperative derivation from this is that most accidents don't happen in the fast zones however they are in the normal speed zones. The number of less severe accidents is relatively very lesser in number.

D. Decision Tree (Manjunath, Nikschal, Mohta & Sindhuja, 2016) to Find the Severity of the Accident Using Consumption of Alcohol and Light Condition as the Various Independent Factors

In this module, the decision tree algorithm was executed to observe the reason for mishaps in the metropolitan regions. The alcohol time was used as the root node, if the liquor is consumed and there is any person on foot on the road, the severity of accidents turns out to be high, if not, it is low. The right side compares to the non-

Figure 17. Analysis of Severity based on the speed zones

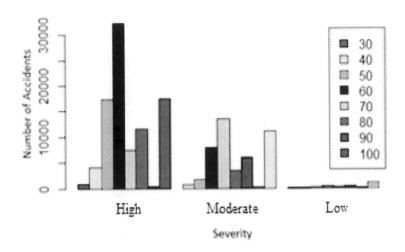

utilization of alcohol. On the off chance that the state of light is 0, which implies that it is totally dark and the severity is high if more than one individual has been injured; in the other case it has low severity. In the event that the light condition is 2, 3 or 4, which implies that amid nightfall, day break and evening, the mishaps are moderately serious.

Figure 18. Decision Tree to find the severity of the accident using consumption of alcohol and light condition

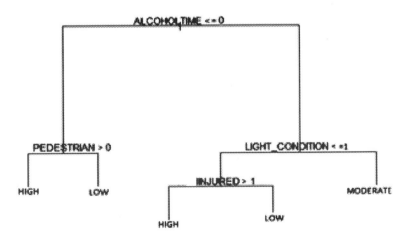

The decision tree algorithm makes use of entropy which is computed utilizing a formula, indicated prior. Utilizing the value of the entropy, we find the largest information gain value. The information gain depicts to only the degree to which the prediction of the events happens appropriately utilizing the technique or algorithm utilized for training the machine. The comparison of the values of the deviations for the module 4.4 is depicted in the table below. The value of the deviations diminished from 0.4337385 to 0.4247297 after performing pruning and optimizing the tree.

CONCLUSION

The analysis of the accident data is performed quantitatively and qualitatively. The sequences of conditions which lead to severe accidents are examined using the decision trees. Also, regions of high density accidents, the severity of the accident and the attributing factors were examined. The project in its early iteration can glean insight into locations which are accident prone and the causes for it. This predictive model can be implemented in several mobile applications which can minimize risk of accidents. It also attempts to research the possible causes of accident and the possible solutions to them. And provides scope for improved traffic scenario and gives users such as daily commuters and ambulances, an option to take alternate routes and save time and life. The initial video generated using Paramics was used as a base case for checking the efficiency of the classifier. The simulated data resulted in an accuracy of above 90% so the next step was to work on a real map and implement a method for finding alternate routes. The map of New BEL Road was imported from OpenStreetMap to SUMO. Dijkstra algorithm, which finds out the shortest routes from a starting point to destination was used along with our ROUTE SELECTIONAL GORITHM, to find out all the alternate routes and select the one with less congestion. This method can be applied at a larger scale to real time traffic data in order to analyse and predict congestion using data from the Traffic Management Centre. The entire process can be made automatic along with deploying sensors at the junctions in order to collect the real time vast data and do the analysis on it. Also, the final output achieved can be either given back to the Traffic Management Centre which they can display on bill boards in order to provide information to the drivers or a mobile app can be designed which allows users to enter their destination and directs them to faster, congestion free routes.

REFERENCES

Al-Ali, Zualkernan, & Aloul. (2010). Mobile GPRS-Sensors Array for Air Pollution Monitoring. IEEE Sensors Journal, 10(10).

Alam. (2015). *Towards Social Internet of Vehicles: Concept, Architecture and Applications*. IEEE.

Ali & Eid. (2015). An Automated System for Accident Detection. *Instrumentation and Measurement Technology Conference, 2015 IEEE Conference*.

Almadani, B.-Y., & Shakshuki. (2015). E-Ambulance: Real-Time Integration Platform for Heterogeneous Medical Telemetry System. *5th International Conference on Current and Future Trends of Information and Communication Technologies in Healthcare*.

Amin, S. (n.d.). [Accident Detection and Reporting System using GPS, GPRS and GSM technology. *Informatics, Electronics & Vision*.]. *Jalil, & Reaz*.

Barai. (2003). *Data Mining Applications In Transport Engineering*. Retrieved from http://tf.nist.gov/seminars/WSTS/PDFs/10_Cisco_FBonomi_ConnectedVehicles.pdf

Chong, Abraham, & Paprzycki. (2004). *Traffic Accident Analysis Using Decision Trees and Neural Networks*. Academic Press.

Der-Horng, Shin-Ting, & Chandrasekar. (2004). Applying data mining techniques for traffic incident analysis. *Journal of The Institution of Engineers, Singapore, 44(2)*.

Gotadki, Mohan, Attarwala, & Gajare. (2014, April). Intelligent Ambulance. *International Journal of Engineering and Technical Research*.

He, Lu, & Wang. (2012). A New Method For Traffic Forecasting Based On Data Mining Technology With Artificial Intelligent Algorithms. *Research Journal of Applied Sciences, Engineering and Technology*.

Jadhav, Satam, & Salvi. (2016, February). An Android-Based Emergency Alarm Message and Healthcare Management System. *International Journal of Advanced Research in Computer and Communication Engineering*.

Krishnaveni & Hemalatha. (2011). *A perspective analysis of traffic accident using data mining techniques*. Academic Press.

Kulkarni & Teja. (2014). Automated System for Air Pollution Detection and Control in Vehicles. *International Journal of Advanced Research in Electrical, Electronics and Instrumentation Engineering, 3*(9).

Liu, Choudhary, Zhou, & Khokhar. (2006). Distributed Stream Mining System for Highway traffic. *Data (København).*

Manjunath, N., & Nikschal, V. M. (2016, May). Design of an Automated Traffic Control System for Emergency Vehicle Clearance. *International Journal of Emerging Research in Management and Technology.*

Megalingam, Nair, & Prakhya. (n.d.). Wireless Vehicular Accident Detection and Reporting System. *Mechanical and Electrical Technology.*

Mell, P., & Grance, T. (2009). *The NIST Definition of Cloud Computing.* Retrieved from http://www.nist.gov/itl/cloud/upload/cloud-def-v15.pdf

Moje, Kumbhar, Shinde, & Korke. (2016, April). Automatic Ambulance Rescue System. *International Journal of Innovative Research in Electrical, Electronics, Instrumentation and Control Engineering.*

Oh, Lee, & Kote. (2003). *Real Time Video Data Mining For Surveillance Video Streams.* Academic Press.

Prabha, Sunitha, & Anitha. (2014). Automatic Vehicle Accident Detection and Messaging System using GSM and GPS modem. *IJAREEIE, 3*(7).

Srinivasa Prasad & Ramakrishna. (n.d.). An Efficient Traffic Forecasting System Based on Spatial Data and Decision Trees. The International Arab Journal of Information Technology, 11(2).

Roseline, Devapriya, & Sumathi. (2013). Pollution Monitoring using Sensors and Wireless Sensor Networks: A Survey. *International Journal of Application or Innovation in Engineering & Management, 2*(7).

Samani & Zhi. (2016, January 4). Robotic Automated External Defibrillator Ambulance for Emergency Medical Service in Smart Cities. *IEEE Access: Practical Innovations, Open Solutions.*

Sangeetha, Archana, Ramya, & Ramya. (2014, February). Automatic Ambulance Rescue with Intelligent Traffic Light System. *IOSR Journal of Engineering.*

Saunier, N. (2011). Investigating Collision Factors by Mining Microscopic Data on Vehicle Conflict and Collisions. Academic Press.

Shanthi & Ramani. (2011). *Classification of Vehicle Collision Patterns in Road Accidents Using Data Mining Algorithms*. Academic Press.

Stankovic, J. A. (2014, February). Research directions for the Internet of Things. *IEEE Internet Things J.*, *1*(1), 3–9. doi:10.1109/JIOT.2014.2312291

Tesma. (2014, March). *Rule Mining And Classification Of Road Traffic Accidents Using Adaptive Regression Trees*. Academic Press.

Vong. (2011). *Framework of Vehicle Emission Inspection and Control through RFID and Traffic Lights*. Proceedings of.

Yu, M., Zhang, D., Cheng, Y., & Wang, M. (2011). An RFID Electronic Tag based Automatic Vehicle Identification System for Traffic IOT Applications. *Chinese Control and Decision Conference (CCDC)*, 4192-4197. 10.1109/CCDC.2011.5968962

Chapter 10
IOT and Data Analytics Solution for Smart Agriculture

Sowmya B. J.
Ramaiah Institute of Technology, India

Chetan Shetty
Ramaiah Institute of Technology, India

Netravati V. Cholappagol
Ramaiah Institute of Technology, India

Seema S.
Ramaiah Institute of Technology, India

ABSTRACT

This chapter gives the real-time solutions to the farmers by providing smart solutions for irrigation, disease monitoring, and decision supporting systems (which involves giving suggestions and solutions to the farmers by monitoring soil conditions, rain, weather, and overall quality of crop growth and the effect on the growth of the crop due to infertile soil or bad climatic conditions). These solutions are provided using the IOT and data analytics technology.

INTRODUCTION

In the farming, field crop necessities management from claiming pesticides, fertilizers. What's more watering system for finer growth, precision agriculture (PA) will be. The idea utilized for the same design. The data for example,. Temperature, humidity, fertilizer, and soil moisture might a chance to be furnished. To provide decision

DOI: 10.4018/978-1-5225-6070-8.ch010

Copyright © 2019, IGI Global. Copying or distributing in print or electronic forms without written permission of IGI Global is prohibited.

support system for maximizing the crop growth development with the optimized utilization of accessible assets and without. Influencing an nature's domain. Those sensor hubs set in the ranch for data gathering ought to dependably think about Vitality utilization. Information sensed by sensors is send with incorporated substance to examination and upgrade and comes about of the Investigation need aid communicated back on to Ranch staff.

We proposed an automated prediction version which analyzes the massive information units of ancient records the use of Big data analytics. Large information analytics is the procedure of inspecting massive amount of facts comes from variety of resources like sensors facts, weather forecasting, and social media information with sort of codecs to find the hidden patterns, unknown correlations and also useful precious information. Economic models generally estimate changes in marketplace developments and situations underneath climate variant. The venture is aiming to discover solutions to troubles, consisting of climate change-precipitated global meals lack of confidence, to predicting and mitigating the impact of severe weather events on worldwide finance. On the grounds that we've sensors everywhere in area which are used to display and degree climate, plants, cloud cowl, ice cover, precipitation, sea floor temperature, and many greater geophysical parameters. those wide-ranging information collections give us an increasing number of deeper and broader coverage of weather trade, both temporally and geospatially.

As smart machines and sensors manifest on farms and cultivate information develop in amount and degree, cultivating procedures will turn out to be progressively data driven and information empowered. Fast improvements in the Internet of Things and Cloud Computing are driving the marvel of what is called smart Farming While Precision Agriculture is simply considering in-field fluctuation, Smart Farming goes past that by constructing administration undertakings with respect to area as well as on information, improved by setting and circumstance mindfulness, activated by constant occasions. Ongoing helping reconfiguration highlights are required to do lithe activities, particularly in instances of all of a sudden changed operational conditions or different conditions (e.g. climate or malady caution). These highlights ordinarily incorporate insightful help in execution, support and utilization of the innovation. Figure 1 condenses the idea of Smart Farming along the administration cycle as a Cyber physical framework, which implies that shrewd gadgets - associated to the Internet - are controlling the ranch framework. Keen gadgets expand regular apparatuses (e.g. rain measure, tractor, scratch pad) by including independent setting mindfulness by all sort of sensors, worked in knowledge, skilled to execute independent activities or doing this remotely. In this photo it is as of now proposed that robots can play an essential part in charge, however it can be normal that the part of people in investigation what's more, arranging is progressively helped by

Figure 1. The cyber-physical management cycle of Smart Farming

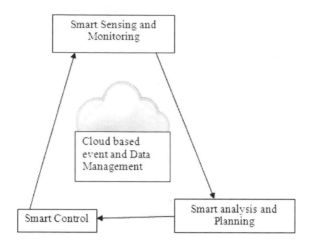

machines so that the cyberphysical cycle turns out to be relatively self-ruling. People will dependably be engaged with the entire procedure yet progressively at a considerably higher knowledge level, leaving most operational exercises to machines.

RELATED WORK

In GSM Based Automated Irrigation Control using Rain gun Irrigation System (Suresh, Gopinath, Govindaraju, Devika, & Vanitha, 2014) utilizing programmed microcontroller based rain weapon water system framework in which the water system will happen just when there will be extraordinary prerequisite of water that spare an expansive amount of water. These framework secured bring down scope of farming area and not monetarily reasonable. The System Supports abundance Amount of water in the land and uses GSM to send message and an android application is been utilized they have utilized a technique to overcome under water system, over water system that causes draining and loss of supplement substance of soil they have additionally guaranteed that Microcontroller utilized can expand System Life and lower the power Consumption. There framework is simply restricted to the robotization of water system framework and needs in additional common highlights.

In GSM based Automatic Irrigation Control System for Efficient Use of Resources and Crop Planning by Using an Android Mobile (Pavithra & Srinath, 2014) describes,

- The framework bolsters water administration choice, utilized for observing the entire framework with GSM(RS-232) module.

- The framework ceaselessly screens the water level (Water level Sensor) in the tank and gives exact measure of water required to the plant or tree (trim).
- The framework checks the temperature, and stickiness of soil to hold the supplement organization of the dirt oversaw for legitimate development of plant.
- Low cost and viable with less power utilization utilizing sensors for remote observing and controlling gadgets which are controlled by means of SMS utilizing a GSM utilizing android portable.

Farming in an India is subject to summer precipitation climate. The impact of precipitation in summer on generation of agribusiness crops is examined in (Kumar, 2004). In this paper, the past harvests information is broken down to analyze trim atmosphere relationship. From the outcomes said in this paper, it can expressed that three elements can specifically make the impact on development of horticulture items in India, for example, storm precipitation, temperature of pacific and Indian seas, and weight of ocean level. Besides, the outcomes demonstrate generation rate and measure of storm precipitation all finished India is consistent, barring a few cases.

For forecast utilizing KF, sensor hubs need to shape set of bunches. The bunch head will get information about various parameters of the condition from leaf hub who is mindful to gather and transmit it to head. In PKF, it is accepted that bunch hcad can anticipate current information sent by leaf hub with adequate mistake utilizing information got by leaf hub already. The PKF disguise discussion between a leaf hub and its group head as for time (Huang, Yu, Osewold & Garcia-Ortiz, 2016). Commonly information gathered by leaf hub is influenced by clamor, so it is required to expel commotion from this information. To expel the clamor from the detected information each leaf hub utilize KF channel and create best comes about. To decrease vitality utilization required for correspondence, bunch head infers Kalman ideal esteems for leaf hub utilizing basic predicator PKF. The leaf hub executes predicator at customary time interim by following perception caught by group head and contrasts those qualities and its ideal incentive to ensure precise predication investigation. In the event that the forecast mistake is more noteworthy than guaranteed edge, the current insignificant esteem is going to the bunch head. The match of predicators with ideal esteem is utilized by PKF. Note that, this indicator is proportional to a k-advance ahead Kalman indicator.

An example space is recursively divided utilizing classifier known as Decision tree. The Decision tree is coordinated tree established tree in which there is one fundamental root hub which has no approaching edges. Every other hub have precisely one approaching edge. To assemble the choice tree, a discrete capacity with the contribution of a quality esteem is utilized where occasion space is isolated into at least two sub-spaces by the inner hub (Rokach & Maimon,n.d.).

In Irrigation Control System Using Android and GSM for Efficient Use of Water and Power (Pasha & Yogesha, 2014). C Automated irrigation system uses valves to turn motor ON and OFF. These valves may be easily automated by using controllers. Automating farm or nursery irrigation allows farmers to apply the right amount of water at the right time, regardless of the availability of labor to turn valves on and off. In addition, farmers using automation equipment are able to reduce runoff from over watering saturated soils, avoid irrigating at the wrong time of day, which will improve crop performance by ensuring adequate water and nutrients when needed. Those valves may be easily automated by using controllers. Automating farm or nursery irrigation allows farmers to apply the right amount of water at the right time, regardless of the availability of labor to turn valves on and off.

They lack in a featured mobile application developed for users with appropriate user interface. It only allows the user to monitor and maintain the moisture level remotely irrespective of time. From the point of view of working at remote place the developed microcontroller based irrigation system can work constantly for indefinite time period, even in certain abnormal circumstances. The factual gauging models can be created to appraise the future climate conditions. The model is basic because of the way that it employments simple mathematical condition utilizing Multiple Linear Relapse (MLR) to anticipate most extreme temperature, least temperature and relative mugginess (Paras & Mathur, 2012). Machine learning strategies accomplished preferable execution over conventional measurable strategies. So present Support Vector Machines (SVM) for climate expectation (Radhika & Shashi, 2009) and improved bolster vector relapse demonstrate with more un-interpretable piece works in the space of estimating the climate conditions (Usha Rani & Rao, 2015). IoT based farming creation framework observing framework to examine edit condition and furthermore gives strategy to enhance the effectiveness of choice making by dissecting harvest measurements, conjecture farming generation utilizing IoT sensors (Lee, Hwang, & Yoe, 2013). Expectation demonstrate in light of large scale atmosphere (Septiawan, Komaruddin, & Budi, 2012) depends on recorded information and an investigative calculation with field observing and traceability display. Neighborhood time arrangement investigation advance factual model furthermore, NWP presents dynamical model of climate forms, another approach joins these two strategies and presenting cross breeds demonstrate. NWP based precise limited here and now climate forecast framework (Corne Dissanayake & Peacock, 2014) foreseeing the estimations of meteorological variable. Another Prediction demonstrate in view of enormous information examination executes cross breed strategy which improves a FCM bunching calculation for complex qualities of the enterprises (Yang & Kim, 2014).

To choose the yield and to anticipate creation rate of the product counterfeit neural system utilize data gathered by sensors from the homestead. This data incorporates parameters, for example, soil, temperature, weight, precipitation, and moistness. The impact of these parameters on trim development is examined, and comes about are assessed in paper (Kumar, Kumar, Ashrit, Deshpande, & Hansen, 2004). It is watched that the climatic parameter, soil write, and soil organization can affect on creation rate of harvest. The strategy examined in this paper moreover predicts reasonable harvest generation rate ahead of time. Artificial neural networks are utilized as viable apparatus for displaying and forecast of product creation rate and enhance the exactness of yield expectation. For anticipating generation of rice trim, an astute apparatus is produced with the assistance of machine learning approach. This apparatus is utilized as a part of arrangement and grouping (Huang, Yu, Osewold, & Garcia-Ortitz, 2016). Rice ranch information are arranged utilizing Bolster vector machine learning method. Part based bunching calculation is utilized for discovering bunch in atmosphere information. To control perplexing, high dimensional and non-straightly distinguishable information Kernel based techniques are relevant. The effects of different impacting parameters on the rice yield are assessed utilizing connection investigation what's more, utilizing relapse investigation forecast about product yield rate is finished. Support vector machine is utilized for uproarious information. Because of every one of these highlights strategy from this paper utilized as a wise framework for foreseeing rice yield.

Irrigation by help of freshwater resources in agricultural areas has a crucial importance. Traditional instrumentation based on discrete and wired solutions, presents many difficulties on measuring and control systems especially over the large geographical areas. Cost effective solar power can be the answer for all our energy needs. Conserves electricity by reducing the usage of grid power and conserves water by reducing water losses. Discourage weeds, saves water and time, statistical data can be used to control diseases and fungal growth, simplest model. This system is just limited to the automation of irrigation system and lacks in extra ordinary features.

IMPLEMENTATION AND RESULTS

Case 1: Weather Forecast Analysis

Different Sensors are used here:

1.   DHT11 Temperature and Humidity Sensor

The DTH11 is a primary, ultra-low-cost digital temperature and humidity sensor. it makes use of a capacitive humidity sensor and a thermistor to degree the surrounding air, and spits out a virtual sign at the information pin (no analog input pins wished).

It's pretty easy to apply, but requires careful timing to seize information. the most effective real drawback of this sensor is you can best get new information from it once each 2 seconds, so whilst using our library, sensor readings can be up to 2 seconds old.

2.   BMP180 Barometric Pressure/Temperature/Altitude Sensor- 5V Ready

This precision sensor from Bosch is the best low-cost sensing solution for measuring barometric pressure and temperature. Because pressure changes with altitude you can also use it as an altimeter! The sensor is soldered onto a PCB with a 3.3V regulator, I2C level shifter and pull-up resistors on the I2C pins.

3.   HC-05 - Bluetooth to Serial Port Module

Serial port Bluetooth, Drop-in replacement for wired serial networks, translucent usage. You can use it simply for a serial port replacement to establish connection between MCU and GPS, PC to your surrounded project and etc. And now, we provide HC-05 and HC-06. HC-05 could be setting to Master or Slave by user. HC-06 has be designed Master or Slave when the factory, user couldn't change the role.

4.   ESP8266 Wi-Fi Module

This component is very low cost, but very simple. It doesn't provision SSL or communication over SPI - just UART! It doesn't have 5V to 3V logic level unstable. so you'll probably want to pick up a logic level shifter, it also doesn't have a regulator on board and it can use big spikes of 300mA or more current at 3.3V so if using with an Arduino, an external 3V regulator is essential

5.   Arduino Ethernet Shield

The Arduino Ethernet Shield permits an Arduino board to attach to the internet. It is based on the Wiznet W5100 ethernet chip (datasheet). The Wiznet W5100 delivers a network (IP) stack accomplished with both TCP and UDP. It supports up to four simultaneous socket connections. Use the Ethernet library to write drawings which connect to the internet by means of the shield. The Ethernet shield joins to an Arduino board using extended wire-wrap headers which extend through the shield. This keeps the pin layout intact and allows another shield to be stacked on top.

This includes c programming with Arduino Uno sensor which is compatible with many packages to implement the project .This employs native interfacing technique to connect components.

1.   Thing Speak API

The user can log into the account on thingspeak. He can revise his channel immediately if he makes his ravine inn for this the use requires any invention such as a pc, laptop etc with an internet association. The use can see the charting of the temperature, moisture and pressure as well as the detail computed by the thingspeak app

2.   Android App

A first-time customer of the mobile request should see a page with two buttons one enables him to list the Bluetooth device in the area of which he can pair with the weather station by selecting it and then he can connect with it using the connect button .when he/she connects the application starts to receive and displays it in the textbox. If the user is satisfied with the reading he/she should be able to disconnect from the device through the disconnect button which now occupies the position previously occupied by connect button. The following is a sample code for the user Interface

```
voidstartEthernet()
{
client. stop();
Serial.println ("Connecting Arduino to network...");
Serial.println ();
delay (1000);
// connect to network and obtain an IP address using DHCP
if (Ethernet.begin(mac) == 0)
{
Serial.println ("DHCP Failed, reset Arduino to try
        Again");
Serial.println ();
}
else
{
Serial.println ("Arduino connected to network using
                DHCP");
Serial.println ();
}
delay(1000);
```

The following Figures 2 and 3 shows the graph which shows the humidity and temperature variation in a particular date using the user interface Thingspeak.

It was found that the latest line of production of the former is Hardware incompatible with the Arduino Uno. This is because the module runs at Baud rate much higher than that compatible with Software Serial Communication. The alternative Ethernet shield is used to communicate over the internet. The Thingspeak API seems to be highly efficient with successful visualization. The communication with the android app also was successful in rendering the sensor data in text format. The following Figure 4 shows the Aurdino interface for the farmers.

Case 2: Smart Agriculture System

In this Information is collected from storage system and field through sensors which are interfaced with raspberry pi, the information acquired is sent to cloud. The data or information is stored in cloud then which is mailed to the farmer.

Figure 2. Graphical Visualization on Thingspeak

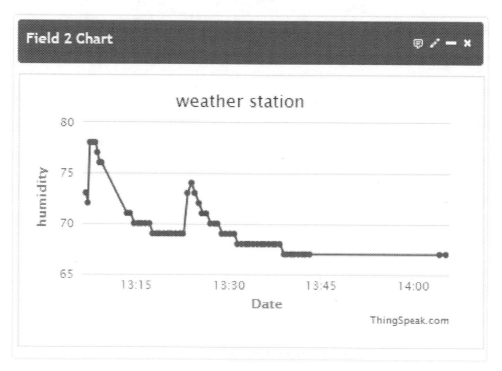

Figure 3. Graphical Visualization on Thingspeak

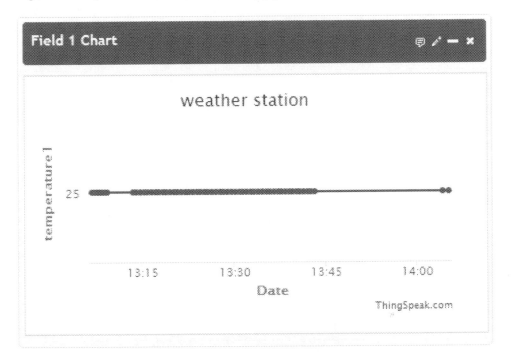

Different Modules

Ubidots

Ubidots offers a REST API through which the Data Sources, Variables and Values, can be generated, read, modified or erased.It is open source application where, which provide us the feature to store data on the cloud and also giving us the feature to send data on the mobile or email to the particular user.

Email

Email is used to receive data from system which is being sent from the cloud and the user could see the message and take appropriate steps.

Putty

PuTTY is a free and open-source terminal emulator, serial console and network file transfer application. It supports many network protocols, including SCP, SSH,

Figure 4. Various parameter information

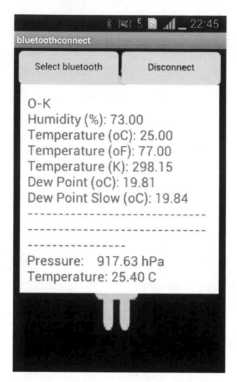

Telnet, login and raw socket connection. It can also provide connection to a serial port. The name "PuTTY" has no definitive meaning. PuTTY was originally written for Microsoft Windows, but it has been ported to various other operating systems. Authorized ports are available for some Unix-likeplatforms, with work-in-progress ports to Classic Mac OS and Mac OS X and unauthorized ports have been contributed to platforms such as Symbian, Windows Mobile and Windows Phone.

Implementation Using the Sensors

The motion detector sensor detects the presence of infrared in its surrounding areas thus detect the presence of the living organism in the field. The soil moisture sensor is being used to detect the presence of the humidity in the soil. The information about the temperature and humidity sensor is given by DTH 11. The data is being analysed and we have used the UBIDOTS where we are creating variables and putting up the condition based on which email is being sent to the user and so that the user is being notified about the environment and its surrounding.

Figure 5. Collection of Information

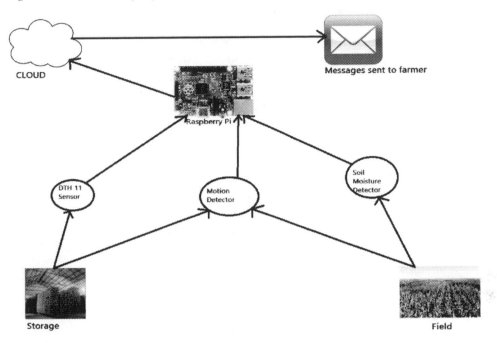

Sample Algorithm for the Implementation

```
Read   temperature_sensor()
Read humidity_sensor()
Read   motion_sensor()
Read soil_moisture_sensor()
```
Upload Data to Cloud
```
If temperature_sensed>20:
                        Notify the user
If motion_sensed ==1:
                    Send email to user about the
intruder
If soil_moisture_sensed ==0
                    Send email to user about the
condition of the land
If humidity_sensed>80
                      Send email to user about the
humidity of storage system
```

In this algorithm we read the data from the sensor and that data is send to the raspberry pi. In raspberry pi we will decide whether or when to send data into the cloud. The data is uploaded to the cloud (ubidots). Ubidot offer us to create some event on the basis of data uploaded on the cloud. On the basis of the condition we will notify the farmer by sending alert message to the cloud.

Information About the Implementation of Modules

In this project we have used four modules in which we are checking the condition on the data received on the cloud. The four modules are:

1. **Sensing Data from the Sensor:** In this module we are checking the pins voltage and based on the data we send data.
2. **Sending the Data to the Cloud:** Checking the condition for the data and sending data to the cloud.
3. **Creating Event:** On the cloud we are creating some event.
4. **Notify the User:** On the basis of event we notify the user.

Figure 6 describes the readings of temperature from the sensors
Figure 7 shows the data acquired from motion sensors.
Figure 8 shows the humidity readings from the sorrounding.
Figure 9 shows the moisture content of the soil.

Figure 6. Reading data from DTH11

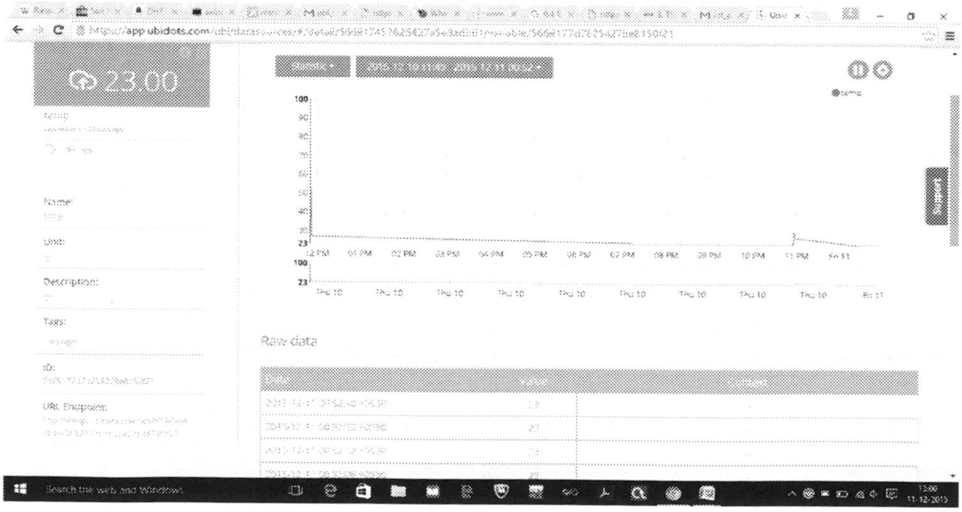

Figure 7. Reading presence of animals

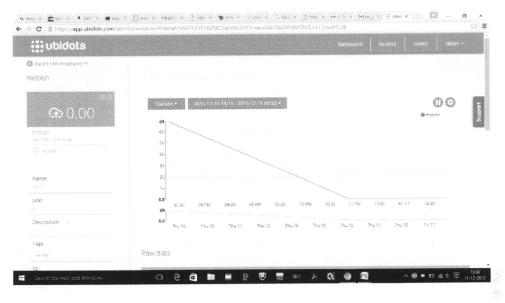

Figure 8. Reading data from DTH11

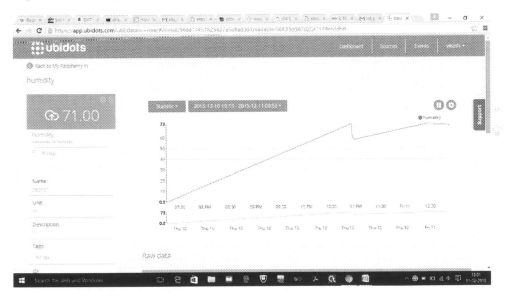

Figure 9. Reading data from Soil

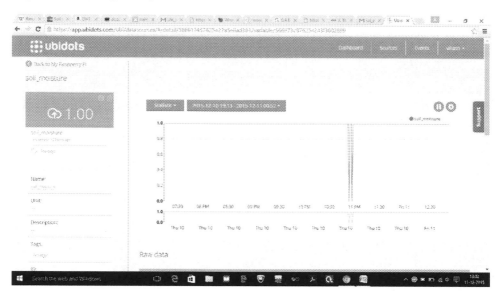

Case 3: IOT Based Smart Irrigation System using Sunflower Tracking Model

The Sunflower Model

Solar tracking will be done with the help of Stepper motor. Microcontroller will be programmed with 1.8 degree step angle to control the rotation of stepper motor. Output of microcontroller sends to buffer for temporary storage, stepper motor driver to drive the stepper motor. Solar panel will be placed upon the stepper motor.

Number of Modules

- Temperature Sensors
- Moisture Sensors
- Conductivity Sensors
- Water Sensors
- DTMF or the Mobile unit
- Solar panel

Modules Description

- **Temperature Sensors:** A Temperature Sensors is a type of controller whose resistance fluctuates significantly with temperature, additionally we require standard resistors. It adapts the crops to appropriate temperature required for its proper growth.

- **Moisture Sensors:** Soil moistness sensors measure the water content in soil. A soil moisture probe is made up of multiple soil moisture sensors. If the soil moisture content is less, then the soil moisture sensor will command the microcontroller to moisturize the soil such that the crops recollects its fertility and stay healthy.

- **Conductivity Sensors:** The Conductivity sensors are located in each and every corner of the field such that it checks whether the land is irrigated entirelyor not and if not, then it will send a message to the concerned user via the microcontroller. In short they are used to check the water conductivity overall the field to be irrigated.

- **Water Sensors:** The Water sensors are used to detect the level of water necessary for the crop. If the level of water is less than required then it commands the microcontroller to provide the necessary water. If the level of water reaches maximum, then it commands the microcontroller to flip a sheet horizontally such that the excess water runs on the sheet and gets collected in a dig.

- **DTMF or The Mobile Unit:** DTMF stands for "Dual Tone Multiple Frequency" signal. The DTMF signal is an arithmetical sum of two different frequencies; those are higher row frequency group and Lower column frequency group. The DTMF technology will be having Encoder and Decoder. The Encoder will be used to convert Digital signal to electrical signal. The Decoder will be used convert the electrical signal to digital signal.

- **Solar Panel:** Solar panel refers to either a photovoltaic module, a solar thermal energy panel, or to a set of solar photovoltaic (PV) modules electrically joined and mounted on a supporting structure. A PV module is a packaged, connected assembly of solar cells.

Irrigation method uses valves to turn irrigation ON and OFF. These valves may be definitely computerized by using checkers and solenoids. Automating farm or nursery irrigation permits farmers to apply the correct amount of water at the accurate time, irrespective of the availability of labor to turn valves on and off. In addition, farmers using automation equipment are able to reduce runoff from over watering saturated soils, avoid irrigating at the wrong time of day, which will improve crop performance by ensuring sufficient water and nutrients when needed. Automatic Drip

Irrigation is a valuable tool for accurate soil moisture regulator in highly specialized greenhouse vegetable production and it is a simple, precise method for irrigation. It also supports in time saving, removal of human error in modifying available soil moisture altitudes and to get the best out of their net profits. Irrigation is the artificial application of water to the soil usually for assisting in growing crops. In crop production it is mainly used in dry areas and in periods of rainfall shortfalls, but also to protect plants against frost. Types of Irrigation are

- Surface Irrigation
- Localized Irrigation
- Drip Irrigation
- Sprinkler Irrigation
- **Power Supply Unit:** This section necessities two voltages viz., +12 V & +5 V, as working voltages. Hence particularly designed power supply is constructed to get controlled power supplies.
- **Temperature Sensor (Thermistor):** A thermistor is a type of regulator whose resistance fluctuates significantly with temperature, more so than in standard resistors. The word is a portmanteau of thermal and resistor.
- **Moisture Sensor:** Soil moisture sensors measure the water content in soil. A soil moisture probe is made up of multiple soil moisture sensors.
- **Solar Panel:** Solar panel refers either to a photovoltaic module, a solar thermal energy panel, or to a set of solar photovoltaic (PV) modules electrically connected and mounted on a supporting structure. A PV module is a packaged, connected assembly of solar cells.
- **DTMF Decoder:** The DTMF decoder used is CM8870. It is used to decode the mobile's audio signal, i.e., the keypad tone. When the user presses a button in the keypad of the mobile, it generates two tones at the same time. These tones are taken from a table comprising of 2 frequency one is row frequency and other is column frequency.
- **Relays:** It is a electromagnetic device which is used to drive the load connected through the relay and the output of relay can be connected to controller or load for further processing.
- **Indicator:** This stage offers visual suggestion of which relay is activated and deactivated, by glowing respective LED or Buzzer.
- **DTMF or The Mobile Unit:** DTMF stands for "Dual Tone Multiple Frequency" signal. The DTMF signal is an algebraic summation of two different frequencies; those are higher row frequency group and Lower column frequency group. The DTMF technology will be having Encoder and Decoder. The Encoder will be used to convert Digital signal to electrical signal. The Decoder will be used convert the electrical signal to digital signal.

This is used to monitor the field to achieve appropriate irrigation by the help of wireless sensors. Temperature sensor, moisture sensor and conductivity sensor is used monitor the field with respect to that specific condition. If any factor of the field varied that will be noticed by individual sensor and sensed signal will be send to buffer for temporary storage, driver to drive the relay and relay for switching via monostable multivibrator. Relay starts the DC engine to irrigate the field properly. Arduino Uno collects the indication which was monitored from sensor, analyses and activates GSM module to send information to concern person as a communication and to update about observed factor to concern person Gmail server to attain IOT. Water sensor will be used to display the water level and if the water content exceeds the requirement then controller starts the flip to achieve rain harvesting. This module will be having mobile component to receive the call from concern person after two rings because that unit will be kept in automatic receive mode. After receiving the call the person has to activate the key to turn ON the motor. That activated indication will be decoded by DTMF decoder and sends to buffer for temporary storage, driver to drive the relay and relay switches the motor to ON situation. Even the concerned person can also turn OFF the motor by activating another key. The Smart Irrigation System Setup is as shown in Figure 10 with the sunflower model

Figure 11 shows the flap system rose to cover the plants at times of heavy rain
Figure 12 shows LCD displays the different conditions sensed by the sensor

Figure 10. Smart irrigation system

Figure 11. Flap over system

Figure 12. Moisture Low message in the Display

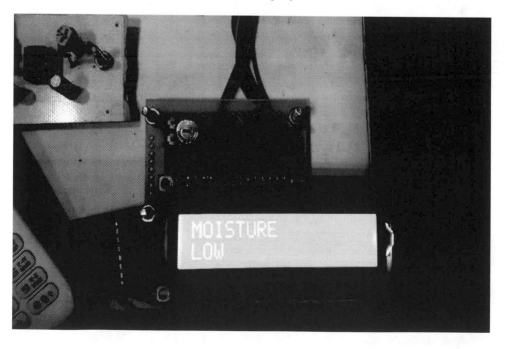

Case 4: Environment Change Prediction to Adapt Climate Smart Agriculture Using Big Data Analytics

The proposed system shown in Figure 13 demonstrate to discover answers for issues, for example, environmental change-initiated worldwide nourishment instability, to foreseeing and moderating the effect of extraordinary climate occasions on worldwide back. Since we have sensors wherever in space which are utilized to screen and measure climate, vegetation, overcast cover, ice cover, precipitation, ocean surface temperature, and some more geophysical parameters. These boundless information accumulations give us progressively more profound and more extensive scope of atmosphere change, both transiently and geospatially. This great sensor conveys an immense rate of unstructured information (petabytes of information from day by day). These gigantic unstructured information require the run of the mill huge information apparatuses for information stockpiling, handling, dissecting, picturing, also, anticipating. The design of the proposed framework in which MapReduce in the utilization of Hadoop to screen and breaking down the enormous information gathered from different sources like climate guaging, sensor information, advertise patterns furthermore, online networking information, at that point result must be displayed to Data researcher for anticipate future climate with high-determination recreations, to help agriculturists in adjusting to environmental change, what's more, to ensure the world's horticulture business.

Implementation

Implementation includes following modules:

Figure 13. Shows the idea of smart agriculture

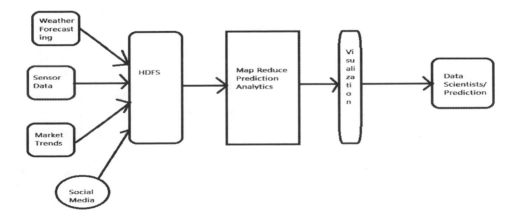

- Data Acquisition Module

This module gathers information from different sources like sensor information, climate determining, online networking information and advertises patterns. These Meteorological information can be issued physically, information can be gained with access of meteorological information procurement hardware, the little gotten information are first put away in a prophet database, at the point when little information are accumulated to a specific number, the little information will be moved into the capacity module, exchanged information will be consequently erased.

- Data Storage Module

It is in charge of capacity of metadata and information sets with repeated duplicate, which give reinforcement office. HDFS is a capacity holder and isn't constrained by an information. Little information in the information procurement module collected to a specific sum will be put in the capacity module all the time.

Figure 14. Integrated working of different modules

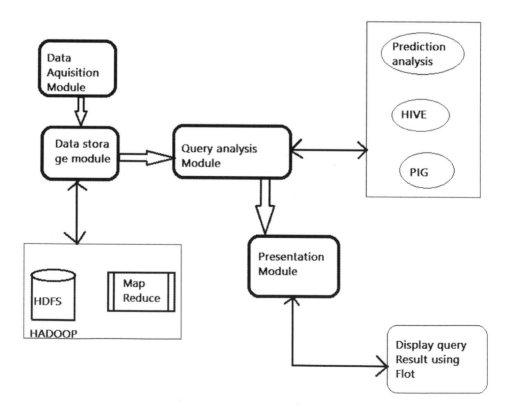

This module is handling stage incorporates two sections of information perusing/breaking down and foundation of conjecture result. The information perusing is done principally by Hive. Hive is a structure for information warehousing over Hadoop. It was made to make it feasible for experts with solid SQL aptitudes to keep running on the immense volumes of information put away in HDFS. Hive keeps running on workstations and change over SQL questions into arrangement of MapReduce occupations for execution on a Hadoop bunch. MapReduce is an execution motor reasonable for expansive information handling and can altogether enhance the reaction speed for returning question comes about. In the second part we actualize forecast work for build up gauge information through k-implies bunch calculation. Here we make utilization of apache mahout. It is an open-source versatile machine learning library. Mahout gives a proficient method for actualizing unsupervised machine learning calculation. The information of recent years are utilized to make forecast about future.

- Query Analysis Module

Query module will be shown in this module in a imagined mode. Speaking to complex information with diagrams what's more, diagrams is a fundamental piece of the information examination process, and we influence utilization of flo tend to instrument to make delightful and one of a kind information visualizations. In the initial step climate datasets will be gathered from different sources and these information things are further pre-processed to make a powerful contribution to forecast calculation. After information cleaning, stack into HDFS at that point apply inquiry utilizing Hive for investigation. We can likewise run Pig content for breaking down this information what's more, result is giving as a contribution to flotend to draw the diagram for examination. We make utilization of strategic relapse calculation for forecast and it can be executed utilizing Apache Mahout Machine learning library. At that point check the exactness of the forecast.

Workflow of Proposed System

Shown in Figure 15.

Prediction Algorithm: Logistic Algorithm

Strategic Regression executes in two noteworthy stages:

Figure 15. Proposed model

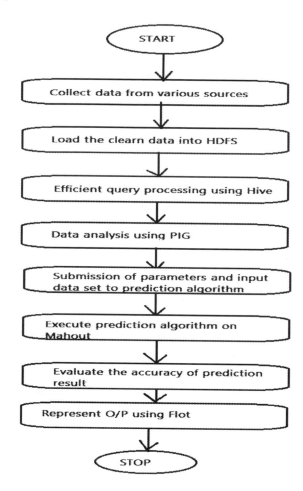

1. **Train the Model**: This progression is tied in with making a show utilizing some prepare information, which can additionally be utilized for the arrangement of any info information rather I would state test information.
2. **Test the Model:** This progression tests the created display in stage 1 by assessing the after effects of grouping of test information, and estimating the exactness, scores and disarray framework.

Supervised Learning algorithm is used for prediction because it provides most accuracy rather than traditional prediction technique.

Model of supervised learning algorithm (Figure 16).

Figure 16. Supervised Learning Methodology

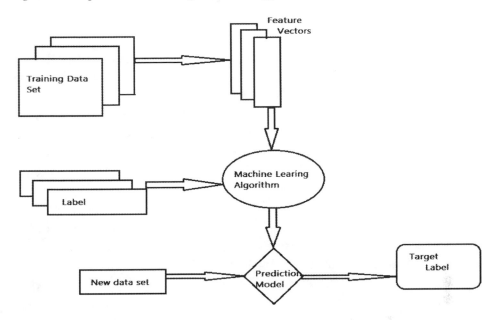

Directed Learning calculation is utilized for expectation since it gives most exactness as opposed to customary forecast strategy Logistic relapse fits an extraordinary s-formed bend by taking the direct relapse, which could create any y-esteem between short unendingness and in addition to boundlessness, and changing it with the capacity:

$$p = Exp(y) / (1 + Exp(y))$$

which produces p-values among 0 (as y approaches minus infinity) and 1 (as y approaches plus infinity). This now becomes a special kind of non-linear regression, which is what this page performs. Online-linear-regression (D, number of iterations)

```
Initialize weights w= (w0, w1, W2 …. Wd)
 For i=1:1: number of iterations
do select a data point from Di=(xi, yi) from D
seta=1/i
updateweight vector
 w<-w + a(yi-f(xi, W))xi
 end for returnweights w
```

The upsides of utilizing on the web straight relapse calculation is anything but difficult to execute, consistent information streams, adapts to changes in the model after some time.

This embraces examination of precipitation and temperature informational index of Tumkur area district over the past 100 years (1901-2000) to lead the determining test and foresee the information of the coming one month from now or year ahead of time, and uses the above climate expectation framework which empowers the strategic relapse calculation to be acknowledged to make predictions. Figure below demonstrates the diagram portrayal of investigation. Here we utilize Pig content to examination what's more, the yield is providing for as a contribution to flo tend code to produce a chart. Here we dissect recent years climate information of Tumkur area and result will be created. Here we examine temperature informational indexes and figure year wise furthermore, month to month normal figuring for Tumkur region. The investigation of various atmosphere factors like greatest temperature, normal temperature, least temperature, precipitation, overcast cover. Here examination depends on authentic information just for Tumkur district. The distinctive parameters utilized as an input variable to run a calculation. Pass is the quantity of times to disregard enters information. Lambda is the measure of coefficient rot to utilize.

Figure 17. Analysis of annual and monthly temperature data of Tumkur region

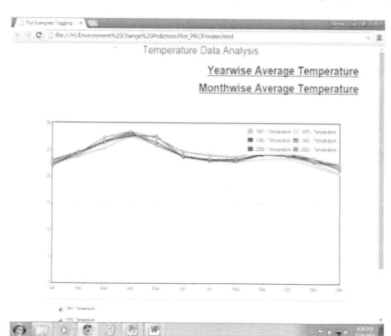

Figure 18. Weather data analysis for Tumkur region

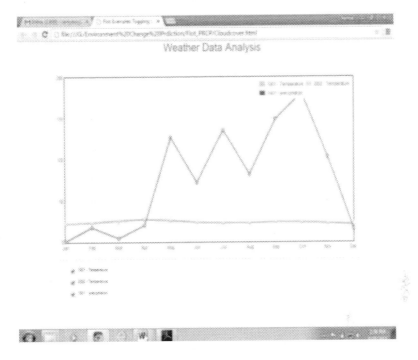

Rate demonstrates Learning rate. Precision will rely upon these parameters. Table underneath demonstrates exactness increments while changing the comparing variable esteem.

CONCLUSION

This system discussed here gives solution for the Smart Agriculture and reduces the water use because it provides irrigation as per the requirement of the crop. This system is automated irrigation system so it reduces the human involvement. This irrigation system was found to be feasible and cost effective for optimizing water resources for agricultural production. The irrigation system can be adjusted to a variety of specific crop needs and requires minimum maintenance. Using this system we can monitor the status of all the sensors (Soil-moisture, Temperature, Water level) and also the ON/OFF status of the motor.

REFERENCES

Corne, D. (2014). *Accurate Localized Short Term Weather Prediction for Renewables Planning*. IEEE.

Dahikar, S. S., & Rode, S. V. (2014). Agricultural crop yield prediction using artificial neural network approach. *Int J Innov Res Electr Electron Instrum Control Eng, 2*(1), 683–686.

Huang, Y., Yu, W., Osewold, C., & Garcia-Ortiz, A. (2016). Analysis of PKF: A communication cost reduction scheme for wireless sensor networks. *IEEE Transactions on Wireless Communications, 15*(2), 843–856. doi:10.1109/TWC.2015.2479234

Kumar, K. K., Kumar, K. R., Ashrit, R. G., Deshpande, N. R., & Hansen, J. W. (2004). Climate impacts on Indian agriculture. *International Journal of Climatology, 24*(11), 1375–1393. doi:10.1002/joc.1081

Lee, M., Hwang, J., & Yoe, H. (2013). Agricultural Production System based on IoT. *IEEE 16th International Conference on Computational Science and Engineering*. 10.1109/CSE.2013.126

Li, L., Ma, Z., & Li, L. (2013). Hadoopbased ARIMA Algorithm and its Application in Weather Forecast. *International Journal of Database Theory and Application, 6*(5), 119-132. 10.14257/ijdta.2013.6.5.11

Paras & Mathur. (2012, September). A Simple Weather Forecasting Model Using Mathematical Regression. *Indian Research Journal of Extension Education*.

Pavithra & Srinath. (2014). GSM based Automatic Irrigation Control System for Efficient Use of Resources and Crop Planning by Using an Android Mobile. *IOSR Journal of Mechanical and Civil Engineering, 11*(1), 49-55.

Radhika & Shashi. (2009). Atmospheric Temperature Prediction using Support Vector Machines. *International Journal of Computer Theory and Engineering, 1*(1).

Rokach & Maimon. (n.d.). Decision trees. In *Data Mining and Knowledge Discovery Handbook*. London: Springer.

Sap, M. N., & Awan, A. M. (2006). Development of an intelligent prediction tool for rice yield based on machine learning techniques. *Jurnal Teknologi Maklumat, 18*(2), 73–93.

Septiawan, Komaruddin, & Budi. (2012). Prediction Model for Chilli Productivity Based on Climate and Productivity Data. *UKSim-AMSS 6th European Modelling Symposium*.

Shabadi, Patil, Nikita, Shruti, Smitha, & Swati. (2014). Irrigation Control System Using Android and GSM for Efficient Use of Water and Power. *International Journal of Advanced Research in Computer Science and Software Engineering, 4*(7).

Shiraz Pasha & Yogesha. (2014). Microcontroller Based Automated Irrigation System. *The International Journal Of Engineering And Science, 3*(7).

Suresh, Gopinath, Govindaraju, Devika, & Vanitha. (2014). GSM based Automated Irrigation Control using Raingun Irrigation System. *International Journal of Advanced Research in Computer and Communication Engineering, 3*(2).

Usha, Rama, & Rao. (2015). An Enhanced Support Vector Regression Model. *International Journal of Advanced Research in Computer Engineering & Technology, 4*(5).

Waga, D. (2014). Environmental Conditions' Big Data Management and Cloud Computing Analytics for Sustainable Agriculture. *World Journal of Computer Application and Technology, 2*(3), 73–81.

Yang & Kim. (2014). A Prediction Model based on Big Data Analysis Using Hybrid FCM Clustering. *The 9th International Conference for Internet Technology and Secured Transactions*.

Compilation of References

Aazam, M., & Huh, E. N. (2014). *Fog computing and smart gateway based communication for cloud of things. In Future Internet of Things and Cloud (FiCloud).* IEEE.

Aazam, M., & Huh, E. N. (2016). Fog computing: The cloud-iot/ioe middleware paradigm. *IEEE Potentials, 35*(3), 40–44. doi:10.1109/MPOT.2015.2456213

Aazam, M., St-Hilaire, M., & Lung, C. H. (2016). Mefore: Qoe based resource estimation at fog to enhance qos in iot. *23rd International Conference on Telecommunications (ICT).* 10.1109/ICT.2016.7500362

Adibi, S. (2014). Biomedical Sensing Analyzer (BSA) for Mobile-Health (m-Health) – LTE. *IEEE Journal of Biomedical and Health Informatics, 18*(1), 345–351. doi:10.1109/JBHI.2013.2262076 PMID:24403433

Ahmed, A., & Ahmed, E. (2016). A Survey on Mobile Edge Computing. *IEEE International Conference on Itelligent System and Control (ISCO 2016).* 10.1109/ISCO.2016.7727082

Ahmed, E., Gani, A., Sookhak, M., Hamid, S. H., & Xia, F. (2015). Application Optimization in Mobile Cloud Computing: Motivation, Taxonomies, and Open Challenges. *Journal of Network and Computer Applications, 2*, 52–68. doi:10.1016/j.jnca.2015.02.003

Ahmed, E., & Rehmani, M. H. (2017). Mobile Edge Computing: Opportunities, Solutions and Challenges. *Future Generation Computer Systems, 70*, 59–63. doi:10.1016/j.future.2016.09.015

Akella & Xiong. (2014). Quality of service (qos)-guaranteed network resource allocation via software defined networking (sdn). In *Dependable, Autonomic and Secure Computing (DASC), 2014 IEEE 12th International Conference on* (pp. 7–13). IEEE.

Al-Ali, Zualkernan, & Aloul. (2010). Mobile GPRS-Sensors Array for Air Pollution Monitoring. IEEE Sensors Journal, 10(10).

Alam. (2015). *Towards Social Internet of Vehicles: Concept, Architecture and Applications*. IEEE.

Ali & Eid. (2015). An Automated System for Accident Detection. *Instrumentation and Measurement Technology Conference, 2015 IEEE Conference*.

Alliance, C. S. (2016). *The Treacherous 12 Cloud Computing Top Threats in 2016*. Retrieved from https://downloads.cloudsecurityalliance.org/assets/ research/top-threats/Treacherous-12_Cloud-Computing_Top-Threats. pdf

Almadani, B.-Y., & Shakshuki. (2015). E-Ambulance: Real-Time Integration Platform for Heterogeneous Medical Telemetry System. *5th International Conference on Current and Future Trends of Information and Communication Technologies in Healthcare*.

Amin, S. (n.d.). [Accident Detection and Reporting System using GPS, GPRS and GSM technology. *Informatics, Electronics & Vision*.]. *Jalil, & Reaz*.

Atzori, L., Iera, A., & Morabito, G. (2010). The internet of things: A survey. *Computer Networks*, *54*(15), 2787–2805. doi:10.1016/j.comnet.2010.05.010

Bahl, P., Han, Y. R., Li, E. L., & Satyanarayanan, M. (2012). Advancing the State of Mobile Cloud Computing. *Proceedings of the 3rd ACM workshop on Mobile cloud computing and services (MCS 2012)*, 21 – 28. 10.1145/2307849.2307856

Baktir, A. C., Ozgovde, A., & Ersoy, C. (2017). How Can Edge Computing Benefit from Software-Defined Networking: A Survey, Use Cases & Future Directions. *IEEE Communications Surveys and Tutorials*, *19*(4), 2359–2391. doi:10.1109/COMST.2017.2717482

Barai. (2003). *Data Mining Applications In Transport Engineering*. Retrieved from http://tf.nist.gov/seminars/WSTS/PDFs/10_Cisco_FBonomi_ConnectedVehicles. pdf

Beck, M., Werner, M., Feld, S., & Schimper, S. (2014). Mobile edge computing: A taxonomy. *Sixth International Conference on Advances in Future Internet*.

Bonomi, Milito, Zhu, & Addepalli. (2012). Fog computing andits role in the internet of things. In *Proceedings of The First Edition of The Mcc Workshop on Mobile Cloud Computing*. ACM.

Bonomi, Milito, Zhu, & Addepalli. (n.d.). *Fog Computing and Its Role in the Internet of Things*. Cisco Systems Inc.

Bonomi, F. (2011). Connected vehicles, the internet of things, and fog computing. *The Eighth ACM International Workshop on Vehicular Inter-Networking (VANET)*.

Bonomi, F. (2014). Fog Computing: A Platform for Internet of Things and Analytics. In N. Bessis & C. Dobre (Eds.), *Big Data and Internet of Things: A Roadmap for Smart Environments* (pp. 169–186). Springer. doi:10.1007/978-3-319-05029-4_7

Bonomi, F., Milito, R., Natarajan, P., & Zhu, J. (2014). *Fog Computing: A Platform for Internet of Things and Analytics*. Springer International Publishing.

Bonomi, F., Milito, R., Zhu, J., & Addepalli, S. (2012). Fog Computing and its Role in the Internet of Things. *Proceedings of the First Edition of the ACM SIGCOMM Workshop on Mobile Cloud Computing (MCC 2012)*. 10.1145/2342509.2342513

Brech, B., Jamison, J., Shao, L., & Wightwick, G. (2013). *The Interconnecting of Everything*. IBM Corp.

Brown, G. (2013). *Converging Telecom and IT in the LTE RAN*. White paper at Heavy Reading on behalf on Samsung Cloud Computing Principles and Paradigms.

Cao, Y. (2015). FAST: A Fog Computing Assisted Distributed Analytics System to Monitor Fall for Stroke Mitigation. *Proc. 10th IEEE Int'l Conf. Networking, Architecture and Storage (NAS 15)*, 2–11. 10.1109/NAS.2015.7255196

Carla, Diala, & Sami, Roch, Glitho, Morrow, & Polakos. (2017). A Comprehensive Survey on Fog Computing: State-of-the-art and Research Challenges. *IEEE Communications Surveys and Tutorials*.

Cervantes, H., & Hall, R. S. (2004). Technical Concepts of Service Orientation. In Service-oriented software system engineering: Challenges and practices. Idea Group Inc. (IGI).

Chang & Srirama. (n.d.). *Indie Fog: An Efficient Fog-Computing Infrastructure for the Internet of Things*. University of Melbourne and Manjrasoft Pty Ltd.

Chavali, L. N. (2014). Cloud Computing in Agriculture. In Agricultural Bioinformatics. Springer. doi:10.1007/978-81-322-1880-7_12

Chen, N., Chen, Y., You, Y., Ling, H., Liang, P., & Zimmermann, R. (2016). Dynamic urban surveillance video stream processing using fog computing. In *Multimedia Big Data (BigMM), 2016 IEEE Second International Conference on*. IEEE. 10.1109/BigMM.2016.53

Chen, R. Y. (2017). An intelligent value stream-based approach to collaboration of food traceability cyber physical system by fog computing. *Food Control, 71*, 124–136. doi:10.1016/j.foodcont.2016.06.042

Chiang, M. (2015). *Fog Networking: An Overview on Research Opportunities*. White Paper.

Chiang, M. (2015, December). *White Paper on Fog Networking: An Overview on Research Opportunities*. Academic Press.

Chiang, M., & Zhang, T. (2016). FogandIoT:Anoverviewofresearchopportunities. *IEEE Internet Things J., 3*(6), 1–11.

Chong, Abraham, & Paprzycki. (2004). *Traffic Accident Analysis Using Decision Trees and Neural Networks*. Academic Press.

Cirani, S., Ferrari, G., Iotti, N., & Picone, M. (2015). The IoT hub: a fog node for seamless management of heterogeneous connected smart objects. *Sensing, Communication, and Networking-Workshops (SECONWorkshops). 12th Annual IEEE International Conference on IEEE*. 10.1109/SECONW.2015.7328145

Cisco IOx and Fog Applications. (2017). Retrieved from https://www.cisco.com/c/en_in/ solutions/internet-of-things/iot-fog-applications.html

Cisco, Tech. Rep. (2014). *Cisco Delivers Vision Of Fog Computing To Accelerate Value From Billions Of Connected Devices*. Cisco.

CISCO. (2015). *Fog computing & the internet of things: extend the cloud to where the things are*. Retrieved from https://www.cisco.com/c/dam/en_us/solutions/trends/iot/docs /computing-overview.pdf

Cisco. (2017). *Fog Computing and Internet of Things: Extend the Cloud to Where the Things Are*. Available: http://www.cisco.com/c/dam/en_us/solutions/trends/iot/docs/computing-overview.pdf

Cisco. (n.d.). *New cisco internet of things (iot) system provides a foundation for the transformation of industries*. Retrieved from https://newsroom.cisco.com

Corne, D. (2014). *Accurate Localized Short Term Weather Prediction for Renewables Planning*. IEEE.

Corser & Aledhari. (2017). *Internet Of Things(IOT)Security Best Practices*. IEEE Internet Technology Policy Community White Paper.

Cristea, V., Dobre, C., & Pop, F. (2013). Context-aware Environments for the Internet of Things. *Internet of Things and Inter-cooperative Computational Technologies for Collective Intelligence Studies in Computational Intelligence, 460*, 25–49.

Dahikar, S. S., & Rode, S. V. (2014). Agricultural crop yield prediction using artificial neural network approach. *Int J Innov Res Electr Electron Instrum Control Eng, 2*(1), 683–686.

Dastjerdi, Gupta, Calheiros, Ghosh, & Buyya. (2016). Fog Computing: Principles, Architectures, and Applications. Internet of Things Principles and Paradigms, 61–75.

Der-Horng, Shin-Ting, & Chandrasekar. (2004). Applying data mining techniques for traffic incident analysis. *Journal of The Institution of Engineers, Singapore, 44*(2).

Dialogic Corporation. (2010). *Introduction to Cloud Computing*. Dialogic Corporation White Paper.

Díaz, M., Martín, C., & Rubio, B. (2016, May). State-of-the-art,challenges,andopen issues in the integration of Internet of Things and cloud computing. *Journal of Network and Computer Applications, 67*, 99–117. doi:10.1016/j.jnca.2016.01.010

Dihn, T. H., Lee, C., Niyato, D., & Wang, P. (2011). A Survey of Mobile Cloud Computing: Architecture, Applications, and Approaches. *Wireless Communications and Mobile Computing, Wiley, 13*(18), 1587–1611.

Do, C. T., Tran, N. H., Pham, C., Alam, M. G. R., Son, J. H., & Hong, C. S. (2015). A proximal algorithm for joint resource allocation and minimizing carbon footprint in geo-distributed fog computing. In *2015 International Conference on Information Networking (ICOIN)*. IEEE. 10.1109/ICOIN.2015.7057905

Dsouza, A., & Taguinod, M. (2014). Policy-driven security management for fog computing: Preliminary framework and a case study. *Information Reuse and Integration (IRI), 2014 IEEE 15th International Conference*, 16-23.

Dsouza, C., Ahn, G. J., & Taguinod, M. (2014, August). Policy-driven security management for fog computing: Preliminary framework and a case study. In *Information Reuse and Integration (IRI), 2014 IEEE 15th International Conference on* (pp. 16-23). IEEE.

Dubey, H., Yang, J., Constant, N., Amiri, A. M., Yang, Q., & Makodiya, K. (2015, October). Fog data: Enhancing telehealth big data through fog computing. In *Proceedings of the ASE BigData & SocialInformatics 2015* (p. 14). ACM.

Ericsson. (2016). *Ericsson Mobility Report on the Pulse of the Networked Society.* Stockholm, Sweden: Ericsson.

European Telecommunications Standards Institute Industry Specifications Group, Mobile-Edge Computing – Service Scenarios. (2017). Retrieved from http://www.etsi.org/deliver/etsi_gs/MEC-IEG/001_099/004/01.01.01_60/gs_MEC-IEG004v010101p.pdf

Evans, D. (2011). The internet of things: How the next evolution of the internet is changing everything. CISCO. *Int. J. Internet, 3*(2), 123–132.

Fakeeh. (2016). Privacy and Security Problems in Fog Computing. Communications on Applied Electronics. *Foundation of Computer Science FCS.*

Farahani, R. Z., & Hekmatfar, M. (2009). *Facility Location, Concepts, Models, Algorithms and Case Studies. Contributions to management science.* Heidelberg, Germany: Physica-Verlag.

Fernández-Lozano, J. J., Martín-Guzmán, M., Martín-Ávila, J., & García-Cerezo, A. (2015). A wireless sensor network for urban traffic characterization and trend monitoring. *Sensors (Basel), 15*(10), 26143–26169. doi:10.3390151026143 PMID:26501278

Fowler, S. (2013). Survey on Mobile Cloud Computing Challenges Ahead. *IEEE CommSoft E-Letters, 2*(1), 13–17.

Gao, L., Luan, T. H., Liu, B. W. Z., & Yu, S. (2017). Fog Computing and Its Applications in 5G. In 5G Mobile Communications (pp. 571-593). Springer International Publishing Switzerland.

Gennaro, R., Gentry, C., & Parno, B. (2010). Non-interactive verifiable computing: Outsourcing computation to untrusted workers. In Advances in Cryptology--CRYPTO 2010. Springer.

Gia, T. N., Jiang, M., Rahmani, A.-M., Westerlund, T., Liljeberg, P., & Tenhunen, H. (2015). Fog Computing in Healthcare Internet of Things: A Case Study on ECG Feature Extraction. In Computer and Information Technology; Ubiquitous Computing and Communications; Dependable, Autonomic and Secure Computing; Pervasive Intelligence and Computing. CIT/IUCC/DASC/PICOM.

Giang, N. K., Blackstock, M., Lea, R., & Leung, V. C. M. (2015). Developing iot applications in the fog: A distributed dataflow approach. *5th International Conference on the Internet of Things (IOT)*. 10.1109/IOT.2015.7356560

Gia, T. N., Jiang, M., Rahmani, A.-M., Westerlund, T., Liljeberg, P., & Tenhunen, H. (2015). Fog Computing in Healthcare Internet-of-Things: A Case Study on ECG Feature Extraction. *15th IEEE International Conference on Computer and Information Technology*, 356-363. 10.1109/CIT/IUCC/DASC/PICOM.2015.51

Goel, Bhagwan, Chaturvedi, Rai, & Pandey. (2015). Application of cloud computing in agricultural sector. *4th International Conference on Agriculture & Horticulture. Agrotechnol*

Gotadki, Mohan, Attarwala, & Gajare. (2014, April). Intelligent Ambulance. *International Journal of Engineering and Technical Research.*

Goyal, S. (2014). Public vs Private vs Hybrid vs Community – Cloud Computing: A Critial Review. *International Journal of Computer Network and Information Security*, 6(3), 20–29. doi:10.5815/ijcnis.2014.03.03

Gu, L., Zeng, D., Guo, S., Barnawi, A., Xiang, Y. (2015). Cost-efficient resource management in fog computing supported medical cps. *IEEE Transactions on Emerging Topics in Computing.*

Gupta, H., Chakraborty, S., Ghosh, K. S., & Buyya, R. (2017). Fog Computing in 5G Networks: An Application Perspective. In Cloud and Fog Computing in 5G Mobile Networks: Emerging advances and applications (pp. 23-54). The Institute of Engineering and Technology (IET), IET Telecommunications Series 70.

Haruna, Manis, Oladipo, & Ariwa. (2017). *User Mobility and Resource Scheduling and Management in Fog Computing to Support IoT Devices.* IEEE.

He, Lu, & Wang. (2012). A New Method For Traffic Forecasting Based On Data Mining Technology With Artificial Intelligent Algorithms. *Research Journal of Applied Sciences, Engineering and Technology.*

Heuser, S., Negro, M., Pendyala, P. K., & Sadeghi, A. R. (2016). Droidauditor: "Forensic analysis of application-layer privilege escalation attacks on android." Technical report. TU Darmstadt.

Hoang, D. B., & Chen, L. (2010). Mobile cloud for assistive healthcare (mocash). *Services Computing Conference (APSCC).*

Hong, K., Lillethun, D., Ramachandran, U., Ottenwälder, B., & Koldehofe, B. (2013). Mobile fog: A programming model for large-scale applications on the internet of things. In *Proceedings of the second ACM SIGCOMM workshop on Mobile cloud computing*. ACM. 10.1145/2491266.2491270

Hossain, M. S., & Atiquzzaman, M. (2013). Cost analysis of mobility protocols. *Telecommunication Systems*, *52*(4), 2271–2285. doi:10.100711235-011-9532-2

Hou, X., Li, Y., Chen, M., Wu, D., Jin, D., & Chen, S. (2016). Vehicular fog computing: A viewpoint of vehicles as the infrastructures. *IEEE Transactions on Vehicular Technology*, *65*(6), 3860–3873. doi:10.1109/TVT.2016.2532863

Huang, Y., Yu, W., Osewold, C., & Garcia-Ortiz, A. (2016). Analysis of PKF: A communication cost reduction scheme for wireless sensor networks. *IEEE Transactions on Wireless Communications*, *15*(2), 843–856. doi:10.1109/TWC.2015.2479234

Intharawijitr, K., Iida, K., & Koga, H. (2016). *Analysis of fog model considering computing and communication latency in 5G cellular networks*. IEEE. doi:10.1109/PERCOMW.2016.7457059

ITU-T. (2013). *Cloud Computing Framework and High Level Requirements*. ITU-T Recommendation Y.3501.

ITU-T. (2013). *Cloud Computing Infrastructure Requirements*. ITU-T Recommendation Y.3510.

Jadhav, Satam, & Salvi. (2016, February). An Android-Based Emergency Alarm Message and Healthcare Management System. *International Journal of Advanced Research in Computer and Communication Engineering*.

Jovović, I., & Forenbacher, I. M. P. (2015). Massive Machine-Type Communications: An Overview and Perspectives Towards 5G. *The 3rd International Virtual Research Conference In Technical Disciplines*.

Kang, K., Wang, C., & Luo, T. (2016). Fog computing for vehicular ad-hoc networks: Paradigms, scenarios, and issues. *Journal of China Universities of Posts and Telecommunications*, *23*(2), 56–96. doi:10.1016/S1005-8885(16)60021-3

Khan, Yongrui, & Qin. (2017). Fog computing security: a review of current applications and security solutions. *Journal of Cloud Computing*.

Khan, A. R., Othman, M., Madani, S. A., & Khan, S. U. (2014). *Survey of Mobile Cloud Computing Application Models. IEEE.*

Kiczales, G., Lamping, J., Mendhekar, A., Maeda, C., Lopes, C., Loingtier, J. M., & Irwin, J. (1997). *Aspect-oriented programming. ECOOP'97. Proceedings of the 11th European Conference on Object-Oriented Programming*, 220–242. 10.1007/BFb0053381

Kirat, D., Vigna, G., & Kruegel, C. (2014), Barecloud: Bare-metal analysis-based evasive malware detection. *USENIX Security Symposium*, 287–301.

Kitanov, S., & Janevski, T. (2014). State of the Art: Mobile Cloud Computing. *Proceedings of the Sixth IEEE International Conference on Computational Intelligence, Communication Systems and Networks 2014 (CICSYN 2014)*, 153-158. 10.1109/CICSyN.2014.41

Kitanov, S., Monteiro, E., & Janevski, T. (2016). 5G and the Fog – Survey of Related Technologies and Research Directions. *Proceedings of the 18th Mediterranean IEEE Electrotechnical Conference MELECON 2016*. 10.1109/MELCON.2016.7495388

Krishnaveni & Hemalatha. (2011). *A perspective analysis of traffic accident using data mining techniques*. Academic Press.

Kulkarni & Teja. (2014). Automated System for Air Pollution Detection and Control in Vehicles. *International Journal of Advanced Research in Electrical, Electronics and Instrumentation Engineering, 3*(9).

Kumar, K. K., Kumar, K. R., Ashrit, R. G., Deshpande, N. R., & Hansen, J. W. (2004). Climate impacts on Indian agriculture. *International Journal of Climatology, 24*(11), 1375–1393. doi:10.1002/joc.1081

Lebied, M. (2017). *6 Cloud Computing Challenges Businesses are facing in these days.* Retrieved from: https://www.datapine.com/blog/top-6-cloud-computing-challenges

Lee, M., Hwang, J., & Yoe, H. (2013). Agricultural Production System based on IoT. *IEEE 16th International Conference on Computational Science and Engineering.* 10.1109/CSE.2013.126

Li, L., Ma, Z., & Li, L. (2013). Hadoopbased ARIMA Algorithm and its Application in Weather Forecast. *International Journal of Database Theory and Application, 6*(5), 119-132. 10.14257/ijdta.2013.6.5.11

Li, J. (2015) EHOPES: Data-Centered Fog Platform for Smart Living. *Int'l Telecommunication Networks and Applications Conf. (ITNAC 15)*, 308–313. 10.1109/ATNAC.2015.7366831

Li, M., Yu, S., Ren, K., & Lou, W. (2010). Securing personal health records in cloud computing: Patient-centric and fine-grained data access control in multi-owner settings. In *International Conference on Security and Privacy in Communication Systems*. Springer. 10.1007/978-3-642-16161-2_6

Liu, Choudhary, Zhou, & Khokhar. (2006). Distributed Stream Mining System for Highway traffic. *Data (København)*.

Liu, G., Hou, X., Jin, J., Wang, F., Wang, Q., Hao, Y., ... Deng, A. (2017). 3-D-MIMO With Massive Antennas Paves the Way to 5G Enhanced Mobile Broadband: From System Design to Field Trials. *IEEE Journal on Selected Areas in Communications*, *35*(6), 1222–1233. doi:10.1109/JSAC.2017.2687998

Liu, Y. J. E., Fieldsend, E. J., & Min, G. (2017). A Framework of Fog Computing: Architecture, Challenges and Optimization. *IEEE Access: Practical Innovations, Open Solutions*, *5*, 25445–25454. doi:10.1109/ACCESS.2017.2766923

Madakam, S., & Date, H. (2016). Security Mechanisms for Connectivity of Smart Devices in the Internet of Things. Springer. doi:10.1007/978-3-319-33124-9_2

Maher. (2015). *IoT, from Cloud to Fog Computing*. Retrieved from https://blogs.cisco.com/ perspectives/iot-from-cloud-to-fog-computing

Mahmud, R., Kotagiri, R., & Buyya, R. (2018). Fog Computing: A Taxonomy, Survey and Future Directions. In B. Di Martino, K. C. Li, L. Yang, & A. Esposito (Eds.), *Internet of Everything. Internet of Things (Technology, Communications and Computing)*. Singapore: Springer. doi:10.1007/978-981-10-5861-5_5

Makwana. (2016). *Introduction to Fog Computing*. AI-eHive.

Manjunath, N., & Nikschal, V. M. (2016, May). Design of an Automated Traffic Control System for Emergency Vehicle Clearance. *International Journal of Emerging Research in Management and Technology*.

Mattern, F., & Floerkemeier, C. (2014). *From the Internet of Computers to the Internet of Things*. ETH Zurich.

Md, S. B. B., & Abu Kassim, R. (2013). Development of Fire Alarm System using Raspberry Pi and Arduino Uno. In *Electrical, Electronics and System Engineering (ICEESE), 2013 International Conference on*. IEEE.

Megalingam, Nair, & Prakhya. (n.d.). Wireless Vehicular Accident Detection and Reporting System. *Mechanical and Electrical Technology*.

Mell, P., & Grance, T. (2009). *The NIST Definition of Cloud Computing*. Retrieved from http://www.nist.gov/itl/cloud/upload/cloud-def-v15.pdf

Meola, A. (2016). *How the Internet of Things will affect the security & privacy?* Retrieved from http://www.businessinsider.com/internet-of-things-security-privacy-2016-8?IR=T

Mitchell, S., Villa, N., Stewart-Weeks, M., & Lange, A. (2013). *The Internet of Everything for Cities Connecting People, Process, Data, and Things to Improve the 'Livability' of Cities and Communities*. CISCO, white paper.

Moje, Kumbhar, Shinde, & Korke. (2016, April). Automatic Ambulance Rescue System. *International Journal of Innovative Research in Electrical, Electronics, Instrumentation and Control Engineering*.

Monteiro, A., Dubey, H., Mahler, L., Yang, Q., & Mankodiya, K. (2016). *Fit a fog computing device for speech tele-treatments*. arXiv preprint arXiv:1605.06236

Mouradian C., Naboulsi D., Yangui S., Glitho H. R., Morrow J. M., & Polakos A. P. (2017). A Comprehensive Survey on Fog Computing: State-of-the-art and Research Challenges. *IEEE Communications Surveys and Tutorials*, 1 – 51.

Munir, A., Kansakar, P., & Khan, S. U. (2017). IFCIoT: Integrated Fog Cloud IoT: A novel architectural paradigm for the future Internet of Things. *IEEE Consumer Electronics Magazine*, 6(3), 74–82. doi:10.1109/MCE.2017.2684981

Nam, T., & Pardo, T. A. (2011, September). Smart city as urban innovation: Focusing on management, policy, and context. In *Proceedings of the 5th international conference on theory and practice of electronic governance* (pp. 185-194). ACM. 10.1145/2072069.2072100

NebbioloTechnologies. (2015). *Fog vs Edge Computing v1.1*. Milpitas, CA: Nebbiolo Technologies Inc.

Ni, Zhang, Lin, & Shen. (n.d.). Securing Fog Computing for Internet of Things Applications: Challenges and Solutions. *IEEE Communications Surveys & Tutorials.* DOI 10.1109/COMST.2017.2762345

Niekamp. (2011). *Software Component Architecture.* Gestión de Congresos - CIMNE/Institute for Scientific Computing, TU Braunschweig.

NIST. (2013). *NIST Cloud Computing Standards Roadmap.* NIST Special Publication 500-291, Version 2.

Oh, Lee, & Kote. (2003). *Real Time Video Data Mining For Surveillance Video Streams.* Academic Press.

Okay, F. Y., & Ozdemir, S. (2016), A Fog Computing based Smart Grid Model, Networks, Computers and Communications (ISNCC). *2016 International Symposium IEEE,* 1-6.

OpenFog Consortium. (2017). *OpenFog Reference Architecture for Fog Computing.* OpenFog Consortium Architecture Working Group.

OpenFog Reference Architecture for Fog Computing, Produced by the OpenFog Consortium Architecture Working Group. (2017, February). Retrieved from http://www.OpenFogConsortium.org

Oueis, J., Strinati, E. C., Sardellitti, S., & Barbarossa, S. (2015). Small cell clustering for efficient distributed fog computing: A multi-user case. In Vehicular Technology Conference (VTC Fall). IEEE. doi:10.1109/VTCFall.2015.7391144

Paras & Mathur. (2012, September). A Simple Weather Forecasting Model Using Mathematical Regression. *Indian Research Journal of Extension Education.*

Pavithra & Srinath. (2014). GSM based Automatic Irrigation Control System for Efficient Use of Resources and Crop Planning by Using an Android Mobile. *IOSR Journal of Mechanical and Civil Engineering, 11*(1), 49-55.

Peng, M., Li, Y., Jiang, J., Li, J., & Wang, C. (2014). Heterogeneous cloud radio access networks: A new perspective for enhancing spectral and energy efficiencies. *IEEE Wireless Communications, 21*(6), 126–135. doi:10.1109/MWC.2014.7000980

Peng, M., Li, Y., Zhao, Z., & Wang, C. (2015). System architecture and key technologies for 5G heterogeneous cloud radio access networks. *IEEE Network, 29*(2), 6–14. doi:10.1109/MNET.2015.7064897 PMID:26504265

Peng, M., Yan, S., Zhang, K., & Wang, C. (2016). Fog Computing based Radio Access Networks: Issues and Challenges. *IEEE Network*, *30*(4), 46–53. doi:10.1109/MNET.2016.7513863

Pfaff, B. J., Pettit, J., & Koponen, T. (2015). *The design and implementation of open vSwitch*. Networked Systems Design and Implementation.

Prabha, Sunitha, & Anitha. (2014). Automatic Vehicle Accident Detection and Messaging System using GSM and GPS modem. *IJAREEIE, 3*(7).

Prieto González, L., Jaedicke, C., Schubert, J., & Stantchev, V. (2016). "Fog computing architectures for healthcare": Wireless performance and semantic opportunities. *J Inf Commun Ethics Soc*, *14*(4), 334–349. doi:10.1108/JICES-05-2016-0014

Qureshi, S. S., Ahmad, T., & Shuja-ul-islam, K. R. (2011). Mobile Cloud Computing as Future for Mobile Applications – Implementation Methods and Challenging Issues. *Proceedings of IEEE Conference on Cloud Computing and Intelligence Systems (CCIS)*.

Quwaider, M., & Jararweh, Y. (2013, December). Cloudlet-based for big data collection in body area networks. In *Internet Technology and Secured Transactions (ICITST), 2013 8th International Conference for* (pp. 137-141). IEEE.

Radhika & Shashi. (2009). Atmospheric Temperature Prediction using Support Vector Machines. *International Journal of Computer Theory and Engineering, 1*(1).

Rauniyar, A., Engelstad, P., Feng, B., & Thanh, D. V. (2016). Crowdsourcing based Disaster Management using Fog Computing in Internet of Things Paradigm. *Collaboration and Internet Computing (CIC), 2016 IEEE 2nd International Conference*, 490-494. 10.1109/CIC.2016.074

Raval, K. (2016). *The Big Data of IoT – Understanding Privacy and Security Threats*. Retrieved from: https://www.letsnurture.com/blog/the-big-data-of-iot-understanding-privacy-and-security-threats.html

Ren, K., Lou, W., & Zhang, Y. (2008). Leds: Providing location-aware end-to-end data security in wireless sensor networks. *IEEE Transactions on Mobile Computing*, *7*(5), 585–598. doi:10.1109/TMC.2007.70753

Rohila & Singla. (2016). An effective review of fog computing using virtualization. *International Journal of Innovation Research of Computer and Communication Engineering, 4*(4).

Rokach & Maimon. (n.d.). Decision trees. In *Data Mining and Knowledge Discovery Handbook*. London: Springer.

Roman, R., Lopez, J., & Manbo, M. (2018). *Mobile Edge Computing, Fog et al.: A Survey and Analysis of Security, Threats and Challenges* (Vol. 78). Futur. Gener. Comp. Syst.

Roseline, Devapriya, & Sumathi. (2013). Pollution Monitoring using Sensors and Wireless Sensor Networks: A Survey. *International Journal of Application or Innovation in Engineering & Management, 2*(7).

Sabarish, K., & Shaji, R. (2014). A Scalable Cloud Enabled Mobile Governance Framework. *Global Humanitarian Technology Conference - South Asia Satellite (GHTC-SAS)*. 10.1109/GHTC-SAS.2014.6967554

Samani & Zhi. (2016, January 4). Robotic Automated External Defibrillator Ambulance for Emergency Medical Service in Smart Cities. *IEEE Access: Practical Innovations, Open Solutions*.

Sangeetha, Archana, Ramya, & Ramya. (2014, February). Automatic Ambulance Rescue with Intelligent Traffic Light System. *IOSR Journal of Engineering*.

Sap, M. N., & Awan, A. M. (2006). Development of an intelligent prediction tool for rice yield based on machine learning techniques. *Jurnal Teknologi Maklumat, 18*(2), 73–93.

Saqib, A., Anwar, R. W., Hussain, O. K., Ahmad, M., Ngadi, M. A., Mohamad, M. M., & .... (2015). Cyber security for cyber physcial systems: A trust-based approach. *J Theor Appl Inf Technol, 71*(2), 144–152.

Sarkar, S., Chatterjee, S., & Misra, S. (Forthcoming). Assessment of the suitability of fog computing in the context of Internet of things. *IEEE Trans. Cloud Comput.*

Satyanarayanan, M., Bahl, P., Caceres, R., & Davies, N. (2009). The Case for VM-based Cloudlets in Mobile Computing. *IEEE Pervasive Computing, 8*(4), 14–23. doi:10.1109/MPRV.2009.82

Satyanarayanan, M., Schuster, R., Ebling, M., Fettweis, G., Flinck, H., Joshi, K., & Sabnani, K. (2015). An open ecosystem for mobile-cloud convergence. *IEEE Communications Magazine, 53*(3), 63–70. doi:10.1109/MCOM.2015.7060484

Saunier, N. (2011). Investigating Collision Factors by Mining Microscopic Data on Vehicle Conflict and Collisions. Academic Press.

Schmidt, D.C. (2006). Model-Driven Engineering. *IEEE Computer, 39*(2).

Sekma, N. C., Dridi, N., & Elleuch, A. (2015). Analyses toward a prediction system for a large-scale volunteer computing system. *2015 World Congress on Information Technology and Computer Applications (WCITCA)*. 10.1109/WCITCA.2015.7367017

Septiawan, Komaruddin, & Budi. (2012). Prediction Model for Chilli Productivity Based on Climate and Productivity Data. *UKSim-AMSS 6th European Modelling Symposium.*

Shabadi, Patil, Nikita, Shruti, Smitha, & Swati. (2014). Irrigation Control System Using Android and GSM for Efficient Use of Water and Power. *International Journal of Advanced Research in Computer Science and Software Engineering, 4*(7).

Shanthi & Ramani. (2011). *Classification of Vehicle Collision Patterns in Road Accidents Using Data Mining Algorithms.* Academic Press.

Shi, Y., Ding, G., Wang, H., Roman, H. E., & Lu, S. (2015). The fog computing service for healthcare. In *Future Information and Communication Technologies for Ubiquitous HealthCare (Ubi-HealthTech), 2015 2nd International Symposium on.* IEEE. 10.1109/Ubi-HealthTech.2015.7203325

Shiraz Pasha & Yogesha. (2014). Microcontroller Based Automated Irrigation System. *The International Journal Of Engineering And Science, 3*(7).

Shi, W., & Dustdar, S. (2016). The promise of edge computing. *Computer, 49*(5), 78–81. doi:10.1109/MC.2016.145

Singh, S., Chiu, Y., & Yang, Y. T. (2016). Mobile Edge Fog Computing in 5G Era: Architecture and Implementation. *2016 International Computer Symposium.*

Sommerville, I. (2011). *Software Engineering* (9th ed.). Academic Press.

Sqalli, H. M., Al-saeedi, M., Binbeshr, F., & Siddiqui, M. (2012). UCloud: Simulated Hybrid Cloud for a University Environment. *IEEE 1st International Conf. on Cloud Networking (CLOUDNET).*

Srinivasa Prasad & Ramakrishna. (n.d.). An Efficient Traffic Forecasting System Based on Spatial Data and Decision Trees. The International Arab Journal of Information Technology, 11(2).

Stankovic, J. A. (2014, February). Research directions for the Internet of Things. *IEEE Internet Things J.*, *1*(1), 3–9. doi:10.1109/JIOT.2014.2312291

Stantchev, V. (2015). Smart Items, Fog and Cloud Computing as Enablers of Servitization in Healthcare. *J. Sensors & Transducers*, *185*(2), 121–128.

Stantchev, V., Barnawi, A., Ghulam, S., Schubert, J., & Tamm, G. (2015). Smart items, fog and cloud computing as enablers of servitization in healthcare. *Sensors Transducers*, *185*(2), 121.

Stojmenovic, I., & Wen, S. (2014). The Fog Computing Paradigm: Scenarios and Security Issues. *Federated Conference on Computer Science and Information Systems, 2*(5).

Stojmenovic, I., & Wen, S. (2014). The fog computing paradigm: Scenarios and security issues. In *Computer Science and Information Systems (FedCSIS), 2014 Federated Conference On*. IEEE. 10.15439/2014F503

Stojmenovic, I. (2014, November). Fog computing: A cloud to the ground support for smart things and machine-to-machine networks. In *Telecommunication Networks and Applications Conference (ATNAC), 2014 Australasian* (pp. 117-122). IEEE. 10.1109/ATNAC.2014.7020884

Stojmenovic, I., Wen, S., Huang, X., & Luan, H. (2015). An overview of fog computing and its security issues. *Concurrency and Computation*.

Stolfo, S. J., Salem, M. B., & Keromytis, A. D. (2012). Fog Computing: Mitigating Insider Data Theft Attacks in the Cloud. *Proceeding of IEEE Symposium on Security and Privacy Workshops (SPW)*. 10.1109/SPW.2012.19

Sun, G., & Shen, J. (2014). Facilitating Social Collaboration in Mobile Cloud-based learning: A Teamwork as a Service (TaaS) Approach. *IEEE Transactions on Learning Technologies*, *7*(3), 207–220. doi:10.1109/TLT.2014.2340402

Suresh, Gopinath, Govindaraju, Devika, & Vanitha. (2014). GSM based Automated Irrigation Control using Raingun Irrigation System. *International Journal of Advanced Research in Computer and Communication Engineering, 3*(2).

Suthar, S. (2016). *How is Security important to IoT devices?* Retrieved from: http://www.cxotoday.com/story/how-is-security-important-to-iot-devices/

Tang, B., Chen, Z., Hefferman, G., Wei, T., He, H., & Yang, Q. (2015, October). A hierarchical distributed fog computing architecture for big data analysis in smart cities. In *Proceedings of the ASE BigData & SocialInformatics 2015* (p. 28). ACM.

Tesma. (2014, March). *Rule Mining And Classification Of Road Traffic Accidents Using Adaptive Regression Trees*. Academic Press.

Usha, Rama, & Rao. (2015). An Enhanced Support Vector Regression Model. *International Journal of Advanced Research in Computer Engineering & Technology, 4*(5).

Vaquero, L. M., & Rodero-Merino, L. (2014). Finding your Way in the Fog: Towards a Comprehensive Definition of Fog Computing. *ACM SIGCOMM Computer Communication Review Newsletter, 44*(5), 27–32. doi:10.1145/2677046.2677052

Varalakshmi, L., Sudha, G. F., & Jaikishan, G. (2014). A selective encryption and energy efficient clustering scheme for video streaming in wireless sensor networks. *Telecommunication Systems, 56*(3), 357–365. doi:10.100711235-013-9849-0

Varshney, P., & Simmhan, Y. (2017). *Demystifying Fog Computing: Characterizing Architectures, Applications and Abstractions*. arXiv:1702.06331

Vong. (2011). *Framework of Vehicle Emission Inspection and Control through RFID and Traffic Lights*. Proceedings of.

Waga, D. (2014). Environmental Conditions' Big Data Management and Cloud Computing Analytics for Sustainable Agriculture. *World Journal of Computer Application and Technology, 2*(3), 73–81.

Wei, X., Gomez, L., Neamtiu, I., & Faloutsos, M. (2012). Malicious android applications in the enterprise: What do they do and how do we fix it? In *Data Engineering Workshops (ICDEW), 2012 IEEE 28th International Conference on*. IEEE. 10.1109/ICDEW.2012.81

Wu, J., Yuen, C., Cheung, N.-M., Chen, J., & Chen, C. (2015). Enabling Adaptive High-frame-rate Video Streaming in Mobile Cloud Gaming Applications. *IEEE Transactions on Circuits and Systems for Video Technology*, 1-1.

Yang & Kim. (2014). A Prediction Model based on Big Data Analysis Using Hybrid FCM Clustering. *The 9th International Conference for Internet Technology and Secured Transactions*.

Yaseen, Q., AlBalas, F., Jararweh, Y., & Al-Ayyoub, M. (2016, September). A fog computing based system for selective forwarding detection in mobile wireless sensor networks. In Foundations and Applications of Self* Systems, IEEE International Workshops on (pp. 256-262). IEEE. doi:10.1109/FAS-W.2016.60

Yilmaz, O. N., Wang, Y.-P. E., & Johansson, N. A. (2015). Analysis of ultra-reliable and low-latency 5G communication for a factory automation use case. *IEEE International Conference on Communication Workshop (ICCW)*. 10.1109/ICCW.2015.7247339

Yi, S., Hao, Z., Qin, Z., & Li, Q. (2015). Fog Computing- Platform and Applications. *IEEE Workshop on Hot Topics in Web Systems and Technologies.*

Yi, S., Qin, Z., & Li, Q. (2015). Security and privacy issues of fog computing: A survey. In *International Conference on Wireless Algorithms, Systems, and Applications*. Springer. 10.1007/978-3-319-21837-3_67

Yi, S., Zi, J. H., Qin, Z., & Li, Q. (2015). Fog Computing: *Platform and Applications. Workshop on Hot Topics in Web Systems and Technologies*. IEEE.

Yu, Ren, & Wenjing. (2010). Achieving secure,scalable,and fine grained data access control in Cloud Computing, Infocom. *2010 Proceedings IEEE,* 1-9.

Yu, M., Zhang, D., Cheng, Y., & Wang, M. (2011). An RFID Electronic Tag based Automatic Vehicle Identification System for Traffic IOT Applications. *Chinese Control and Decision Conference (CCDC)*, 4192-4197. 10.1109/CCDC.2011.5968962

Yu, Y. (2016). Mobile Edge Computing Towards 5G: Vision, Recent Progress, and Open Challenges. *China Communications*, *13*(Supplement No. 2), 89–99. doi:10.1109/CC.2016.7833463

Zao, J. (2014) Augmented Brain Computer Interaction Based on Fog Computing and Linked Data. *Proc. 10th IEEE Int'l Conf. Intelligent Environments (IE 14)*, 374–377. 10.1109/IE.2014.54

Zeng, D., Gu, L., Guo, S., Cheng, Z., & Yu, S. (2016). Joint optimization of task scheduling and image placement in fog computing supported software-defined embedded system. *IEEE Transactions on Computers*, *65*(12), 3702–3712. doi:10.1109/TC.2016.2536019

Zhang, Z., Zhang, J., & Ying, L. (n.d.). *Multimedia streaming in cooperative mobile social networks*. Academic Press.

Zhang, S., Zhang, S., Chen, X., & Huo, X. (2010). Cloud Computing, Research and Development Trend. *Proceedings of the 2nd IEEE International Conference on Future Networks*.

Zhang, W., Lin, B., Yin, Q., & Zhao, T. (2016). *Infrastructure deployment and optimization of fog network based on microdc and lrpon integration*. Peer-to-Peer Networking and Applications Springer.

Zhang, Y., Niyato, D., Wang, P., & Dong, I. K. (2016). Optimal energy management policy of mobile energy gateway. *IEEE Transactions on Vehicular Technology*, 65(5), 3685–3699. doi:10.1109/TVT.2015.2445833

Zhu, J. (2013). Improving web sites performance using edge servers in fog computing architecture. In *Service Oriented System Engineering (SOSE), 2013 IEEE 7th International Symposium on*. IEEE.

Zhu, J., Chan, D. S., Prabhu, M. S., Natarajan, P., Hu, H., & Bonomi, F. (2013). Improving Web Sites Performance Using Edge Servers in Fog Computing Architecture. *Service Oriented System Engineering (SOSE), IEEE 7th International Symposium*, 320-323.

Related References

To continue our tradition of advancing information science and technology research, we have compiled a list of recommended IGI Global readings. These references will provide additional information and guidance to further enrich your knowledge and assist you with your own research and future publications.

Aasi, P., Rusu, L., & Vieru, D. (2017). The Role of Culture in IT Governance Five Focus Areas: A Literature Review. *International Journal of IT/Business Alignment and Governance, 8*(2), 42-61. doi:10.4018/IJITBAG.2017070103

Abdrabo, A. A. (2018). Egypt's Knowledge-Based Development: Opportunities, Challenges, and Future Possibilities. In A. Alraouf (Ed.), *Knowledge-Based Urban Development in the Middle East* (pp. 80–101). Hershey, PA: IGI Global. doi:10.4018/978-1-5225-3734-2.ch005

Abu Doush, I., & Alhami, I. (2018). Evaluating the Accessibility of Computer Laboratories, Libraries, and Websites in Jordanian Universities and Colleges. *International Journal of Information Systems and Social Change, 9*(2), 44–60. doi:10.4018/IJISSC.2018040104

Adeboye, A. (2016). Perceived Use and Acceptance of Cloud Enterprise Resource Planning (ERP) Implementation in the Manufacturing Industries. *International Journal of Strategic Information Technology and Applications, 7*(3), 24–40. doi:10.4018/IJSITA.2016070102

Adegbore, A. M., Quadri, M. O., & Oyewo, O. R. (2018). A Theoretical Approach to the Adoption of Electronic Resource Management Systems (ERMS) in Nigerian University Libraries. In A. Tella & T. Kwanya (Eds.), *Handbook of Research on Managing Intellectual Property in Digital Libraries* (pp. 292–311). Hershey, PA: IGI Global. doi:10.4018/978-1-5225-3093-0.ch015

Adhikari, M., & Roy, D. (2016). Green Computing. In G. Deka, G. Siddesh, K. Srinivasa, & L. Patnaik (Eds.), *Emerging Research Surrounding Power Consumption and Performance Issues in Utility Computing* (pp. 84–108). Hershey, PA: IGI Global. doi:10.4018/978-1-4666-8853-7.ch005

Afolabi, O. A. (2018). Myths and Challenges of Building an Effective Digital Library in Developing Nations: An African Perspective. In A. Tella & T. Kwanya (Eds.), *Handbook of Research on Managing Intellectual Property in Digital Libraries* (pp. 51–79). Hershey, PA: IGI Global. doi:10.4018/978-1-5225-3093-0.ch004

Agarwal, R., Singh, A., & Sen, S. (2016). Role of Molecular Docking in Computer-Aided Drug Design and Development. In S. Dastmalchi, M. Hamzeh-Mivehroud, & B. Sokouti (Eds.), *Applied Case Studies and Solutions in Molecular Docking-Based Drug Design* (pp. 1–28). Hershey, PA: IGI Global. doi:10.4018/978-1-5225-0362-0.ch001

Ali, O., & Soar, J. (2016). Technology Innovation Adoption Theories. In L. Al-Hakim, X. Wu, A. Koronios, & Y. Shou (Eds.), *Handbook of Research on Driving Competitive Advantage through Sustainable, Lean, and Disruptive Innovation* (pp. 1–38). Hershey, PA: IGI Global. doi:10.4018/978-1-5225-0135-0.ch001

Alsharo, M. (2017). Attitudes Towards Cloud Computing Adoption in Emerging Economies. *International Journal of Cloud Applications and Computing*, 7(3), 44–58. doi:10.4018/IJCAC.2017070102

Amer, T. S., & Johnson, T. L. (2016). Information Technology Progress Indicators: Temporal Expectancy, User Preference, and the Perception of Process Duration. *International Journal of Technology and Human Interaction*, 12(4), 1–14. doi:10.4018/IJTHI.2016100101

Amer, T. S., & Johnson, T. L. (2017). Information Technology Progress Indicators: Research Employing Psychological Frameworks. In A. Mesquita (Ed.), *Research Paradigms and Contemporary Perspectives on Human-Technology Interaction* (pp. 168–186). Hershey, PA: IGI Global. doi:10.4018/978-1-5225-1868-6.ch008

Anchugam, C. V., & Thangadurai, K. (2016). Introduction to Network Security. In D. G., M. Singh, & M. Jayanthi (Eds.), Network Security Attacks and Countermeasures (pp. 1-48). Hershey, PA: IGI Global. doi:10.4018/978-1-4666-8761-5.ch001

Anchugam, C. V., & Thangadurai, K. (2016). Classification of Network Attacks and Countermeasures of Different Attacks. In D. G., M. Singh, & M. Jayanthi (Eds.), Network Security Attacks and Countermeasures (pp. 115-156). Hershey, PA: IGI Global. doi:10.4018/978-1-4666-8761-5.ch004

Anohah, E. (2016). Pedagogy and Design of Online Learning Environment in Computer Science Education for High Schools. *International Journal of Online Pedagogy and Course Design*, 6(3), 39–51. doi:10.4018/IJOPCD.2016070104

Anohah, E. (2017). Paradigm and Architecture of Computing Augmented Learning Management System for Computer Science Education. *International Journal of Online Pedagogy and Course Design*, 7(2), 60–70. doi:10.4018/IJOPCD.2017040105

Anohah, E., & Suhonen, J. (2017). Trends of Mobile Learning in Computing Education from 2006 to 2014: A Systematic Review of Research Publications. *International Journal of Mobile and Blended Learning*, 9(1), 16–33. doi:10.4018/IJMBL.2017010102

Assis-Hassid, S., Heart, T., Reychav, I., & Pliskin, J. S. (2016). Modelling Factors Affecting Patient-Doctor-Computer Communication in Primary Care. *International Journal of Reliable and Quality E-Healthcare*, 5(1), 1–17. doi:10.4018/IJRQEH.2016010101

Bailey, E. K. (2017). Applying Learning Theories to Computer Technology Supported Instruction. In M. Grassetti & S. Brookby (Eds.), *Advancing Next-Generation Teacher Education through Digital Tools and Applications* (pp. 61–81). Hershey, PA: IGI Global. doi:10.4018/978-1-5225-0965-3.ch004

Balasubramanian, K. (2016). Attacks on Online Banking and Commerce. In K. Balasubramanian, K. Mala, & M. Rajakani (Eds.), *Cryptographic Solutions for Secure Online Banking and Commerce* (pp. 1–19). Hershey, PA: IGI Global. doi:10.4018/978-1-5225-0273-9.ch001

Baldwin, S., Opoku-Agyemang, K., & Roy, D. (2016). Games People Play: A Trilateral Collaboration Researching Computer Gaming across Cultures. In K. Valentine & L. Jensen (Eds.), *Examining the Evolution of Gaming and Its Impact on Social, Cultural, and Political Perspectives* (pp. 364–376). Hershey, PA: IGI Global. doi:10.4018/978-1-5225-0261-6.ch017

Banerjee, S., Sing, T. Y., Chowdhury, A. R., & Anwar, H. (2018). Let's Go Green: Towards a Taxonomy of Green Computing Enablers for Business Sustainability. In M. Khosrow-Pour (Ed.), *Green Computing Strategies for Competitive Advantage and Business Sustainability* (pp. 89–109). Hershey, PA: IGI Global. doi:10.4018/978-1-5225-5017-4.ch005

Basham, R. (2018). Information Science and Technology in Crisis Response and Management. In M. Khosrow-Pour, D.B.A. (Ed.), Encyclopedia of Information Science and Technology, Fourth Edition (pp. 1407-1418). Hershey, PA: IGI Global. doi:10.4018/978-1-5225-2255-3.ch121

Batyashe, T., & Iyamu, T. (2018). Architectural Framework for the Implementation of Information Technology Governance in Organisations. In M. Khosrow-Pour, D.B.A. (Ed.), Encyclopedia of Information Science and Technology, Fourth Edition (pp. 810-819). Hershey, PA: IGI Global. doi:10.4018/978-1-5225-2255-3.ch070

Bekleyen, N., & Çelik, S. (2017). Attitudes of Adult EFL Learners towards Preparing for a Language Test via CALL. In D. Tafazoli & M. Romero (Eds.), *Multiculturalism and Technology-Enhanced Language Learning* (pp. 214–229). Hershey, PA: IGI Global. doi:10.4018/978-1-5225-1882-2.ch013

Bennett, A., Eglash, R., Lachney, M., & Babbitt, W. (2016). Design Agency: Diversifying Computer Science at the Intersections of Creativity and Culture. In M. Raisinghani (Ed.), *Revolutionizing Education through Web-Based Instruction* (pp. 35–56). Hershey, PA: IGI Global. doi:10.4018/978-1-4666-9932-8.ch003

Bergeron, F., Croteau, A., Uwizeyemungu, S., & Raymond, L. (2017). A Framework for Research on Information Technology Governance in SMEs. In S. De Haes & W. Van Grembergen (Eds.), *Strategic IT Governance and Alignment in Business Settings* (pp. 53–81). Hershey, PA: IGI Global. doi:10.4018/978-1-5225-0861-8.ch003

Bhatt, G. D., Wang, Z., & Rodger, J. A. (2017). Information Systems Capabilities and Their Effects on Competitive Advantages: A Study of Chinese Companies. *Information Resources Management Journal*, *30*(3), 41–57. doi:10.4018/IRMJ.2017070103

Bogdanoski, M., Stoilkovski, M., & Risteski, A. (2016). Novel First Responder Digital Forensics Tool as a Support to Law Enforcement. In M. Hadji-Janev & M. Bogdanoski (Eds.), *Handbook of Research on Civil Society and National Security in the Era of Cyber Warfare* (pp. 352–376). Hershey, PA: IGI Global. doi:10.4018/978-1-4666-8793-6.ch016

Boontarig, W., Papasratorn, B., & Chutimaskul, W. (2016). The Unified Model for Acceptance and Use of Health Information on Online Social Networks: Evidence from Thailand. *International Journal of E-Health and Medical Communications*, 7(1), 31–47. doi:10.4018/IJEHMC.2016010102

Brown, S., & Yuan, X. (2016). Techniques for Retaining Computer Science Students at Historical Black Colleges and Universities. In C. Prince & R. Ford (Eds.), *Setting a New Agenda for Student Engagement and Retention in Historically Black Colleges and Universities* (pp. 251–268). Hershey, PA: IGI Global. doi:10.4018/978-1-5225-0308-8.ch014

Burcoff, A., & Shamir, L. (2017). Computer Analysis of Pablo Picasso's Artistic Style. *International Journal of Art, Culture and Design Technologies*, 6(1), 1–18. doi:10.4018/IJACDT.2017010101

Byker, E. J. (2017). I Play I Learn: Introducing Technological Play Theory. In C. Martin & D. Polly (Eds.), *Handbook of Research on Teacher Education and Professional Development* (pp. 297–306). Hershey, PA: IGI Global. doi:10.4018/978-1-5225-1067-3.ch016

Calongne, C. M., Stricker, A. G., Truman, B., & Arenas, F. J. (2017). Cognitive Apprenticeship and Computer Science Education in Cyberspace: Reimagining the Past. In A. Stricker, C. Calongne, B. Truman, & F. Arenas (Eds.), *Integrating an Awareness of Selfhood and Society into Virtual Learning* (pp. 180–197). Hershey, PA: IGI Global. doi:10.4018/978-1-5225-2182-2.ch013

Carlton, E. L., Holsinger, J. W. Jr, & Anunobi, N. (2016). Physician Engagement with Health Information Technology: Implications for Practice and Professionalism. *International Journal of Computers in Clinical Practice*, 1(2), 51–73. doi:10.4018/IJCCP.2016070103

Carneiro, A. D. (2017). Defending Information Networks in Cyberspace: Some Notes on Security Needs. In M. Dawson, D. Kisku, P. Gupta, J. Sing, & W. Li (Eds.), Developing Next-Generation Countermeasures for Homeland Security Threat Prevention (pp. 354-375). Hershey, PA: IGI Global. doi:10.4018/978-1-5225-0703-1.ch016

Cavalcanti, J. C. (2016). The New "ABC" of ICTs (Analytics + Big Data + Cloud Computing): A Complex Trade-Off between IT and CT Costs. In J. Martins & A. Molnar (Eds.), *Handbook of Research on Innovations in Information Retrieval, Analysis, and Management* (pp. 152–186). Hershey, PA: IGI Global. doi:10.4018/978-1-4666-8833-9.ch006

Chase, J. P., & Yan, Z. (2017). Affect in Statistics Cognition. In *Assessing and Measuring Statistics Cognition in Higher Education Online Environments: Emerging Research and Opportunities* (pp. 144–187). Hershey, PA: IGI Global. doi:10.4018/978-1-5225-2420-5.ch005

Chen, C. (2016). Effective Learning Strategies for the 21st Century: Implications for the E-Learning. In M. Anderson & C. Gavan (Eds.), *Developing Effective Educational Experiences through Learning Analytics* (pp. 143–169). Hershey, PA: IGI Global. doi:10.4018/978-1-4666-9983-0.ch006

Chen, E. T. (2016). Examining the Influence of Information Technology on Modern Health Care. In P. Manolitzas, E. Grigoroudis, N. Matsatsinis, & D. Yannacopoulos (Eds.), *Effective Methods for Modern Healthcare Service Quality and Evaluation* (pp. 110–136). Hershey, PA: IGI Global. doi:10.4018/978-1-4666-9961-8.ch006

Cimermanova, I. (2017). Computer-Assisted Learning in Slovakia. In D. Tafazoli & M. Romero (Eds.), *Multiculturalism and Technology-Enhanced Language Learning* (pp. 252–270). Hershey, PA: IGI Global. doi:10.4018/978-1-5225-1882-2.ch015

Cipolla-Ficarra, F. V., & Cipolla-Ficarra, M. (2018). Computer Animation for Ingenious Revival. In F. Cipolla-Ficarra, M. Ficarra, M. Cipolla-Ficarra, A. Quiroga, J. Alma, & J. Carré (Eds.), *Technology-Enhanced Human Interaction in Modern Society* (pp. 159–181). Hershey, PA: IGI Global. doi:10.4018/978-1-5225-3437-2.ch008

Cockrell, S., Damron, T. S., Melton, A. M., & Smith, A. D. (2018). Offshoring IT. In M. Khosrow-Pour, D.B.A. (Ed.), Encyclopedia of Information Science and Technology, Fourth Edition (pp. 5476-5489). Hershey, PA: IGI Global. doi:10.4018/978-1-5225-2255-3.ch476

Coffey, J. W. (2018). Logic and Proof in Computer Science: Categories and Limits of Proof Techniques. In J. Horne (Ed.), *Philosophical Perceptions on Logic and Order* (pp. 218–240). Hershey, PA: IGI Global. doi:10.4018/978-1-5225-2443-4.ch007

Dale, M. (2017). Re-Thinking the Challenges of Enterprise Architecture Implementation. In M. Tavana (Ed.), *Enterprise Information Systems and the Digitalization of Business Functions* (pp. 205–221). Hershey, PA: IGI Global. doi:10.4018/978-1-5225-2382-6.ch009

Das, A., Dasgupta, R., & Bagchi, A. (2016). Overview of Cellular Computing-Basic Principles and Applications. In J. Mandal, S. Mukhopadhyay, & T. Pal (Eds.), *Handbook of Research on Natural Computing for Optimization Problems* (pp. 637–662). Hershey, PA: IGI Global. doi:10.4018/978-1-5225-0058-2.ch026

De Maere, K., De Haes, S., & von Kutzschenbach, M. (2017). CIO Perspectives on Organizational Learning within the Context of IT Governance. *International Journal of IT/Business Alignment and Governance, 8*(1), 32-47. doi:10.4018/IJITBAG.2017010103

Demir, K., Çaka, C., Yaman, N. D., İslamoğlu, H., & Kuzu, A. (2018). Examining the Current Definitions of Computational Thinking. In H. Ozcinar, G. Wong, & H. Ozturk (Eds.), *Teaching Computational Thinking in Primary Education* (pp. 36–64). Hershey, PA: IGI Global. doi:10.4018/978-1-5225-3200-2.ch003

Deng, X., Hung, Y., & Lin, C. D. (2017). Design and Analysis of Computer Experiments. In S. Saha, A. Mandal, A. Narasimhamurthy, S. V, & S. Sangam (Eds.), Handbook of Research on Applied Cybernetics and Systems Science (pp. 264-279). Hershey, PA: IGI Global. doi:10.4018/978-1-5225-2498-4.ch013

Denner, J., Martinez, J., & Thiry, H. (2017). Strategies for Engaging Hispanic/Latino Youth in the US in Computer Science. In Y. Rankin & J. Thomas (Eds.), *Moving Students of Color from Consumers to Producers of Technology* (pp. 24–48). Hershey, PA: IGI Global. doi:10.4018/978-1-5225-2005-4.ch002

Devi, A. (2017). Cyber Crime and Cyber Security: A Quick Glance. In R. Kumar, P. Pattnaik, & P. Pandey (Eds.), *Detecting and Mitigating Robotic Cyber Security Risks* (pp. 160–171). Hershey, PA: IGI Global. doi:10.4018/978-1-5225-2154-9.ch011

Dores, A. R., Barbosa, F., Guerreiro, S., Almeida, I., & Carvalho, I. P. (2016). Computer-Based Neuropsychological Rehabilitation: Virtual Reality and Serious Games. In M. Cruz-Cunha, I. Miranda, R. Martinho, & R. Rijo (Eds.), *Encyclopedia of E-Health and Telemedicine* (pp. 473–485). Hershey, PA: IGI Global. doi:10.4018/978-1-4666-9978-6.ch037

Doshi, N., & Schaefer, G. (2016). Computer-Aided Analysis of Nailfold Capillaroscopy Images. In D. Fotiadis (Ed.), *Handbook of Research on Trends in the Diagnosis and Treatment of Chronic Conditions* (pp. 146–158). Hershey, PA: IGI Global. doi:10.4018/978-1-4666-8828-5.ch007

Doyle, D. J., & Fahy, P. J. (2018). Interactivity in Distance Education and Computer-Aided Learning, With Medical Education Examples. In M. Khosrow-Pour, D.B.A. (Ed.), Encyclopedia of Information Science and Technology, Fourth Edition (pp. 5829-5840). Hershey, PA: IGI Global. doi:10.4018/978-1-5225-2255-3.ch507

Elias, N. I., & Walker, T. W. (2017). Factors that Contribute to Continued Use of E-Training among Healthcare Professionals. In F. Topor (Ed.), *Handbook of Research on Individualism and Identity in the Globalized Digital Age* (pp. 403–429). Hershey, PA: IGI Global. doi:10.4018/978-1-5225-0522-8.ch018

Eloy, S., Dias, M. S., Lopes, P. F., & Vilar, E. (2016). Digital Technologies in Architecture and Engineering: Exploring an Engaged Interaction within Curricula. In D. Fonseca & E. Redondo (Eds.), *Handbook of Research on Applied E-Learning in Engineering and Architecture Education* (pp. 368–402). Hershey, PA: IGI Global. doi:10.4018/978-1-4666-8803-2.ch017

Estrela, V. V., Magalhães, H. A., & Saotome, O. (2016). Total Variation Applications in Computer Vision. In N. Kamila (Ed.), *Handbook of Research on Emerging Perspectives in Intelligent Pattern Recognition, Analysis, and Image Processing* (pp. 41–64). Hershey, PA: IGI Global. doi:10.4018/978-1-4666-8654-0.ch002

Filipovic, N., Radovic, M., Nikolic, D. D., Saveljic, I., Milosevic, Z., Exarchos, T. P., ... Parodi, O. (2016). Computer Predictive Model for Plaque Formation and Progression in the Artery. In D. Fotiadis (Ed.), *Handbook of Research on Trends in the Diagnosis and Treatment of Chronic Conditions* (pp. 279–300). Hershey, PA: IGI Global. doi:10.4018/978-1-4666-8828-5.ch013

Fisher, R. L. (2018). Computer-Assisted Indian Matrimonial Services. In M. Khosrow-Pour, D.B.A. (Ed.), Encyclopedia of Information Science and Technology, Fourth Edition (pp. 4136-4145). Hershey, PA: IGI Global. doi:10.4018/978-1-5225-2255-3.ch358

Fleenor, H. G., & Hodhod, R. (2016). Assessment of Learning and Technology: Computer Science Education. In V. Wang (Ed.), *Handbook of Research on Learning Outcomes and Opportunities in the Digital Age* (pp. 51–78). Hershey, PA: IGI Global. doi:10.4018/978-1-4666-9577-1.ch003

García-Valcárcel, A., & Mena, J. (2016). Information Technology as a Way To Support Collaborative Learning: What In-Service Teachers Think, Know and Do. *Journal of Information Technology Research*, 9(1), 1–17. doi:10.4018/JITR.2016010101

Gardner-McCune, C., & Jimenez, Y. (2017). Historical App Developers: Integrating CS into K-12 through Cross-Disciplinary Projects. In Y. Rankin & J. Thomas (Eds.), *Moving Students of Color from Consumers to Producers of Technology* (pp. 85–112). Hershey, PA: IGI Global. doi:10.4018/978-1-5225-2005-4.ch005

Garvey, G. P. (2016). Exploring Perception, Cognition, and Neural Pathways of Stereo Vision and the Split–Brain Human Computer Interface. In A. Ursyn (Ed.), *Knowledge Visualization and Visual Literacy in Science Education* (pp. 28–76). Hershey, PA: IGI Global. doi:10.4018/978-1-5225-0480-1.ch002

Ghafele, R., & Gibert, B. (2018). Open Growth: The Economic Impact of Open Source Software in the USA. In M. Khosrow-Pour (Ed.), *Optimizing Contemporary Application and Processes in Open Source Software* (pp. 164–197). Hershey, PA: IGI Global. doi:10.4018/978-1-5225-5314-4.ch007

Ghobakhloo, M., & Azar, A. (2018). Information Technology Resources, the Organizational Capability of Lean-Agile Manufacturing, and Business Performance. *Information Resources Management Journal, 31*(2), 47–74. doi:10.4018/IRMJ.2018040103

Gianni, M., & Gotzamani, K. (2016). Integrated Management Systems and Information Management Systems: Common Threads. In P. Papajorgji, F. Pinet, A. Guimarães, & J. Papathanasiou (Eds.), *Automated Enterprise Systems for Maximizing Business Performance* (pp. 195–214). Hershey, PA: IGI Global. doi:10.4018/978-1-4666-8841-4.ch011

Gikandi, J. W. (2017). Computer-Supported Collaborative Learning and Assessment: A Strategy for Developing Online Learning Communities in Continuing Education. In J. Keengwe & G. Onchwari (Eds.), *Handbook of Research on Learner-Centered Pedagogy in Teacher Education and Professional Development* (pp. 309–333). Hershey, PA: IGI Global. doi:10.4018/978-1-5225-0892-2.ch017

Gokhale, A. A., & Machina, K. F. (2017). Development of a Scale to Measure Attitudes toward Information Technology. In L. Tomei (Ed.), *Exploring the New Era of Technology-Infused Education* (pp. 49–64). Hershey, PA: IGI Global. doi:10.4018/978-1-5225-1709-2.ch004

Grace, A., O'Donoghue, J., Mahony, C., Heffernan, T., Molony, D., & Carroll, T. (2016). Computerized Decision Support Systems for Multimorbidity Care: An Urgent Call for Research and Development. In M. Cruz-Cunha, I. Miranda, R. Martinho, & R. Rijo (Eds.), *Encyclopedia of E-Health and Telemedicine* (pp. 486–494). Hershey, PA: IGI Global. doi:10.4018/978-1-4666-9978-6.ch038

Gupta, A., & Singh, O. (2016). Computer Aided Modeling and Finite Element Analysis of Human Elbow. *International Journal of Biomedical and Clinical Engineering*, *5*(1), 31–38. doi:10.4018/IJBCE.2016010104

H., S. K. (2016). Classification of Cybercrimes and Punishments under the Information Technology Act, 2000. In S. Geetha, & A. Phamila (Eds.), *Combating Security Breaches and Criminal Activity in the Digital Sphere* (pp. 57-66). Hershey, PA: IGI Global. doi:10.4018/978-1-5225-0193-0.ch004

Hafeez-Baig, A., Gururajan, R., & Wickramasinghe, N. (2017). Readiness as a Novel Construct of Readiness Acceptance Model (RAM) for the Wireless Handheld Technology. In N. Wickramasinghe (Ed.), *Handbook of Research on Healthcare Administration and Management* (pp. 578–595). Hershey, PA: IGI Global. doi:10.4018/978-1-5225-0920-2.ch035

Hanafizadeh, P., Ghandchi, S., & Asgarimehr, M. (2017). Impact of Information Technology on Lifestyle: A Literature Review and Classification. *International Journal of Virtual Communities and Social Networking*, *9*(2), 1–23. doi:10.4018/IJVCSN.2017040101

Harlow, D. B., Dwyer, H., Hansen, A. K., Hill, C., Iveland, A., Leak, A. E., & Franklin, D. M. (2016). Computer Programming in Elementary and Middle School: Connections across Content. In M. Urban & D. Falvo (Eds.), *Improving K-12 STEM Education Outcomes through Technological Integration* (pp. 337–361). Hershey, PA: IGI Global. doi:10.4018/978-1-4666-9616-7.ch015

Haseski, H. İ., Ilic, U., & Tuğtekin, U. (2018). Computational Thinking in Educational Digital Games: An Assessment Tool Proposal. In H. Ozcinar, G. Wong, & H. Ozturk (Eds.), *Teaching Computational Thinking in Primary Education* (pp. 256–287). Hershey, PA: IGI Global. doi:10.4018/978-1-5225-3200-2.ch013

Hee, W. J., Jalleh, G., Lai, H., & Lin, C. (2017). E-Commerce and IT Projects: Evaluation and Management Issues in Australian and Taiwanese Hospitals. *International Journal of Public Health Management and Ethics*, *2*(1), 69–90. doi:10.4018/IJPHME.2017010104

Hernandez, A. A. (2017). Green Information Technology Usage: Awareness and Practices of Philippine IT Professionals. *International Journal of Enterprise Information Systems*, *13*(4), 90–103. doi:10.4018/IJEIS.2017100106

Related References

Hernandez, A. A., & Ona, S. E. (2016). Green IT Adoption: Lessons from the Philippines Business Process Outsourcing Industry. *International Journal of Social Ecology and Sustainable Development, 7*(1), 1–34. doi:10.4018/IJSESD.2016010101

Hernandez, M. A., Marin, E. C., Garcia-Rodriguez, J., Azorin-Lopez, J., & Cazorla, M. (2017). Automatic Learning Improves Human-Robot Interaction in Productive Environments: A Review. *International Journal of Computer Vision and Image Processing, 7*(3), 65–75. doi:10.4018/IJCVIP.2017070106

Horne-Popp, L. M., Tessone, E. B., & Welker, J. (2018). If You Build It, They Will Come: Creating a Library Statistics Dashboard for Decision-Making. In L. Costello & M. Powers (Eds.), *Developing In-House Digital Tools in Library Spaces* (pp. 177–203). Hershey, PA: IGI Global. doi:10.4018/978-1-5225-2676-6.ch009

Hossan, C. G., & Ryan, J. C. (2016). Factors Affecting e-Government Technology Adoption Behaviour in a Voluntary Environment. *International Journal of Electronic Government Research, 12*(1), 24–49. doi:10.4018/IJEGR.2016010102

Hu, H., Hu, P. J., & Al-Gahtani, S. S. (2017). User Acceptance of Computer Technology at Work in Arabian Culture: A Model Comparison Approach. In M. Khosrow-Pour (Ed.), *Handbook of Research on Technology Adoption, Social Policy, and Global Integration* (pp. 205–228). Hershey, PA: IGI Global. doi:10.4018/978-1-5225-2668-1.ch011

Huie, C. P. (2016). Perceptions of Business Intelligence Professionals about Factors Related to Business Intelligence input in Decision Making. *International Journal of Business Analytics, 3*(3), 1–24. doi:10.4018/IJBAN.2016070101

Hung, S., Huang, W., Yen, D. C., Chang, S., & Lu, C. (2016). Effect of Information Service Competence and Contextual Factors on the Effectiveness of Strategic Information Systems Planning in Hospitals. *Journal of Global Information Management, 24*(1), 14–36. doi:10.4018/JGIM.2016010102

Ifinedo, P. (2017). Using an Extended Theory of Planned Behavior to Study Nurses' Adoption of Healthcare Information Systems in Nova Scotia. *International Journal of Technology Diffusion, 8*(1), 1–17. doi:10.4018/IJTD.2017010101

Ilie, V., & Sneha, S. (2018). A Three Country Study for Understanding Physicians' Engagement With Electronic Information Resources Pre and Post System Implementation. *Journal of Global Information Management, 26*(2), 48–73. doi:10.4018/JGIM.2018040103

Inoue-Smith, Y. (2017). Perceived Ease in Using Technology Predicts Teacher Candidates' Preferences for Online Resources. *International Journal of Online Pedagogy and Course Design*, 7(3), 17–28. doi:10.4018/IJOPCD.2017070102

Islam, A. A. (2016). Development and Validation of the Technology Adoption and Gratification (TAG) Model in Higher Education: A Cross-Cultural Study Between Malaysia and China. *International Journal of Technology and Human Interaction*, 12(3), 78–105. doi:10.4018/IJTHI.2016070106

Islam, A. Y. (2017). Technology Satisfaction in an Academic Context: Moderating Effect of Gender. In A. Mesquita (Ed.), *Research Paradigms and Contemporary Perspectives on Human-Technology Interaction* (pp. 187–211). Hershey, PA: IGI Global. doi:10.4018/978-1-5225-1868-6.ch009

Jamil, G. L., & Jamil, C. C. (2017). Information and Knowledge Management Perspective Contributions for Fashion Studies: Observing Logistics and Supply Chain Management Processes. In G. Jamil, A. Soares, & C. Pessoa (Eds.), *Handbook of Research on Information Management for Effective Logistics and Supply Chains* (pp. 199–221). Hershey, PA: IGI Global. doi:10.4018/978-1-5225-0973-8.ch011

Jamil, G. L., Jamil, L. C., Vieira, A. A., & Xavier, A. J. (2016). Challenges in Modelling Healthcare Services: A Study Case of Information Architecture Perspectives. In G. Jamil, J. Poças Rascão, F. Ribeiro, & A. Malheiro da Silva (Eds.), *Handbook of Research on Information Architecture and Management in Modern Organizations* (pp. 1–23). Hershey, PA: IGI Global. doi:10.4018/978-1-4666-8637-3.ch001

Janakova, M. (2018). Big Data and Simulations for the Solution of Controversies in Small Businesses. In M. Khosrow-Pour, D.B.A. (Ed.), Encyclopedia of Information Science and Technology, Fourth Edition (pp. 6907-6915). Hershey, PA: IGI Global. doi:10.4018/978-1-5225-2255-3.ch598

Jha, D. G. (2016). Preparing for Information Technology Driven Changes. In S. Tiwari & L. Nafees (Eds.), *Innovative Management Education Pedagogies for Preparing Next-Generation Leaders* (pp. 258–274). Hershey, PA: IGI Global. doi:10.4018/978-1-4666-9691-4.ch015

Jhawar, A., & Garg, S. K. (2018). Logistics Improvement by Investment in Information Technology Using System Dynamics. In A. Azar & S. Vaidyanathan (Eds.), *Advances in System Dynamics and Control* (pp. 528–567). Hershey, PA: IGI Global. doi:10.4018/978-1-5225-4077-9.ch017

Related References

Kalelioğlu, F., Gülbahar, Y., & Doğan, D. (2018). Teaching How to Think Like a Programmer: Emerging Insights. In H. Ozcinar, G. Wong, & H. Ozturk (Eds.), *Teaching Computational Thinking in Primary Education* (pp. 18–35). Hershey, PA: IGI Global. doi:10.4018/978-1-5225-3200-2.ch002

Kamberi, S. (2017). A Girls-Only Online Virtual World Environment and its Implications for Game-Based Learning. In A. Stricker, C. Calongne, B. Truman, & F. Arenas (Eds.), *Integrating an Awareness of Selfhood and Society into Virtual Learning* (pp. 74–95). Hershey, PA: IGI Global. doi:10.4018/978-1-5225-2182-2. ch006

Kamel, S., & Rizk, N. (2017). ICT Strategy Development: From Design to Implementation – Case of Egypt. In C. Howard & K. Hargiss (Eds.), *Strategic Information Systems and Technologies in Modern Organizations* (pp. 239–257). Hershey, PA: IGI Global. doi:10.4018/978-1-5225-1680-4.ch010

Kamel, S. H. (2018). The Potential Role of the Software Industry in Supporting Economic Development. In M. Khosrow-Pour, D.B.A. (Ed.), Encyclopedia of Information Science and Technology, Fourth Edition (pp. 7259-7269). Hershey, PA: IGI Global. doi:10.4018/978-1-5225-2255-3.ch631

Karon, R. (2016). Utilisation of Health Information Systems for Service Delivery in the Namibian Environment. In T. Iyamu & A. Tatnall (Eds.), *Maximizing Healthcare Delivery and Management through Technology Integration* (pp. 169–183). Hershey, PA: IGI Global. doi:10.4018/978-1-4666-9446-0.ch011

Kawata, S. (2018). Computer-Assisted Parallel Program Generation. In M. Khosrow-Pour, D.B.A. (Ed.), Encyclopedia of Information Science and Technology, Fourth Edition (pp. 4583-4593). Hershey, PA: IGI Global. doi:10.4018/978-1-5225-2255-3. ch398

Khanam, S., Siddiqui, J., & Talib, F. (2016). A DEMATEL Approach for Prioritizing the TQM Enablers and IT Resources in the Indian ICT Industry. *International Journal of Applied Management Sciences and Engineering, 3*(1), 11–29. doi:10.4018/ IJAMSE.2016010102

Khari, M., Shrivastava, G., Gupta, S., & Gupta, R. (2017). Role of Cyber Security in Today's Scenario. In R. Kumar, P. Pattnaik, & P. Pandey (Eds.), *Detecting and Mitigating Robotic Cyber Security Risks* (pp. 177–191). Hershey, PA: IGI Global. doi:10.4018/978-1-5225-2154-9.ch013

Khouja, M., Rodriguez, I. B., Ben Halima, Y., & Moalla, S. (2018). IT Governance in Higher Education Institutions: A Systematic Literature Review. *International Journal of Human Capital and Information Technology Professionals*, *9*(2), 52–67. doi:10.4018/IJHCITP.2018040104

Kim, S., Chang, M., Choi, N., Park, J., & Kim, H. (2016). The Direct and Indirect Effects of Computer Uses on Student Success in Math. *International Journal of Cyber Behavior, Psychology and Learning*, *6*(3), 48–64. doi:10.4018/IJCBPL.2016070104

Kiourt, C., Pavlidis, G., Koutsoudis, A., & Kalles, D. (2017). Realistic Simulation of Cultural Heritage. *International Journal of Computational Methods in Heritage Science*, *1*(1), 10–40. doi:10.4018/IJCMHS.2017010102

Korikov, A., & Krivtsov, O. (2016). System of People-Computer: On the Way of Creation of Human-Oriented Interface. In V. Mkrttchian, A. Bershadsky, A. Bozhday, M. Kataev, & S. Kataev (Eds.), *Handbook of Research on Estimation and Control Techniques in E-Learning Systems* (pp. 458–470). Hershey, PA: IGI Global. doi:10.4018/978-1-4666-9489-7.ch032

Köse, U. (2017). An Augmented-Reality-Based Intelligent Mobile Application for Open Computer Education. In G. Kurubacak & H. Altinpulluk (Eds.), *Mobile Technologies and Augmented Reality in Open Education* (pp. 154–174). Hershey, PA: IGI Global. doi:10.4018/978-1-5225-2110-5.ch008

Lahmiri, S. (2018). Information Technology Outsourcing Risk Factors and Provider Selection. In M. Gupta, R. Sharman, J. Walp, & P. Mulgund (Eds.), *Information Technology Risk Management and Compliance in Modern Organizations* (pp. 214–228). Hershey, PA: IGI Global. doi:10.4018/978-1-5225-2604-9.ch008

Landriscina, F. (2017). Computer-Supported Imagination: The Interplay Between Computer and Mental Simulation in Understanding Scientific Concepts. In I. Levin & D. Tsybulsky (Eds.), *Digital Tools and Solutions for Inquiry-Based STEM Learning* (pp. 33–60). Hershey, PA: IGI Global. doi:10.4018/978-1-5225-2525-7.ch002

Lau, S. K., Winley, G. K., Leung, N. K., Tsang, N., & Lau, S. Y. (2016). An Exploratory Study of Expectation in IT Skills in a Developing Nation: Vietnam. *Journal of Global Information Management*, *24*(1), 1–13. doi:10.4018/JGIM.2016010101

Lavranos, C., Kostagiolas, P., & Papadatos, J. (2016). Information Retrieval Technologies and the "Realities" of Music Information Seeking. In I. Deliyannis, P. Kostagiolas, & C. Banou (Eds.), *Experimental Multimedia Systems for Interactivity and Strategic Innovation* (pp. 102–121). Hershey, PA: IGI Global. doi:10.4018/978-1-4666-8659-5.ch005

Lee, W. W. (2018). Ethical Computing Continues From Problem to Solution. In M. Khosrow-Pour, D.B.A. (Ed.), Encyclopedia of Information Science and Technology, Fourth Edition (pp. 4884-4897). Hershey, PA: IGI Global. doi:10.4018/978-1-5225-2255-3.ch423

Lehto, M. (2016). Cyber Security Education and Research in the Finland's Universities and Universities of Applied Sciences. *International Journal of Cyber Warfare & Terrorism, 6*(2), 15–31. doi:10.4018/IJCWT.2016040102

Lin, C., Jalleh, G., & Huang, Y. (2016). Evaluating and Managing Electronic Commerce and Outsourcing Projects in Hospitals. In A. Dwivedi (Ed.), *Reshaping Medical Practice and Care with Health Information Systems* (pp. 132–172). Hershey, PA: IGI Global. doi:10.4018/978-1-4666-9870-3.ch005

Lin, S., Chen, S., & Chuang, S. (2017). Perceived Innovation and Quick Response Codes in an Online-to-Offline E-Commerce Service Model. *International Journal of E-Adoption, 9*(2), 1–16. doi:10.4018/IJEA.2017070101

Liu, M., Wang, Y., Xu, W., & Liu, L. (2017). Automated Scoring of Chinese Engineering Students' English Essays. *International Journal of Distance Education Technologies, 15*(1), 52 –68. doi:10.4018/IJDET.2017010104

Luciano, E. M., Wiedenhöft, G. C., Macadar, M. A., & Pinheiro dos Santos, F. (2016). Information Technology Governance Adoption: Understanding its Expectations Through the Lens of Organizational Citizenship. *International Journal of IT/Business Alignment and Governance, 7*(2), 22-32. doi:10.4018/IJITBAG.2016070102

Mabe, L. K., & Oladele, O. I. (2017). Application of Information Communication Technologies for Agricultural Development through Extension Services: A Review. In T. Tossy (Ed.), *Information Technology Integration for Socio-Economic Development* (pp. 52–101). Hershey, PA: IGI Global. doi:10.4018/978-1-5225-0539-6.ch003

Manogaran, G., Thota, C., & Lopez, D. (2018). Human-Computer Interaction With Big Data Analytics. In D. Lopez & M. Durai (Eds.), *HCI Challenges and Privacy Preservation in Big Data Security* (pp. 1–22). Hershey, PA: IGI Global. doi:10.4018/978-1-5225-2863-0.ch001

Margolis, J., Goode, J., & Flapan, J. (2017). A Critical Crossroads for Computer Science for All: "Identifying Talent" or "Building Talent," and What Difference Does It Make? In Y. Rankin & J. Thomas (Eds.), *Moving Students of Color from Consumers to Producers of Technology* (pp. 1–23). Hershey, PA: IGI Global. doi:10.4018/978-1-5225-2005-4.ch001

Mbale, J. (2018). Computer Centres Resource Cloud Elasticity-Scalability (CRECES): Copperbelt University Case Study. In S. Aljawarneh & M. Malhotra (Eds.), *Critical Research on Scalability and Security Issues in Virtual Cloud Environments* (pp. 48–70). Hershey, PA: IGI Global. doi:10.4018/978-1-5225-3029-9.ch003

McKee, J. (2018). The Right Information: The Key to Effective Business Planning. In *Business Architectures for Risk Assessment and Strategic Planning: Emerging Research and Opportunities* (pp. 38–52). Hershey, PA: IGI Global. doi:10.4018/978-1-5225-3392-4.ch003

Mensah, I. K., & Mi, J. (2018). Determinants of Intention to Use Local E-Government Services in Ghana: The Perspective of Local Government Workers. *International Journal of Technology Diffusion*, *9*(2), 41–60. doi:10.4018/IJTD.2018040103

Mohamed, J. H. (2018). Scientograph-Based Visualization of Computer Forensics Research Literature. In J. Jeyasekar & P. Saravanan (Eds.), *Innovations in Measuring and Evaluating Scientific Information* (pp. 148–162). Hershey, PA: IGI Global. doi:10.4018/978-1-5225-3457-0.ch010

Moore, R. L., & Johnson, N. (2017). Earning a Seat at the Table: How IT Departments Can Partner in Organizational Change and Innovation. *International Journal of Knowledge-Based Organizations*, *7*(2), 1–12. doi:10.4018/IJKBO.2017040101

Mtebe, J. S., & Kissaka, M. M. (2016). Enhancing the Quality of Computer Science Education with MOOCs in Sub-Saharan Africa. In J. Keengwe & G. Onchwari (Eds.), *Handbook of Research on Active Learning and the Flipped Classroom Model in the Digital Age* (pp. 366–377). Hershey, PA: IGI Global. doi:10.4018/978-1-4666-9680-8.ch019

Mukul, M. K., & Bhattaharyya, S. (2017). Brain-Machine Interface: Human-Computer Interaction. In E. Noughabi, B. Raahemi, A. Albadvi, & B. Far (Eds.), *Handbook of Research on Data Science for Effective Healthcare Practice and Administration* (pp. 417–443). Hershey, PA: IGI Global. doi:10.4018/978-1-5225-2515-8.ch018

Na, L. (2017). Library and Information Science Education and Graduate Programs in Academic Libraries. In L. Ruan, Q. Zhu, & Y. Ye (Eds.), *Academic Library Development and Administration in China* (pp. 218–229). Hershey, PA: IGI Global. doi:10.4018/978-1-5225-0550-1.ch013

Nabavi, A., Taghavi-Fard, M. T., Hanafizadeh, P., & Taghva, M. R. (2016). Information Technology Continuance Intention: A Systematic Literature Review. *International Journal of E-Business Research*, *12*(1), 58–95. doi:10.4018/IJEBR.2016010104

Nath, R., & Murthy, V. N. (2018). What Accounts for the Differences in Internet Diffusion Rates Around the World? In M. Khosrow-Pour, D.B.A. (Ed.), Encyclopedia of Information Science and Technology, Fourth Edition (pp. 8095-8104). Hershey, PA: IGI Global. doi:10.4018/978-1-5225-2255-3.ch705

Nedelko, Z., & Potocan, V. (2018). The Role of Emerging Information Technologies for Supporting Supply Chain Management. In M. Khosrow-Pour, D.B.A. (Ed.), Encyclopedia of Information Science and Technology, Fourth Edition (pp. 5559-5569). Hershey, PA: IGI Global. doi:10.4018/978-1-5225-2255-3.ch483

Ngafeeson, M. N. (2018). User Resistance to Health Information Technology. In M. Khosrow-Pour, D.B.A. (Ed.), Encyclopedia of Information Science and Technology, Fourth Edition (pp. 3816-3825). Hershey, PA: IGI Global. doi:10.4018/978-1-5225-2255-3.ch331

Nozari, H., Najafi, S. E., Jafari-Eskandari, M., & Aliahmadi, A. (2016). Providing a Model for Virtual Project Management with an Emphasis on IT Projects. In C. Graham (Ed.), *Strategic Management and Leadership for Systems Development in Virtual Spaces* (pp. 43–63). Hershey, PA: IGI Global. doi:10.4018/978-1-4666-9688-4.ch003

Nurdin, N., Stockdale, R., & Scheepers, H. (2016). Influence of Organizational Factors in the Sustainability of E-Government: A Case Study of Local E-Government in Indonesia. In I. Sodhi (Ed.), *Trends, Prospects, and Challenges in Asian E-Governance* (pp. 281–323). Hershey, PA: IGI Global. doi:10.4018/978-1-4666-9536-8.ch014

Odagiri, K. (2017). Introduction of Individual Technology to Constitute the Current Internet. In *Strategic Policy-Based Network Management in Contemporary Organizations* (pp. 20–96). Hershey, PA: IGI Global. doi:10.4018/978-1-68318-003-6.ch003

Okike, E. U. (2018). Computer Science and Prison Education. In I. Biao (Ed.), *Strategic Learning Ideologies in Prison Education Programs* (pp. 246–264). Hershey, PA: IGI Global. doi:10.4018/978-1-5225-2909-5.ch012

Olelewe, C. J., & Nwafor, I. P. (2017). Level of Computer Appreciation Skills Acquired for Sustainable Development by Secondary School Students in Nsukka LGA of Enugu State, Nigeria. In C. Ayo & V. Mbarika (Eds.), *Sustainable ICT Adoption and Integration for Socio-Economic Development* (pp. 214–233). Hershey, PA: IGI Global. doi:10.4018/978-1-5225-2565-3.ch010

Oliveira, M., Maçada, A. C., Curado, C., & Nodari, F. (2017). Infrastructure Profiles and Knowledge Sharing. *International Journal of Technology and Human Interaction*, *13*(3), 1–12. doi:10.4018/IJTHI.2017070101

Otarkhani, A., Shokouhyar, S., & Pour, S. S. (2017). Analyzing the Impact of Governance of Enterprise IT on Hospital Performance: Tehran's (Iran) Hospitals – A Case Study. *International Journal of Healthcare Information Systems and Informatics*, *12*(3), 1–20. doi:10.4018/IJHISI.2017070101

Otunla, A. O., & Amuda, C. O. (2018). Nigerian Undergraduate Students' Computer Competencies and Use of Information Technology Tools and Resources for Study Skills and Habits' Enhancement. In M. Khosrow-Pour, D.B.A. (Ed.), Encyclopedia of Information Science and Technology, Fourth Edition (pp. 2303-2313). Hershey, PA: IGI Global. doi:10.4018/978-1-5225-2255-3.ch200

Özçınar, H. (2018). A Brief Discussion on Incentives and Barriers to Computational Thinking Education. In H. Ozcinar, G. Wong, & H. Ozturk (Eds.), *Teaching Computational Thinking in Primary Education* (pp. 1–17). Hershey, PA: IGI Global. doi:10.4018/978-1-5225-3200-2.ch001

Pandey, J. M., Garg, S., Mishra, P., & Mishra, B. P. (2017). Computer Based Psychological Interventions: Subject to the Efficacy of Psychological Services. *International Journal of Computers in Clinical Practice*, *2*(1), 25–33. doi:10.4018/IJCCP.2017010102

Parry, V. K., & Lind, M. L. (2016). Alignment of Business Strategy and Information Technology Considering Information Technology Governance, Project Portfolio Control, and Risk Management. *International Journal of Information Technology Project Management*, *7*(4), 21–37. doi:10.4018/IJITPM.2016100102

Patro, C. (2017). Impulsion of Information Technology on Human Resource Practices. In P. Ordóñez de Pablos (Ed.), *Managerial Strategies and Solutions for Business Success in Asia* (pp. 231–254). Hershey, PA: IGI Global. doi:10.4018/978-1-5225-1886-0.ch013

Patro, C. S., & Raghunath, K. M. (2017). Information Technology Paraphernalia for Supply Chain Management Decisions. In M. Tavana (Ed.), *Enterprise Information Systems and the Digitalization of Business Functions* (pp. 294–320). Hershey, PA: IGI Global. doi:10.4018/978-1-5225-2382-6.ch014

Paul, P. K. (2016). Cloud Computing: An Agent of Promoting Interdisciplinary Sciences, Especially Information Science and I-Schools – Emerging Techno-Educational Scenario. In L. Chao (Ed.), *Handbook of Research on Cloud-Based STEM Education for Improved Learning Outcomes* (pp. 247–258). Hershey, PA: IGI Global. doi:10.4018/978-1-4666-9924-3.ch016

Paul, P. K. (2018). The Context of IST for Solid Information Retrieval and Infrastructure Building: Study of Developing Country. *International Journal of Information Retrieval Research, 8*(1), 86–100. doi:10.4018/IJIRR.2018010106

Paul, P. K., & Chatterjee, D. (2018). iSchools Promoting "Information Science and Technology" (IST) Domain Towards Community, Business, and Society With Contemporary Worldwide Trend and Emerging Potentialities in India. In M. Khosrow-Pour, D.B.A. (Ed.), Encyclopedia of Information Science and Technology, Fourth Edition (pp. 4723-4735). Hershey, PA: IGI Global. doi:10.4018/978-1-5225-2255-3.ch410

Pessoa, C. R., & Marques, M. E. (2017). Information Technology and Communication Management in Supply Chain Management. In G. Jamil, A. Soares, & C. Pessoa (Eds.), *Handbook of Research on Information Management for Effective Logistics and Supply Chains* (pp. 23–33). Hershey, PA: IGI Global. doi:10.4018/978-1-5225-0973-8.ch002

Pineda, R. G. (2016). Where the Interaction Is Not: Reflections on the Philosophy of Human-Computer Interaction. *International Journal of Art, Culture and Design Technologies, 5*(1), 1–12. doi:10.4018/IJACDT.2016010101

Pineda, R. G. (2018). Remediating Interaction: Towards a Philosophy of Human-Computer Relationship. In M. Khosrow-Pour (Ed.), *Enhancing Art, Culture, and Design With Technological Integration* (pp. 75–98). Hershey, PA: IGI Global. doi:10.4018/978-1-5225-5023-5.ch004

Poikela, P., & Vuojärvi, H. (2016). Learning ICT-Mediated Communication through Computer-Based Simulations. In M. Cruz-Cunha, I. Miranda, R. Martinho, & R. Rijo (Eds.), *Encyclopedia of E-Health and Telemedicine* (pp. 674–687). Hershey, PA: IGI Global. doi:10.4018/978-1-4666-9978-6.ch052

Qian, Y. (2017). Computer Simulation in Higher Education: Affordances, Opportunities, and Outcomes. In P. Vu, S. Fredrickson, & C. Moore (Eds.), *Handbook of Research on Innovative Pedagogies and Technologies for Online Learning in Higher Education* (pp. 236–262). Hershey, PA: IGI Global. doi:10.4018/978-1-5225-1851-8.ch011

Radant, O., Colomo-Palacios, R., & Stantchev, V. (2016). Factors for the Management of Scarce Human Resources and Highly Skilled Employees in IT-Departments: A Systematic Review. *Journal of Information Technology Research*, *9*(1), 65–82. doi:10.4018/JITR.2016010105

Rahman, N. (2016). Toward Achieving Environmental Sustainability in the Computer Industry. *International Journal of Green Computing*, *7*(1), 37–54. doi:10.4018/IJGC.2016010103

Rahman, N. (2017). Lessons from a Successful Data Warehousing Project Management. *International Journal of Information Technology Project Management*, *8*(4), 30–45. doi:10.4018/IJITPM.2017100103

Rahman, N. (2018). Environmental Sustainability in the Computer Industry for Competitive Advantage. In M. Khosrow-Pour (Ed.), *Green Computing Strategies for Competitive Advantage and Business Sustainability* (pp. 110–130). Hershey, PA: IGI Global. doi:10.4018/978-1-5225-5017-4.ch006

Rajh, A., & Pavetic, T. (2017). Computer Generated Description as the Required Digital Competence in Archival Profession. *International Journal of Digital Literacy and Digital Competence*, *8*(1), 36–49. doi:10.4018/IJDLDC.2017010103

Raman, A., & Goyal, D. P. (2017). Extending IMPLEMENT Framework for Enterprise Information Systems Implementation to Information System Innovation. In M. Tavana (Ed.), *Enterprise Information Systems and the Digitalization of Business Functions* (pp. 137–177). Hershey, PA: IGI Global. doi:10.4018/978-1-5225-2382-6.ch007

Rao, Y. S., Rauta, A. K., Saini, H., & Panda, T. C. (2017). Mathematical Model for Cyber Attack in Computer Network. *International Journal of Business Data Communications and Networking*, *13*(1), 58–65. doi:10.4018/IJBDCN.2017010105

Rapaport, W. J. (2018). Syntactic Semantics and the Proper Treatment of Computationalism. In M. Danesi (Ed.), *Empirical Research on Semiotics and Visual Rhetoric* (pp. 128–176). Hershey, PA: IGI Global. doi:10.4018/978-1-5225-5622-0.ch007

Raut, R., Priyadarshinee, P., & Jha, M. (2017). Understanding the Mediation Effect of Cloud Computing Adoption in Indian Organization: Integrating TAM-TOE- Risk Model. *International Journal of Service Science, Management, Engineering, and Technology*, *8*(3), 40–59. doi:10.4018/IJSSMET.2017070103

Regan, E. A., & Wang, J. (2016). Realizing the Value of EHR Systems Critical Success Factors. *International Journal of Healthcare Information Systems and Informatics, 11*(3), 1–18. doi:10.4018/IJHISI.2016070101

Rezaie, S., Mirabedini, S. J., & Abtahi, A. (2018). Designing a Model for Implementation of Business Intelligence in the Banking Industry. *International Journal of Enterprise Information Systems, 14*(1), 77–103. doi:10.4018/IJEIS.2018010105

Rezende, D. A. (2016). Digital City Projects: Information and Public Services Offered by Chicago (USA) and Curitiba (Brazil). *International Journal of Knowledge Society Research, 7*(3), 16–30. doi:10.4018/IJKSR.2016070102

Rezende, D. A. (2018). Strategic Digital City Projects: Innovative Information and Public Services Offered by Chicago (USA) and Curitiba (Brazil). In M. Lytras, L. Daniela, & A. Visvizi (Eds.), *Enhancing Knowledge Discovery and Innovation in the Digital Era* (pp. 204–223). Hershey, PA: IGI Global. doi:10.4018/978-1-5225-4191-2.ch012

Riabov, V. V. (2016). Teaching Online Computer-Science Courses in LMS and Cloud Environment. *International Journal of Quality Assurance in Engineering and Technology Education, 5*(4), 12–41. doi:10.4018/IJQAETE.2016100102

Ricordel, V., Wang, J., Da Silva, M. P., & Le Callet, P. (2016). 2D and 3D Visual Attention for Computer Vision: Concepts, Measurement, and Modeling. In R. Pal (Ed.), *Innovative Research in Attention Modeling and Computer Vision Applications* (pp. 1–44). Hershey, PA: IGI Global. doi:10.4018/978-1-4666-8723-3.ch001

Rodriguez, A., Rico-Diaz, A. J., Rabuñal, J. R., & Gestal, M. (2017). Fish Tracking with Computer Vision Techniques: An Application to Vertical Slot Fishways. In M. S., & V. V. (Eds.), Multi-Core Computer Vision and Image Processing for Intelligent Applications (pp. 74-104). Hershey, PA: IGI Global. doi:10.4018/978-1-5225-0889-2.ch003

Romero, J. A. (2018). Sustainable Advantages of Business Value of Information Technology. In M. Khosrow-Pour, D.B.A. (Ed.), Encyclopedia of Information Science and Technology, Fourth Edition (pp. 923-929). Hershey, PA: IGI Global. doi:10.4018/978-1-5225-2255-3.ch079

Romero, J. A. (2018). The Always-On Business Model and Competitive Advantage. In N. Bajgoric (Ed.), *Always-On Enterprise Information Systems for Modern Organizations* (pp. 23–40). Hershey, PA: IGI Global. doi:10.4018/978-1-5225-3704-5.ch002

Rosen, Y. (2018). Computer Agent Technologies in Collaborative Learning and Assessment. In M. Khosrow-Pour, D.B.A. (Ed.), Encyclopedia of Information Science and Technology, Fourth Edition (pp. 2402-2410). Hershey, PA: IGI Global. doi:10.4018/978-1-5225-2255-3.ch209

Rosen, Y., & Mosharraf, M. (2016). Computer Agent Technologies in Collaborative Assessments. In Y. Rosen, S. Ferrara, & M. Mosharraf (Eds.), *Handbook of Research on Technology Tools for Real-World Skill Development* (pp. 319–343). Hershey, PA: IGI Global. doi:10.4018/978-1-4666-9441-5.ch012

Roy, D. (2018). Success Factors of Adoption of Mobile Applications in Rural India: Effect of Service Characteristics on Conceptual Model. In M. Khosrow-Pour (Ed.), *Green Computing Strategies for Competitive Advantage and Business Sustainability* (pp. 211–238). Hershey, PA: IGI Global. doi:10.4018/978-1-5225-5017-4.ch010

Ruffin, T. R. (2016). Health Information Technology and Change. In V. Wang (Ed.), *Handbook of Research on Advancing Health Education through Technology* (pp. 259–285). Hershey, PA: IGI Global. doi:10.4018/978-1-4666-9494-1.ch012

Ruffin, T. R. (2016). Health Information Technology and Quality Management. *International Journal of Information Communication Technologies and Human Development*, 8(4), 56–72. doi:10.4018/IJICTHD.2016100105

Ruffin, T. R., & Hawkins, D. P. (2018). Trends in Health Care Information Technology and Informatics. In M. Khosrow-Pour, D.B.A. (Ed.), Encyclopedia of Information Science and Technology, Fourth Edition (pp. 3805-3815). Hershey, PA: IGI Global. doi:10.4018/978-1-5225-2255-3.ch330

Safari, M. R., & Jiang, Q. (2018). The Theory and Practice of IT Governance Maturity and Strategies Alignment: Evidence From Banking Industry. *Journal of Global Information Management*, 26(2), 127–146. doi:10.4018/JGIM.2018040106

Sahin, H. B., & Anagun, S. S. (2018). Educational Computer Games in Math Teaching: A Learning Culture. In E. Toprak & E. Kumtepe (Eds.), *Supporting Multiculturalism in Open and Distance Learning Spaces* (pp. 249–280). Hershey, PA: IGI Global. doi:10.4018/978-1-5225-3076-3.ch013

Sanna, A., & Valpreda, F. (2017). An Assessment of the Impact of a Collaborative Didactic Approach and Students' Background in Teaching Computer Animation. *International Journal of Information and Communication Technology Education*, 13(4), 1–16. doi:10.4018/IJICTE.2017100101

Related References

Savita, K., Dominic, P., & Ramayah, T. (2016). The Drivers, Practices and Outcomes of Green Supply Chain Management: Insights from ISO14001 Manufacturing Firms in Malaysia. *International Journal of Information Systems and Supply Chain Management*, *9*(2), 35–60. doi:10.4018/IJISSCM.2016040103

Scott, A., Martin, A., & McAlear, F. (2017). Enhancing Participation in Computer Science among Girls of Color: An Examination of a Preparatory AP Computer Science Intervention. In Y. Rankin & J. Thomas (Eds.), *Moving Students of Color from Consumers to Producers of Technology* (pp. 62–84). Hershey, PA: IGI Global. doi:10.4018/978-1-5225-2005-4.ch004

Shahsavandi, E., Mayah, G., & Rahbari, H. (2016). Impact of E-Government on Transparency and Corruption in Iran. In I. Sodhi (Ed.), *Trends, Prospects, and Challenges in Asian E-Governance* (pp. 75–94). Hershey, PA: IGI Global. doi:10.4018/978-1-4666-9536-8.ch004

Siddoo, V., & Wongsai, N. (2017). Factors Influencing the Adoption of ISO/IEC 29110 in Thai Government Projects: A Case Study. *International Journal of Information Technologies and Systems Approach*, *10*(1), 22–44. doi:10.4018/IJITSA.2017010102

Sidorkina, I., & Rybakov, A. (2016). Computer-Aided Design as Carrier of Set Development Changes System in E-Course Engineering. In V. Mkrttchian, A. Bershadsky, A. Bozhday, M. Kataev, & S. Kataev (Eds.), *Handbook of Research on Estimation and Control Techniques in E-Learning Systems* (pp. 500–515). Hershey, PA: IGI Global. doi:10.4018/978-1-4666-9489-7.ch035

Sidorkina, I., & Rybakov, A. (2016). Creating Model of E-Course: As an Object of Computer-Aided Design. In V. Mkrttchian, A. Bershadsky, A. Bozhday, M. Kataev, & S. Kataev (Eds.), *Handbook of Research on Estimation and Control Techniques in E-Learning Systems* (pp. 286–297). Hershey, PA: IGI Global. doi:10.4018/978-1-4666-9489-7.ch019

Simões, A. (2017). Using Game Frameworks to Teach Computer Programming. In R. Alexandre Peixoto de Queirós & M. Pinto (Eds.), *Gamification-Based E-Learning Strategies for Computer Programming Education* (pp. 221–236). Hershey, PA: IGI Global. doi:10.4018/978-1-5225-1034-5.ch010

Sllame, A. M. (2017). Integrating LAB Work With Classes in Computer Network Courses. In H. Alphin Jr, R. Chan, & J. Lavine (Eds.), *The Future of Accessibility in International Higher Education* (pp. 253–275). Hershey, PA: IGI Global. doi:10.4018/978-1-5225-2560-8.ch015

Smirnov, A., Ponomarev, A., Shilov, N., Kashevnik, A., & Teslya, N. (2018). Ontology-Based Human-Computer Cloud for Decision Support: Architecture and Applications in Tourism. *International Journal of Embedded and Real-Time Communication Systems*, *9*(1), 1–19. doi:10.4018/IJERTCS.2018010101

Smith-Ditizio, A. A., & Smith, A. D. (2018). Computer Fraud Challenges and Its Legal Implications. In M. Khosrow-Pour, D.B.A. (Ed.), Encyclopedia of Information Science and Technology, Fourth Edition (pp. 4837-4848). Hershey, PA: IGI Global. doi:10.4018/978-1-5225-2255-3.ch419

Sohani, S. S. (2016). Job Shadowing in Information Technology Projects: A Source of Competitive Advantage. *International Journal of Information Technology Project Management*, *7*(1), 47–57. doi:10.4018/IJITPM.2016010104

Sosnin, P. (2018). Figuratively Semantic Support of Human-Computer Interactions. In *Experience-Based Human-Computer Interactions: Emerging Research and Opportunities* (pp. 244–272). Hershey, PA: IGI Global. doi:10.4018/978-1-5225-2987-3.ch008

Spinelli, R., & Benevolo, C. (2016). From Healthcare Services to E-Health Applications: A Delivery System-Based Taxonomy. In A. Dwivedi (Ed.), *Reshaping Medical Practice and Care with Health Information Systems* (pp. 205–245). Hershey, PA: IGI Global. doi:10.4018/978-1-4666-9870-3.ch007

Srinivasan, S. (2016). Overview of Clinical Trial and Pharmacovigilance Process and Areas of Application of Computer System. In P. Chakraborty & A. Nagal (Eds.), *Software Innovations in Clinical Drug Development and Safety* (pp. 1–13). Hershey, PA: IGI Global. doi:10.4018/978-1-4666-8726-4.ch001

Srisawasdi, N. (2016). Motivating Inquiry-Based Learning Through a Combination of Physical and Virtual Computer-Based Laboratory Experiments in High School Science. In M. Urban & D. Falvo (Eds.), *Improving K-12 STEM Education Outcomes through Technological Integration* (pp. 108–134). Hershey, PA: IGI Global. doi:10.4018/978-1-4666-9616-7.ch006

Stavridi, S. V., & Hamada, D. R. (2016). Children and Youth Librarians: Competencies Required in Technology-Based Environment. In J. Yap, M. Perez, M. Ayson, & G. Entico (Eds.), *Special Library Administration, Standardization and Technological Integration* (pp. 25–50). Hershey, PA: IGI Global. doi:10.4018/978-1-4666-9542-9.ch002

Related References

Sung, W., Ahn, J., Kai, S. M., Choi, A., & Black, J. B. (2016). Incorporating Touch-Based Tablets into Classroom Activities: Fostering Children's Computational Thinking through iPad Integrated Instruction. In D. Mentor (Ed.), *Handbook of Research on Mobile Learning in Contemporary Classrooms* (pp. 378–406). Hershey, PA: IGI Global. doi:10.4018/978-1-5225-0251-7.ch019

Syväjärvi, A., Leinonen, J., Kivivirta, V., & Kesti, M. (2017). The Latitude of Information Management in Local Government: Views of Local Government Managers. *International Journal of Electronic Government Research, 13*(1), 69–85. doi:10.4018/IJEGR.2017010105

Tanque, M., & Foxwell, H. J. (2018). Big Data and Cloud Computing: A Review of Supply Chain Capabilities and Challenges. In A. Prasad (Ed.), *Exploring the Convergence of Big Data and the Internet of Things* (pp. 1–28). Hershey, PA: IGI Global. doi:10.4018/978-1-5225-2947-7.ch001

Teixeira, A., Gomes, A., & Orvalho, J. G. (2017). Auditory Feedback in a Computer Game for Blind People. In T. Issa, P. Kommers, T. Issa, P. Isaías, & T. Issa (Eds.), *Smart Technology Applications in Business Environments* (pp. 134–158). Hershey, PA: IGI Global. doi:10.4018/978-1-5225-2492-2.ch007

Thompson, N., McGill, T., & Murray, D. (2018). Affect-Sensitive Computer Systems. In M. Khosrow-Pour, D.B.A. (Ed.), Encyclopedia of Information Science and Technology, Fourth Edition (pp. 4124-4135). Hershey, PA: IGI Global. doi:10.4018/978-1-5225-2255-3.ch357

Trad, A., & Kalpić, D. (2016). The E-Business Transformation Framework for E-Commerce Control and Monitoring Pattern. In I. Lee (Ed.), *Encyclopedia of E-Commerce Development, Implementation, and Management* (pp. 754–777). Hershey, PA: IGI Global. doi:10.4018/978-1-4666-9787-4.ch053

Triberti, S., Brivio, E., & Galimberti, C. (2018). On Social Presence: Theories, Methodologies, and Guidelines for the Innovative Contexts of Computer-Mediated Learning. In M. Marmon (Ed.), *Enhancing Social Presence in Online Learning Environments* (pp. 20–41). Hershey, PA: IGI Global. doi:10.4018/978-1-5225-3229-3.ch002

Tripathy, B. K. T. R., S., & Mohanty, R. K. (2018). Memetic Algorithms and Their Applications in Computer Science. In S. Dash, B. Tripathy, & A. Rahman (Eds.), Handbook of Research on Modeling, Analysis, and Application of Nature-Inspired Metaheuristic Algorithms (pp. 73-93). Hershey, PA: IGI Global. doi:10.4018/978-1-5225-2857-9.ch004

Turulja, L., & Bajgoric, N. (2017). Human Resource Management IT and Global Economy Perspective: Global Human Resource Information Systems. In M. Khosrow-Pour (Ed.), *Handbook of Research on Technology Adoption, Social Policy, and Global Integration* (pp. 377–394). Hershey, PA: IGI Global. doi:10.4018/978-1-5225-2668-1.ch018

Unwin, D. W., Sanzogni, L., & Sandhu, K. (2017). Developing and Measuring the Business Case for Health Information Technology. In K. Moahi, K. Bwalya, & P. Sebina (Eds.), *Health Information Systems and the Advancement of Medical Practice in Developing Countries* (pp. 262–290). Hershey, PA: IGI Global. doi:10.4018/978-1-5225-2262-1.ch015

Vadhanam, B. R. S., M., Sugumaran, V., V., V., & Ramalingam, V. V. (2017). Computer Vision Based Classification on Commercial Videos. In M. S., & V. V. (Eds.), Multi-Core Computer Vision and Image Processing for Intelligent Applications (pp. 105-135). Hershey, PA: IGI Global. doi:10.4018/978-1-5225-0889-2.ch004

Valverde, R., Torres, B., & Motaghi, H. (2018). A Quantum NeuroIS Data Analytics Architecture for the Usability Evaluation of Learning Management Systems. In S. Bhattacharyya (Ed.), *Quantum-Inspired Intelligent Systems for Multimedia Data Analysis* (pp. 277–299). Hershey, PA: IGI Global. doi:10.4018/978-1-5225-5219-2.ch009

Vassilis, E. (2018). Learning and Teaching Methodology: "1:1 Educational Computing. In K. Koutsopoulos, K. Doukas, & Y. Kotsanis (Eds.), *Handbook of Research on Educational Design and Cloud Computing in Modern Classroom Settings* (pp. 122–155). Hershey, PA: IGI Global. doi:10.4018/978-1-5225-3053-4.ch007

Wadhwani, A. K., Wadhwani, S., & Singh, T. (2016). Computer Aided Diagnosis System for Breast Cancer Detection. In Y. Morsi, A. Shukla, & C. Rathore (Eds.), *Optimizing Assistive Technologies for Aging Populations* (pp. 378–395). Hershey, PA: IGI Global. doi:10.4018/978-1-4666-9530-6.ch015

Wang, L., Wu, Y., & Hu, C. (2016). English Teachers' Practice and Perspectives on Using Educational Computer Games in EIL Context. *International Journal of Technology and Human Interaction*, *12*(3), 33–46. doi:10.4018/IJTHI.2016070103

Watfa, M. K., Majeed, H., & Salahuddin, T. (2016). Computer Based E-Healthcare Clinical Systems: A Comprehensive Survey. *International Journal of Privacy and Health Information Management*, *4*(1), 50–69. doi:10.4018/IJPHIM.2016010104

Weeger, A., & Haase, U. (2016). Taking up Three Challenges to Business-IT Alignment Research by the Use of Activity Theory. *International Journal of IT/ Business Alignment and Governance, 7*(2), 1-21. doi:10.4018/IJITBAG.2016070101

Wexler, B. E. (2017). Computer-Presented and Physical Brain-Training Exercises for School Children: Improving Executive Functions and Learning. In B. Dubbels (Ed.), *Transforming Gaming and Computer Simulation Technologies across Industries* (pp. 206–224). Hershey, PA: IGI Global. doi:10.4018/978-1-5225-1817-4.ch012

Williams, D. M., Gani, M. O., Addo, I. D., Majumder, A. J., Tamma, C. P., Wang, M., ... Chu, C. (2016). Challenges in Developing Applications for Aging Populations. In Y. Morsi, A. Shukla, & C. Rathore (Eds.), *Optimizing Assistive Technologies for Aging Populations* (pp. 1–21). Hershey, PA: IGI Global. doi:10.4018/978-1-4666-9530-6.ch001

Wimble, M., Singh, H., & Phillips, B. (2018). Understanding Cross-Level Interactions of Firm-Level Information Technology and Industry Environment: A Multilevel Model of Business Value. *Information Resources Management Journal, 31*(1), 1–20. doi:10.4018/IRMJ.2018010101

Wimmer, H., Powell, L., Kilgus, L., & Force, C. (2017). Improving Course Assessment via Web-based Homework. *International Journal of Online Pedagogy and Course Design, 7*(2), 1–19. doi:10.4018/IJOPCD.2017040101

Wong, Y. L., & Siu, K. W. (2018). Assessing Computer-Aided Design Skills. In M. Khosrow-Pour, D.B.A. (Ed.), Encyclopedia of Information Science and Technology, Fourth Edition (pp. 7382-7391). Hershey, PA: IGI Global. doi:10.4018/978-1-5225-2255-3.ch642

Wongsurawat, W., & Shrestha, V. (2018). Information Technology, Globalization, and Local Conditions: Implications for Entrepreneurs in Southeast Asia. In P. Ordóñez de Pablos (Ed.), *Management Strategies and Technology Fluidity in the Asian Business Sector* (pp. 163–176). Hershey, PA: IGI Global. doi:10.4018/978-1-5225-4056-4.ch010

Yang, Y., Zhu, X., Jin, C., & Li, J. J. (2018). Reforming Classroom Education Through a QQ Group: A Pilot Experiment at a Primary School in Shanghai. In H. Spires (Ed.), *Digital Transformation and Innovation in Chinese Education* (pp. 211–231). Hershey, PA: IGI Global. doi:10.4018/978-1-5225-2924-8.ch012

Yilmaz, R., Sezgin, A., Kurnaz, S., & Arslan, Y. Z. (2018). Object-Oriented Programming in Computer Science. In M. Khosrow-Pour, D.B.A. (Ed.), Encyclopedia of Information Science and Technology, Fourth Edition (pp. 7470-7480). Hershey, PA: IGI Global. doi:10.4018/978-1-5225-2255-3.ch650

Yu, L. (2018). From Teaching Software Engineering Locally and Globally to Devising an Internationalized Computer Science Curriculum. In S. Dikli, B. Etheridge, & R. Rawls (Eds.), *Curriculum Internationalization and the Future of Education* (pp. 293–320). Hershey, PA: IGI Global. doi:10.4018/978-1-5225-2791-6.ch016

Yuhua, F. (2018). Computer Information Library Clusters. In M. Khosrow-Pour, D.B.A. (Ed.), Encyclopedia of Information Science and Technology, Fourth Edition (pp. 4399-4403). Hershey, PA: IGI Global. doi:10.4018/978-1-5225-2255-3.ch382

Zare, M. A., Taghavi Fard, M. T., & Hanafizadeh, P. (2016). The Assessment of Outsourcing IT Services using DEA Technique: A Study of Application Outsourcing in Research Centers. *International Journal of Operations Research and Information Systems*, 7(1), 45–57. doi:10.4018/IJORIS.2016010104

Zhao, J., Wang, Q., Guo, J., Gao, L., & Yang, F. (2016). An Overview on Passive Image Forensics Technology for Automatic Computer Forgery. *International Journal of Digital Crime and Forensics*, 8(4), 14–25. doi:10.4018/IJDCF.2016100102

Zimeras, S. (2016). Computer Virus Models and Analysis in M-Health IT Systems: Computer Virus Models. In A. Moumtzoglou (Ed.), *M-Health Innovations for Patient-Centered Care* (pp. 284–297). Hershey, PA: IGI Global. doi:10.4018/978-1-4666-9861-1.ch014

Zlatanovska, K. (2016). Hacking and Hacktivism as an Information Communication System Threat. In M. Hadji-Janev & M. Bogdanoski (Eds.), *Handbook of Research on Civil Society and National Security in the Era of Cyber Warfare* (pp. 68–101). Hershey, PA: IGI Global. doi:10.4018/978-1-4666-8793-6.ch004

Index

Purchase Print, E-Book, or Print + E-Book

IGI Global books can now be purchased from three unique pricing formats:
Print Only, E-Book Only, or Print + E-Book. Shipping fees apply.

www.igi-global.com

Recommended Reference Books

ISBN: 978-1-4666-9834-5
© 2016; 314 pp.
List Price: $195

ISBN: 978-1-4666-9770-6
© 2016; 485 pp.
List Price: $200

ISBN: 978-1-4666-6539-2
© 2015; 2,388 pp.
List Price: $2,435

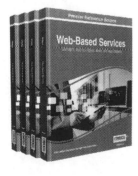

ISBN: 978-1-4666-9466-8
© 2016; 2,418 pp.
List Price: $2,300

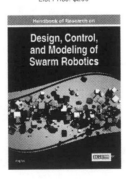

ISBN: 978-1-4666-9572-6
© 2016; 854 pp.
List Price: $465

ISBN: 978-1-5225-0058-2
© 2016; 1,015 pp.
List Price: $465

Looking for free content, product updates, news, and special offers?
Join IGI Global's mailing list today and start enjoying exclusive perks sent only to IGI Global members.
Add your name to the list at **www.igi-global.com/newsletters**.

Publishing Information Science and Technology Research Since 1988

IGI Global
DISSEMINATOR OF KNOWLEDGE

www.igi-global.com   ✉ Sign up at www.igi-global.com/newsletters   f facebook.com/igiglobal   t twitter.com/igiglobal

Stay Current on the Latest Emerging Research Developments

Become an IGI Global Reviewer for Authored Book Projects

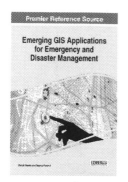

Premier Reference Source

Emerging GIS Applications for Emergency and Disaster Management

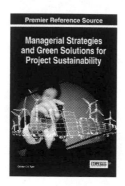

Premier Reference Source

Managerial Strategies and Green Solutions for Project Sustainability

Premier Reference Source

Comparative Approaches to Using R and Python for Statistical Data Analysis

Premier Reference Source

Solutions for High-Touch Communications in a High-Tech World

The overall success of an authored book project is dependent on quality and timely reviews.

In this competitive age of scholarly publishing, constructive and timely feedback significantly decreases the turnaround time of manuscripts from submission to acceptance, allowing the publication and discovery of progressive research at a much more expeditious rate. Several IGI Global authored book projects are currently seeking highly qualified experts in the field to fill vacancies on their respective editorial review boards:

Applications may be sent to:
development@igi-global.com

Applicants must have a doctorate (or an equivalent degree) as well as publishing and reviewing experience. Reviewers are asked to write reviews in a timely, collegial, and constructive manner. All reviewers will begin their role on an ad-hoc basis for a period of one year, and upon successful completion of this term can be considered for full editorial review board status, with the potential for a subsequent promotion to Associate Editor.

If you have a colleague that may be interested in this opportunity, we encourage you to share this information with them.

www.igi-global.com

InfoSci®-Books
A Database for Information Science and Technology Research

Maximize Your Library's Book Collection!

Invest in IGI Global's InfoSci®-Books database and gain access to hundreds of reference books at a fraction of their individual list price.

The InfoSci®-Books database offers unlimited simultaneous users the ability to precisely return search results through more than 80,000 full-text chapters from nearly 3,900 reference books in the following academic research areas:

Business & Management Information Science & Technology • Computer Science & Information Technology
Educational Science & Technology • Engineering Science & Technology • Environmental Science & Technology
Government Science & Technology • Library Information Science & Technology • Media & Communication Science & Technology
Medical, Healthcare & Life Science & Technology • Security & Forensic Science & Technology • Social Sciences & Online Behavior

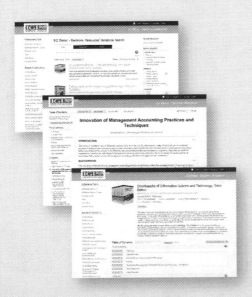

Peer-Reviewed Content:
• Cutting-edge research
• No embargoes
• Scholarly and professional
• Interdisciplinary

Award-Winning Platform:
• Unlimited simultaneous users
• Full-text in XML and PDF
• Advanced search engine
• No DRM

Librarian-Friendly:
• Free MARC records
• Discovery services
• COUNTER4/SUSHI compliant
• Training available

To find out more or request a free trial, visit:
www.igi-global.com/eresources

IGI Global
DISSEMINATOR OF KNOWLEDGE
www.igi-global.com

www.igi-global.com

IGI Global Proudly Partners with

Enhance Your Manuscript with
eContent Pro International's Professional
Copy Editing Service

Expert Copy Editing

eContent Pro International copy editors, with over 70 years of combined experience, will provide complete and comprehensive care for your document by resolving all issues with spelling, punctuation, grammar, terminology, jargon, semantics, syntax, consistency, flow, and more. In addition, they will format your document to the style you specify (APA, Chicago, etc.). All edits will be performed using Microsoft Word's Track Changes feature, which allows for fast and simple review and management of edits.

Additional Services

eContent Pro International also offers fast and affordable proofreading to enhance the readability of your document, professional translation in over 100 languages, and market localization services to help businesses and organizations localize their content and grow into new markets around the globe.

IGI Global Authors Save 25% on eContent Pro International's Services!

Scan the QR Code to Receive Your 25% Discount

The 25% discount is applied directly to your eContent Pro International shopping cart when placing an order through IGI Global's referral link. Use the QR code to access this referral link. eContent Pro International has the right to end or modify any promotion at any time.

Email: customerservice@econtentpro.com

econtentpro.com

Information Resources Management Association

Advancing the Concepts & Practices of Information Resources Management in Modern Organizations

Become an IRMA Member

Members of the **Information Resources Management Association (IRMA)** understand the importance of community within their field of study. The Information Resources Management Association is an ideal venue through which professionals, students, and academicians can convene and share the latest industry innovations and scholarly research that is changing the field of information science and technology. Become a member today and enjoy the benefits of membership as well as the opportunity to collaborate and network with fellow experts in the field.

IRMA Membership Benefits:

- **One FREE Journal Subscription**

- **30% Off Additional Journal Subscriptions**

- **20% Off Book Purchases**

- Updates on the latest events and research on Information Resources Management through the IRMA-L listserv.

- Updates on new open access and downloadable content added to Research IRM.

- A copy of the Information Technology Management Newsletter twice a year.

- A certificate of membership.

IRMA Membership $195

Scan code or visit **irma-international.org** and begin by selecting your free journal subscription.

Membership is good for one full year.

www.irma-international.org

www.igi-global.com

Available to Order Now

Order through www.igi-global.com with Free Standard Shipping.

The Premier Reference for Information Science & Information Technology

Encyclopedia of
Information Science
and Technology
Fourth Edition

100% Original Content
Contains 705 new, peer-reviewed articles with color figures covering over 80 categories in 11 subject areas

Diverse Contributions
More than 1,100 experts from 74 unique countries contributed their specialized knowledge

Easy Navigation
Includes two tables of content and a comprehensive index in each volume for the user's convenience

Highly-Cited
Embraces a complete list of references and additional reading sections to allow for further research

Included in:
InfoSci®-Books

Encyclopedia of Information Science and Technology Fourth Edition

A Comprehensive 10-Volume Set

Mehdi Khosrow-Pour, D.B.A. (Information Resources Management Association, USA)
ISBN: 978-1-5225-2255-3; © 2018; Pg: 8,104; Release Date: July 31, 2017

The **Encyclopedia of Information Science and Technology, Fourth Edition** is a 10-volume set which includes 705 original and previously unpublished research articles covering a full range of perspectives, applications, and techniques contributed by thousands of experts and researchers from around the globe. This authoritative encyclopedia is an all-encompassing, well-established reference source that is ideally designed to disseminate the most forward-thinking and diverse research findings. With critical perspectives on the impact of information science management and new technologies in modern settings, including but not limited to computer science, education, healthcare, government, engineering, business, and natural and physical sciences, it is a pivotal and relevant source of knowledge that will benefit every professional within the field of information science and technology and is an invaluable addition to every academic and corporate library.

Scan for
Online Bookstore

Pricing Information
Hardcover: **$5,695**   E-Book: **$5,695**   Hardcover + E-Book: **$6,895**

Recommend this Title to Your Institution's Library: www.igi-global.com/books

www.igi-global.com/infosci-ondemand

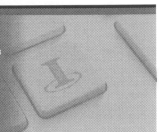

InfoSci®-OnDemand

Continuously updated with new material on a weekly basis, InfoSci®-OnDemand offers the ability to search through thousands of quality full-text research papers. Users can narrow each search by identifying key topic areas of interest, then display a complete listing of relevant papers, and purchase materials specific to their research needs.

Comprehensive Service

- Over 81,600+ journal articles, book chapters, and case studies.
- All content is downloadable in PDF format and can be stored locally for future use.

No Subscription Fees

- One time fee of $37.50 per PDF download.

Instant Access

- Receive a download link immediately after order completion!

Database Platform Features:

- Comprehensive Pay-Per-View Service
- Written by Prominent International Experts/Scholars
- Precise Search and Retrieval
- Updated With New Material on a Weekly Basis
- Immediate Access to Full-Text PDFs
- No Subscription Needed
- Purchased Research Can Be Stored Locally for Future Use

"It really provides an excellent entry into the research literature of the field. It presents a manageable number of highly relevant sources on topics of interest to a wide range of researchers. The sources are scholarly, but also accessible to 'practitioners'."

– Lisa Stimatz, MLS, University of North Carolina at Chapel Hill, USA

"It is an excellent and well designed database which will facilitate research, publication and teaching. It is a very very useful tool to have."

– George Ditsa, PhD, University of Wollongong, Australia

"I have accessed the database and find it to be a valuable tool to the IT/IS community. I found valuable articles meeting my search criteria 95% of the time."

– Lynda Louis, Xavier University of Louisiana, USA

Recommended for use by researchers who wish to immediately download PDFs of individual chapters or articles.

www.igi-global.com/e-resources/infosci-ondemand

IGI Global
DISSEMINATOR OF KNOWLEDGE

www.igi-global.com

Printed in the United States
By Bookmasters